THE FIRST
TIP-OFF

The Incredible Story
of the Birth of the NBA

Charley Rosen

New York   Chicago   San Francisco   Lisbon   London   Madrid   Mexico City
Milan   New Delhi   San Juan   Seoul   Singapore   Sydney   Toronto

The McGraw·Hill Companies

Library of Congress Cataloging-in-Publication Data

Rosen, Charles.
    The first tip-off : the incredible story of the birth of the NBA / Charley Rosen.
        p.   cm.
    ISBN 978-0-07-148785-6 (alk. paper)
    1. National Basketball Association—History.   2. Basketball—United States—History.
    I. Title.

  GV885.515.N37R67   2009
  796.323'640973—dc22   2008005360

1 2 3 4 5 6 7 8 9 10 11 12 13 14 15 16 17 18 19 20 21 22 23 24   FGR/FGR 0 9 8

ISBN 978-0-07-148785-6
MHID   0-07-148785-9

Interior design by Think Design Group

McGraw-Hill books are available at special quantity discounts to use as premiums and sales promotions or for use in corporate training programs. To contact a representative, please visit the Contact Us pages at www.mhprofessional.com.

This book is printed on acid-free paper.

For Michael Rakosi, the keeper of the flame

And for Phil Berger, whose passion for the game
(on the court and off) will rarely be equaled

Other Books by Charley Rosen

The Wizard of Odds
The Pivotal Season
Players and Pretenders
God, Man, and Basketball Jones
Chocolate Thunder (with Darryl Dawkins)
Scandals of '51

With Phil Jackson

Maverick
More Than a Game

Novels

No Blood, No Foul
Barney Polan's Game
The House of Moses All-Stars
Have Jump Shot, Will Travel
The Cockroach Basketball League
A Mile Above the Rim

CONTENTS

FOREWORD

Phil Jackson

The history of professional basketball is a tall tale. Basketball by its nature is a game that can be very competitive with two, four, six, eight, or ten players and played anywhere from outdoor swimming pools (the Globetrotters did this in my home state of Montana) to church auditoriums, the site of many early games. There would be a time for the game to come of age as a professional sport, but that time had a slipshod beginning. Charley Rosen, the foremost writer of basketball novels, has undertaken the challenge of documenting the latest and greatest history of the game professionally—and has done so to great success. The NBA has a slim amount of archives of the early games, but Rosen has dredged up a tremendous amount of material about the difficult decisions made in bringing this recreational sport into the professional entertainment business. And it's all quite fascinating.

The National Basketball Association is such a young league that in my initial season it was celebrating its twenty-fifth year in the business. Before our opening game of that 1967 season we honored members of the "old" Knickerbockers. The man who scored the first goal, Ossie Schectman, was there—he's a featured interview in Rosen's book, and I can vouch for his enthusiasm for the game of basketball. Bud Palmer and Butch van Breda Kolff, former Princeton Tigers, were also on that first Knicks team. Rosen has a colorful way of portraying these young players and their footloose-and-free approach to the game. There are plenty of laughs about the irregularities of playing for an incipient professional league, the characters that made the league colorful, and the hardships that were shared by these early pioneers of this profession that has become a big business. The interviews with members of each team from that initial season, which he inherited from Phil Berger, give readers an insight into the individual franchises as well as the game itself, and by combining their firsthand perspective with information from old sports pages and game stat sheets, Charley has re-created the origin story for each of the twelve old BAA teams (later renamed the NBA). Rosen then summarizes the season, giving the final statistics of the players on the roster and some highlights in a postscript that includes the team's total attendance, net receipts, and estimated losses. Looking at the numbers for each team, it is a wonder that professional basketball took root and survived those first years.

People with an interest in basketball genealogy will see quite a few familiar names in those stat sheets, including players like Bones McKinney and Press Maravich, who both became famous college coaches. There is also Chuck Connors, who played the game more for fun than for money. Fans of the Celtics' famous coach Red Auerbach will not like the portrait drawn of his first season as a twenty-nine-year-old coach of the Washington Capitols, but the depiction given certainly matches the feisty character who became the general of the most successful franchise in the NBA's first thirty years. It is my opinion that cutting his teeth during those early years with the Capitols gave Red the understanding of what it would take to create a winning team in Boston.

The First Tip-Off finishes with a flurry of descriptions about the first playoffs. Philadelphia turned out to be the winner, with the creative scoring champion, Joe Fulks, leading the way after the favorites, Washington and Chicago, faltered. When I finished the book it seemed as if I had gone through another season, injuries and all. Sometimes it's great to look back at where you've been and where all the skeletons are buried, and sometimes it's exciting to look ahead at the wonderful things that might be possible; but in the end the truth remains: the joy is in the journey. Charley Rosen skillfully leads readers through the NBA's first steps along its journey toward what it has become today.

PREFACE

Here we are, living game by game amid the delightful turmoil of still another NBA season rushing headlong to judgment. Even here in Sports America—where fuel prices are rocketing out of sight, where the dogs of war have been set loose, where disappointed idealists (like me) try with all their might to be hopeful in the face of a game (and a culture) increasingly distorted by money, power, and rampant egomania—there is an understandable danger that every one of us may become terminally cynical. So now, before it's too late, we need a brief pause to revive our minds and spirits. More than ever, we need a time-out.

In other words, we could learn much from a return to the very beginnings, when things were much purer, simpler, and more innocent; when basketball players wore knee pads and itchy woolen jerseys and considered themselves fortunate to be supplied with sliced oranges to suck on during the halftime intermission and dry towels and hot showers after the game; when TV was a mere oddity and the players played in relative obscurity; when winning was all that mattered.

If the child is indeed the father of the man, then we must understand the wacky workaday world of the Basketball Association of America to fully appreciate how very special are the modern-day NBA and its supremely talented athletes.

ACKNOWLEDGMENTS

Phil Berger was a fine writer who penned several top-notch books—his best being *Miracle on 33rd Street*, with *The Last Laugh* a close second. In addition to possessing considerable journalistic gifts, Berger was a willing and extremely thorough researcher of any topic that interested him and that he thought might someday turn into a full-fledged book project.

In 1982, Berger scripted a four-part story, "The History of the NBA," for *NBA Today*, a now-defunct magazine. In preparing for the piece, Berger became convinced that a book delineating the NBA's first season was a terrific idea, so he greatly expanded his investigations. Unfortunately, a bout with stomach cancer (that eventually proved fatal) seriously compromised his health and rendered him unable to bring this vision to completion.

Phil was in the last phase of this tragic illness when I first met him at a story-pitching conference for a national magazine. We were familiar with each other's work, and our mutual regard was refreshing in a business in which rival freelancers are most often sworn enemies. At the time, and until his death, I was completely unaware of his deteriorated condition.

Meanwhile, and totally independent of Phil's piece for *NBA Today* (which I didn't even know existed), I was also nurturing a plan to do a book about that same inaugural NBA season. About two years ago, I chanced to bring up the subject to Michael Rakosi, a basketball aficionado and accomplished amateur historian. Rakosi had been a close friend of Berger's, and just before Phil's untimely passing, we had also struck up what turned out to be a lasting friendship.

Imagine my surprise and delight when Rakosi informed me that Phil had had the same plan in mind—and that he had possession of all of Phil's pertinent notes, clippings, and, most important, several taped interviews with players and coaches from that long-ago season.

In all, there were about forty-five hours of interviews dating from 1981–82, none of which had been transcribed. What made these interviews so precious was that most of the subjects were long-since deceased. While some of the cassettes were warped or broken and therefore unusable, the majority survived, and the first-person testimonies of these pioneers (ably prompted by Berger's acute questioning) were both fascinating and enlightening. These tapes became the backbone of my version of the book that Phil never had the chance to write.

So, I offer heartfelt thanks for Phil's friendship and diligence, as well as for Michael's friendship and largesse.

Here's a complete listing of the interview subjects on those tapes:

PLAYERS: Brooms Abramovic, Frank Baumholtz, Moe Becker, Al Brightman, Chuck Connors, Howie Dallmar, Dutch Garfinkel, Matt Goukas, Chuck Halbert, Sonny Hertzberg, Tony Kappen, Tom King, John Mahnken, Press Maravich, Don Martin, Mike McCarron, Bones McKinney, Ed Melvin, Stan Miasek, George Munroe, Angelo Musi, John Norlander, Stan Noszka, Bud Palmer, Petey Rosenberg, Kenny Sailors, Fred Scolari, George Senesky, Johnny Simmons, Belus Smawley, and Irv Torgoff.

COACHES: Red Auerbach, Paul Birch, and Roy Clifford.

OTHERS: Sid Alpert (team photographer of Washington Caps), Sid Borgia (referee), Howie McHugh (public relations director for Boston), Maurice Podoloff (president of the league), Harvey Pollack (statistician for Philadelphia), and Dave Zinkoff (public announcer for Philadelphia).

My profound gratitude also to Matt Zeysing, librarian and archivist at the Basketball Hall of Fame, for granting me access to several scrapbooks, box scores, and team programs as well as the minutes of the BAA's board of governors meetings. Also from Zeysing's collection was an unpublished term paper, "The Toronto Huskies," by R. Mark Stephen, which collated the history of professional basketball in Toronto.

The First Basket and the First Basketeer

On January 25, 1988, Rickey Green unfurled a twenty-four-foot jumper just before the buzzer terminated the third quarter of a game between the Utah Jazz and the visiting Cleveland Cavaliers. The shot dropped through the hoop but was barely noticed in the wake of Utah's overwhelming 119–96 win. Several days later, a computer registered the fact that Green's three-pointer constituted the five-millionth point scored since the NBA's inception forty-two years before.

Only then was the question asked: Who scored the first point?

When I contacted him in the spring of 2002, eighty-six-year-old Ossie Schectman had to turn up his hearing aid to participate in a telephone conversation, and many of his recollections of that historic score have likewise dimmed. Back then, Schectman was a sturdy guard for the New York Knickerbockers, and he clearly recalled that the inaugural game was played against the Huskies in Toronto. "I scored on a two-handed underhand layup," he said, "which was the standard chippy shot back then. I also remember that the basket came on the receiving end of a give-and-go, but I can't remember who I received the pass from."

In 1996, the surviving players of that historic game were honored at a reunion that kicked off the NBA's season-long fiftieth-anniversary celebration. "That's when a teammate of mine," said Schectman, "a guy named Nat Militzok, told me that he had made the pass, but I'm positive that Nat wasn't one of the starters."

Yet Schectman does recall other salient information: "I was the Knicks' third-leading scorer [8.1 points per game]; I also finished third in the league in assists [2.0], and my salary worked out to about sixty dollars a game. Ha! These days, the players make about three times that every second of every game. Don't get me wrong, though. I have no jealousy or resentment over how much money these guys make today. I think they're the best athletes in the world, and they're worth every red cent. I'm just proud to have been one of the NBA's pioneers."

Ossie Schectman was a joyful survivor from another generation, a visitor from another world, where athletes played basketball at the highest level, unconcerned about vying with one another for the biggest contract or the costliest neck ice or the biggest posse, where $60 was just fine, where somebody could do something (anything) just for the intrinsic joy of doing it.

How refreshing to listen to Schectman talk about the differences between the players and the game then and now. "The ball was made of leather, and it was darker colored, larger, and much heavier. Nobody could even think of palming it. There was a rubber bladder inside that would have to be pumped full of air, usually at a gas station. And the outside of the ball was sealed tight with leather laces. The laces were slightly raised from the rest of the surface, so that if you were dribbling and the ball landed on the laces, it wouldn't bounce straight up, and you could easily lose control."

Schectman and his boyhood chums all grew up in poverty on New York's Lower East Side, where the cost of a legitimate basketball was far beyond their means. "Sometimes somebody gave us a worn-out ball," he recalled, "all thin-skinned and shiny. We just taped up all the holes and used it as long as we could. When we didn't have a ball, we used to tape some rags together in the shape of a ball. The gyms in the settlement houses were the only places that had baskets, and when we wanted to play on our own, we had to improvise."

The hoop might be an old laundry basket, a bent-wire clothes hanger nailed to a telephone pole, or, most often, the bottom slot of a fire-escape ladder. "We didn't mind that this goal was square-shaped, vertical to the sidewalk, and perpendicular to the brick wall that served as a backboard," said Schectman. "We were just happy to have someplace to play."

Schectman's peers were the best hoopers of their generation, yet he cited only a handful who would conceivably be able to compete in the modern game. "Joe Fulks, for sure—maybe Connie Simmons and Bud Palmer. We didn't have the size, the agility, or the physicality. Players today also have to be ambidextrous, and we never were. I was a point guard, one of the best ball handlers in the league, and I went left maybe once every game."

Dunking was out of the question. "Who could do such a thing?" Schectman wondered. "Maybe Fulks? George Mikan didn't come into the league until after I was through, but I doubt if he could ever dunk. Besides, if you did dunk the ball, the refs would call you for basket interference."

Schectman also noted other vast differences between those early days and now. "We all ran some form of a figure-eight offense that was predicated on movement, picks, and changes of direction. Before Mikan, most of the centers played the high post and were good shooters and passers. The best pivotman I ever played with was Dolly King, but back then, no blacks were allowed in the league."

Although he didn't categorically criticize young whippersnappers, Schectman did reflect on some basics of the game that the old-timers performed on a higher level. "We moved better without the ball, and we played much smarter. Back then, a good defender could stop a good scorer one-on-one, but that's not possible anymore. I think the way the women play in the WNBA is comparable to the way we played."

Even so, Schectman was a big fan of NBA action and watched the march of the seasons with a joyful heart. "We had a thirty-foot range with our set shots," he said, "so I love the three-point line. I also like the zone defenses, because they force quick ball movement. And I think that the NBA offenses are just terrific. Why go through all the motions when they can get right to the shooting and the one-on-one situations? We needed all the cutting and running around to get open shots, but these guys don't. That's why the present game is so much more exciting."

His hearing might have been diminished, but the years had not darkened his luminous sense of wonder. "When I watch the games on the TV," he said, "I can't help projecting myself into the action. Naturally, I concentrate on the point guards, since that was my position. And it's a thrill to see guys like Mike Bibby and Steve Nash. Their fundamentals are outstanding—footwork, balance, shooting techniques, ballhandling skills. Contrary to what some other old fogies might say, I think their fundamental skills are much better than ours ever were."

Schectman apologized for cutting short the conversation: "There's a game on the TV that I don't want to miss—Sacramento versus Phoenix, my two favorite teams. Believe me, the golden years are terrific as long as it's game time."

Before he hung up, he answered one last question. "Sure, I have regrets," he said. "I wish I could have known how to do a crossover dribble. That really looks like a lot of fun."

Anything else?

"Not really. I always thought I wanted to be able to dribble between my legs, but that's something that started happening on its own about five years ago."

The First Game

dvertisements in the local media hailed the inauguration of "big-league" basketball in Toronto as being the greatest development in Canadian sports since the recent patenting of the Zamboni ice-resurfacing machine.

The blitz began on Monday, October 28, 1946—four days before the Toronto Huskies were scheduled to make their maiden appearance—when a full-page notice appeared in the *Toronto Globe and Mail* encouraging readers to purchase season tickets for all of the Huskies' games while they were still available. "Make no mistake," the ad advised, the Huskies were destined to be the latest sports craze, eventually rivaling the Maple Leafs and the Argonauts, the city's beloved entries in the National Hockey League and the Canadian Football League, respectively. "Get your seats early."

Ticket prices ranged from seventy-five cents to $2.50. But an even bigger notice in Tuesday's *Globe and Mail* presented a photo, spread over three columns, of the Huskies' tallest player, 6′8″ George Nostrand, under a headline asking "Can You Top This?" The come-on was that all fans taller than Nostrand would be admitted to the game free of charge.

Charles Watson represented the corporate owners of the Huskies, a group who also directed the fortunes of the Maple Leaf Gardens as well as the nationally celebrated ice hockey team that played there. To Watson and his bosses, a professional basketball franchise in Toronto seemed like a fabulous idea. After all, wasn't Dr. James Naismith, the inventor of the game, a Canadian? And hadn't he been born in nearby Almonte, Ontario? And wouldn't the Huskies' home schedule add thirty more (hopefully) lucrative dates for the Gardens?

Besides, the war was over. Hitler was dead, and the A-bomb had blown Japan to smithereens. The economy was still booming, the vets were back home, and just about everybody had plenty of spare change to spend on fun and games.

Also, since the Argos and the Leafs always played to standing-room-only crowds, the Huskies offered the only readily available "big-league" sports ticket in town. Even more promising was the fact that the rest of the teams in the newly hatched Basketball Association of America wouldn't commence playing until the following night, November 2, 1946, a prized Saturday date that was already co-opted in Toronto by the Leafs. So, not only would the upcoming roundball contest showcase the first professional basketball game in Toronto (or, for that matter, in Canada), but also it would mark the official onset of the BAA.

How could the Huskies miss?

But even before the visiting New York Knickerbockers crossed the border, they already had their doubts. October 30, 1946, was cold and brisk when their train was halted at the Niagara Falls crossing the routine customs-and-immigration inspections. After completing a cursory check of the Knickerbockers' traveling party, the uniformed officer couldn't help noting their extraordinary size, and he asked one of the players, "What are you?"

The team's coach, Neil Cohalan, proudly responded: "We're the New York Knicks."

The inspector was perplexed. "I'm familiar with the New York Rangers," he said. "Are you anything like them?"

Instantly deflated, Cohalan said, "They play hockey. We play basketball."

Before moving on to the next car, the inspector offered his opinion. "I don't imagine you'll find many people up this way who understand your game—or have an interest in it, either."

Even so, the advance advertising paid immediate dividends, as the opening crowd at the Maple Leaf Gardens numbered an impressive 7,090 (none of whom was taller than Nostrand). Also on hand were Ned Irish, the influential boss of the Knicks, and Maurice Podoloff, the BAA's commissioner.

At eight o'clock, after both teams completed their warm-ups, the Huskies conducted an educational miniclinic wherein they demonstrated the variety of shots the novice fans would be seeing. The repertoire consisted of right- and left-handed layups and hook shots, two-handed set shots, and underhanded free throws. Since none of the players on either team was a practitioner of the newfangled one-handed shots, these were totally ignored.

Adding to the problem that all elements of the game were new to most of the fans on hand, the hometown team was unfamiliar with the court itself. The only time the Huskies had seen the court had been during a brief morning practice, and both the see-through Plexiglas backboards and the playing surface were unusual.

Only a handful of on-campus courts in the States were similarly equipped with the latest development in backboards. Even if they were a boon to the spectators stationed high up in the baseline seats, the glare and lack of a solid shooting background was profoundly distracting to the players.

The court itself was a portable apparatus that had been laid directly on the ice surface. The footing in the practice session had been adequate, but with so large a crowd, the elevated temperature in the building created some condensation on the floorboards, and the surface could be treacherous, particularly near the out-of-bounds lines.

After a few welcoming words from the mayor, the opening tip-off took place on schedule at eight thirty.

The Knicks' coach, Neil Cohalan, was a fixture in New York basketball circles. He'd been a star player at Manhattan College (which was actually situated in the northwestern corner of the Bronx) and had coached the Jaspers from 1929 until he enlisted in the army in 1942. Still, it was common knowledge that Cohalan was only keeping the Knicks' command seat warm until the season was over, when the legendary Joe Lapchick would take over after completing his contractual obligations at St. John's University. Cohalan's drinking problems were no secret either, but since his father was a prestigious member of New York's judiciary, his caretaking assignment was deemed to be a politically savvy move by Ned Irish.

Cohalan's counterpart was "Big Ed" Sadowski, a player-coach who measured an imposing 6'5" and weighed 270 pounds. The small coterie of basketball experts who cared about such things expected that Sadowski, a veteran of several fly-by-night pro leagues that preceded the BAA, would be one of the best players (if not *the* best) in the new league. A scowling brute of a man with close-cropped hair and a game face as belligerent as a clenched fist, Big Ed tallied most of his points with a sweeping right-handed hook shot that was virtually unstoppable. For sure, he was relatively immobile and could shoot only with his right hand; the word was that if Sadowski ever had to feed himself with only his left hand, he'd starve to death. Moreover, playing defense and passing the ball were aspects of the game that Sadowski generally left to his teammates. Still, when he assumed his favorite position deep along the right side of the three-second lane, he was as hard to uproot as the Statue of Liberty.

Indeed, once Sadowski got more familiar with the home team's basketball apparatus, he made two subtle alterations designed to enhance his influence on the game at hand. First, he arranged for the bolts that secured the rims to the backboards to be slightly loosened. Subsequently, the hoops in the Maple Leaf Gardens became renowned as "sewers," where any shot that caught a considerable arc of the rim tended to flop through. Sadowski didn't care that every shot was so generously altered, as long as his were too.

Second, the lower sections of both nets were sufficiently tightened so as to delay the rapid passage of all successful shots. This was done to give Sadowski sufficient time to transport his bulky body to the defensive end of the court, and also to prevent his teammates from quickly inbounding the ball and racing into the attack zone after yielding a score. Instead, they were compelled to play a slowdown style and allow Sadowski to settle into the pivot.

When one of the refs eventually complained about the illegal alterations, Sadowski shrugged and said, "I'm the coach, not the maintenance man."

Since both Cohalan and Sadowski hailed from New York, their teams played similar styles: passing, screening, cutting either to or away from the ball, slicing off the pivot for the old give-and-go, and shooting only the traditional set shots, hooks, and layups. Accordingly, after the Huskies captured the opening tip-off (with the oafish, 6'10" Bob Cluggish failing to outjump Nostrand), the standard weave offense was implemented as each of the Huskies handled the ball (with the notable exception of Sadowski). Round and round the ball went, propelled by simple handoffs or the most basic chest and bounce passes.

Since the basketball was much larger and moved more slowly than a hockey puck, the fans were immediately captivated by the intricate choreography. As in their beloved national game, it was only fitting that the ball/puck was in constant motion while the offense sought to induce the defenders into committing a slight misstep or off-balance reaction.

The Huskies worked the ball for nearly a minute before it wound up in Big Ed's hands. But his inevitable hook shot misfired! The Knickerbockers were quick to snatch the rebound, carefully move the ball across the time line, and then initiate their own version of what was referred to as the "East Coast offense."

Within seconds, Ossie Schectman passed the ball to Leo "Ace" Gottlieb, who executed a convincing up-fake and then bounced a nifty give-and-go pass to a back-cutting Schectman. Ossie needed only one dribble to approach the basket and convert an easy two-handed scoop shot.

It was a historic event, the very first of more than six million points that would eventually be tallied by thousands of BAA-cum-NBA players who would be bigger, better, and richer than Schectman. "All I cared about," Schectman said years later, "was that we were up two to nothing. I mean, it was just another layup."

The Knicks soon extended to a 6–0 lead and led 16–12 at the quarter.

"It was interesting playing before Canadians," said Sonny Hertzberg, a ballhandling whiz in New York's backcourt. "The fans really didn't understand what was going on at first. To them, a jump ball was like a face-off in hockey. But they started to catch on and seemed to like the action."

Part of the action was the antics of the two referees, Pat Kennedy and Nat Messenger. Kennedy was an old-timer, and his energetic miming of the infractions he called was sure to rouse even the most casual fans. To demonstrate a blocking foul, Kennedy would place his hands on his hips and do a bunny hop. "Oh, no you don't!" he'd holler whenever he caught a player committing a particularly egregious violation.

While Messenger wasn't quite the showman that his partner was, he did have his own dramatic flair. Messenger's specialty was to forcefully whack his forearm to illustrate a hacking foul. Later in the season, however, several players would come to suspect that Messenger was fixing the outcome of games in league with big-time gamblers.

The visitors widened their margin to 33–18 in the second quarter, but then Sadowski found the range, and the Huskies rallied to trail by only 37–29 at halftime. Toronto seemed doomed to defeat when Sadowski was whistled for his fifth foul and was thereby disqualified only three minutes into the second half. (Despite the fact that BAA games were eight minutes longer than the forty-minute collegiate contests, the board of directors voted to duplicate the NCAA's five-foul limit. Their reasoning was that increasing the number of allowable fouls would lead to indiscriminant mayhem.)

The elongated Nostrand replaced Sadowski and led the Huskies in a stirring comeback that ignited the crowd. His layup provided the Huskies' initial lead of the game at 44–43, and Toronto actually forged ahead 48–44 at the next quarter break.

The final period was both ragged and rugged, primarily because the refs decided to silently suck on their whistles and let the players play. As the game raced to the wire, the fans began chanting the name of the only Canadian on the Huskies' roster. "Bi-a-satti! Bi-a-satti!"

In truth, Hank Biasatti was a 6'4", 200-pound graduate of nearby Assumption College who had played briefly in several local amateur basketball leagues but gained a certain degree of fame thereabouts as a hard-hitting first baseman for Windsor (Ontario) in a low-level pro baseball league. Yielding to the fans' wishes, however, Sadowski inserted Biasatti into the fray with three minutes remaining.

This turned out to be a bad idea. Biasatti's only contribution was some inadequate defense as the Knicks rallied behind a pair of field goals by Dick Murphy and a free throw by Tommy Byrnes in the final two and a half minutes.

At the buzzer, the Knicks had won by 68–66. Gottlieb led the victors with 14 points, and despite his abbreviated playing time, Sadowski registered a game-high total of 18 points.

The Toronto sportswriters were puzzled by the game, identifying Sadowski's fouls as "roughing" and "cross-checking." Even so, the Huskies' management counted the gate receipts and dared to hope that both their franchise and the fledgling league would be a huge success.

Genesis

Elsewhere in the sports world, the start of the BAA roused little enthusiasm. That's because the basketball landscape had been littered with the tattered remains of flimsy professional leagues for nearly fifty years.

The first identifiable play-for-pay outfit was the Trenton Basket Ball Team. Making their inaugural appearance on November 7, 1896, nearly five years after the original Dr. J, James Naismith, had invented the game, the Trentons beat the amateur Brooklyn YMCA, 16–1, and were probably paid $5 each.

After barnstorming the Northeast competing against club, YMCA, college, and various pro-come-lately teams, the Trentons became a charter member of what was the first all-pro organization, the National Basketball League (1898–1904). The other teams were based in Pennsylvania, Delaware, and New Jersey, along with the New York Wanderers, who played all of their games on the road.

Playing as the Trenton Nationals, these pioneer pros were famous for their passing and overall teamwork. None of the league's aficionados were surprised when Trenton won the first championship with a record of 18–2.

Other pro leagues were soon organized in the Northeast corridor, the most prestigious being the Philadelphia Basket Ball League (1902–1909), the Central Basket Ball League (1906–1912), the Eastern League (1909–1918, 1919–1923), the Hudson River League (1909–1912), the New York State League (1911–1917, 1919–1923), the Pennsylvania State League (1914–1918, 1919–1921), the Interstate Basket Ball League (1915–1917, 1919–1920), the Metropolitan Basketball League (1921–1928, 1932–1933), and the first incarnation of the American Basketball League (1926–1931).

These ephemeral leagues were plagued with profound difficulties, mostly arising from poor organization and insufficient funding. For example, in the absence of binding contracts, players routinely jumped from team to team, selling themselves to the highest bidder, oftentimes right before a game. Within the same league, some players performed for as many as five different teams each season. Nor was it unusual for entire teams to jump from one league to another. The most damaging result of the unstable rosters was that fans were unable to maintain a rooting interest in their local ball clubs, and attendance inevitably dwindled as each season progressed.

The early pro rules allowed two-handed discontinued dribbles, which enabled players to simply bull their way to the basket. Head-butting a defender was deemed a savvy move. Also, with the aim of speeding up the game and preventing hometown fans sitting courtside from abusing visiting players with cigar butts and hat pins, most venues surrounded the court with some type of wire enclosure—either a self-supporting fence or a metal or rope "cage" that hung from the ceiling. Shoving an opponent into the fence was standard operating procedure. And since the ball was therefore always in bounds, the action was continuous and continually brutal—so much so that the lone referee who worked these games often chose to remain outside the cage, entering only to hand the ball to free-throw shooters before making a hasty exit. In lieu of handling the ball for center jumps after each score, the ball would be tossed into the cage just as a zookeeper might throw a chunk of meat to caged lions.

Adding to the mayhem was the fact that free throws were awarded only if a player was fouled while shooting. All other fouls resulted in side-outs, with the player who was inbounding the ball being compelled to have his back against the cage while making his pass—a risky undertaking for visiting players.

Overall, the pro game was mostly an exercise in brute force and dirty tricks that appealed only to the most bloodthirsty of sports fans. Old-timers compared it to ice hockey played on wood and without skates. The college game, on the other hand, was cleaner and, because of the emphasis on finesse, was considered to be much more skillful than the pro version.

The inauguration of the BAA was also largely ignored in the sports media because two other quasi-stable pro leagues were already in operation: a resurrection of the ABL (which resumed play in 1933) and the much more popular National Basketball League (which had been reincarnated in 1937).

In any case, the vast majority of Sports America viewed professional cagers as at best mercenaries and at worse prostitutes, especially when compared with the squeaky-clean, boola-boola college players. How ironic, then, that the increasing popularity of the college game ultimately provided the impetus for the creation of the BAA.

In January 1931, during the darkest days of the Depression, Mayor Jimmy Walker's Committee for the Relief of the Unemployed and Needy asked several New York sportswriters to find a way to raise some money. The result was a basketball triple-header at the relatively new Madison Square Garden (it opened for business in 1925 with a seating capacity of 18,000) involving six metropolitan colleges. The event drew 14,500 and raised $24,000 for the cause. The rousing success created a mild sensation but was considered to be a onetime event (although private promoters subsequently staged a handful of triple-headers for their own profit).

At the time, Ned Irish was a twenty-seven-year-old sportswriter for the *New York World-Telegram* earning $48.60 per week. Even though his arched eyebrows gave the impression that he was perpetually on the verge of astonishment, Irish was a hardheaded realist with an incisive mind.

Although he was never even a modest athlete, sports always fascinated Irish. He began writing about fun and games as a freshman in Erasmus Hall High School, in his native Brooklyn. By his senior year, he was the Brooklyn correspondent for so many metropolitan newspapers that his income often approached $100 a week.

Irish's next stop was the University of Pennsylvania, where his ambition began to expand even more. Among his part-time activities were the creation of a student employment agency; writing for the daily on-campus newspaper, *The Pennsylvanian*, as well as the undergraduate literary publication, *The Red and the Blue*; plus serving as the Philadelphia sports correspondent for most of the New York papers. He joined the *World-Telegram* immediately after graduating from Penn's Wharton School of Finance in 1928.

But Irish's ambitions were an itch that still needed scratching. Simultaneous with his duties at the *World-Telegram*, he held two other jobs—as publicity director for what was then referred to as the New York Football Giants, and as the lead man in the National Football League Press Bureau. All kinds of big-time schemes were dancing in and out of his dreams, when one chilly evening in February 1933, Irish was assigned to cover a basketball game between Manhattan and NYU at the Jaspers' tiny gym high on a hill overlooking Van Cortland Park.

Irish and several of his peers arrived at the gym an hour before game time, only to find that 1,800 fans had already filled the stands, and there were a like number clamoring for entrance. The only response the harassed

Manhattan authorities could think of was to lock the front door. When the scribes' pounding and shouts proved fruitless, Irish had an idea: "Maybe we could sneak in through a window in the athletic office."

They all scrambled to the far side of the building and rapped on the appropriate window and were soon pleased to see several of their safely ensconced compatriots come over to investigate the racket. Faces were recognized, laughter ensued, and the window was quickly pried open from the inside. However, as Irish clambered through the small opening, he ripped his pants on a protruding screw. Even worse, the only perch he could find from which to watch the game was atop a steaming radiator. Even though he twitched, fidgeted, and tried changing positions throughout the game, his pants suffered the further indignity of being scorched.

Everett Morris reported on sports for the *Herald-Tribune* and was renowned for his temper. Noting the damage done to Irish's trousers, Morris finally erupted. "This fool game is getting too big for its britches," he thundered. "Every gym in the city is hopelessly inadequate. Someone ought to do something about it."

His compatriots all raised their voices in agreement, but it was Irish who had sufficient daring, acumen, and resourcefulness to make a move. Shortly thereafter, he called upon General John Reed Kilpatrick, the president of Madison Square Garden, and presented his case for renting the arena and staging a college doubleheader.

Irish had no difficulty in convincing Kilpatrick of the popularity of college basketball. He further reasoned that New York's entertainment seekers were used to baseball and hockey games, Broadway shows, and downtown movies that lasted up to three hours. A college basketball game ran only ninety minutes tops, but a doubleheader would give the patrons a satisfactory value for their money. Irish also argued that triple-headers were unwieldy, took too long, and would quickly exhaust the intracity rivalries.

The General was won over and, after some juggling of dates, agreed to rent the facility to Irish for the bargain price of $4,000. As part of the deal, the four colleges would split 50 percent of the net proceeds, while Irish and the Garden would share the rest.

Tim Mara, the owner of the Giants, bowed to the same arguments and readily advanced Irish the necessary front money. Irish immediately quit the newspaper, yet he held fast to his football jobs.

Irish's first promotion occurred on December 29, 1934, and eventuated in NYU's beating Notre Dame by 25–18, and Westminster's (Pennsylvania) downing St. John's, 37–33. More significantly, 16,180 fans came through the turnstiles. Irish's profit was estimated as being in the neighborhood of $3,000—a hefty return in the depths of the Depression.

His buddies in press row dubbed Irish "the boy promoter," even as they resented his suddenly terminating whatever personal friendships that had developed over the years. Sure, Irish was a genius destined for who knew what heights of organizational and financial celebrity, but he had also become a snob.

In the next few years, Irish was staging as many as seven doubleheaders per season with the same lucrative results. Irish's particular brainstorm was to import the best teams nationwide to compete against powerful local squads from NYU, CCNY, St. John's, Fordham, and LIU. Not that intersectional games hadn't been played before—Yale had toured the Midwest in the late nineteenth century—but Irish organized and glamorized the process. His pairing of LIU and Stanford University in December 1936 was historic. That's because the visitors' star player was Angelo "Hank" Luisetti, who scored points in bunches with a radical one-handed push shot that alarmed basketball traditionalists. With Luisetti registering 15 points, Stanford terminated LIU's forty-three-game winning streak with a rousing 45–31 victory.

Encouraged by his burgeoning successes, Irish branched out and began booking doubleheaders at Convention Hall in Philadelphia and in the Convention Center in Buffalo. To no surprise, promoters in Boston and Cleveland sought to duplicate Irish's box-office bonanzas. So it was that college squads from the outlands could make lengthy cross-country tours for considerable guaranteed fees. In fact, shortly after stunning the Garden crowd, Stanford played in Cleveland, where, under coach Johnny Bunn's order, Luisetti was force-fed the ball by his cooperative teammates and tallied an outlandish total of 50 points.

In addition to the universal banishment of the cages in the early twenties (which led to the addition of a second referee), two other subsequent developments succeeded in lifting the popularity of the college game into orbit. Prior to 1937, each made basket was followed by a center jump, during which the game clock kept running. The delays encountered by all the players and referees convening at center court and jockeying for position greatly limited and slowed the available action. The elimination of the center jump quickened the pace, encouraged fast breaks, and gave trailing teams more of an opportunity to close their deficit.

The following year, the Metropolitan Basketball Writers Association purloined one of Irish's long-standing concepts and sponsored a postseason championship tournament that featured six out-of-town teams along with NYU and LIU. Played entirely at MSG, this initial National Invitational Tournament was won by Temple, 60–36, over a Colorado squad that starred Byron "Whizzer" White, an all-American football player and future Supreme Court justice. The NIT was such a hit that the National Collegiate Athletic Association (NCAA) followed suit a year later, playing its tournament in the more collegial environs of Evanston, Illinois.

When General Kilpatrick was recalled to active duty in 1946, Irish succeeded him as president of "the World's Greatest Arena." Indeed, the lure and aura of the Garden were so strong that the NCAA moved its championship contests there in 1943 (where they remained until the betting scandals erupted in 1951).

Concurrent with this ascension, Irish was now the most powerful sports promoter in the most important city in the country. His ambitions sated, Irish was content to defend his perimeter and continue to do business as usual.

Meanwhile, Max Kase, the sports editor of the *New York Journal-American*, watched the growth of Irish's empire with a keen eye and a greedy fascination. Kase was born in Yonkers in 1898 (only seven years after basketball was invented), and his longtime residence in the fourth estate included stints at the *New York Mail*, the International News Service, the *Havana Telegram*, and the *Boston American*. During his career, his trademark widow's peak and devilish smile were seen at every conceivable sporting event from basketball to baseball, from football to ice hockey, from rodeos to bullfights, from six-day bicycle races to flagpole-sitting contests, as well as boxing and wrestling matches, dog shows, and track meets. Along the way, he'd met and befriended everybody who was worth knowing.

Nor was Kase afraid to go against the grain. Ever since he'd eyeballed that historic triple-header at MSG back in 1931, Kase harbored the idea that, properly organized, advertised, and financed, professional basketball could likewise be a big winner. In 1944, he had gone so far as to become involved in promoting a matchup between two outstanding barnstorming outfits at Manhattan Center, a small auditorium on Thirty-fourth Street whose modest seating capacity was augmented with folding chairs. The proceeds were donated to war relief, but even Kase was astounded at the huge overflow crowd. The event finally convinced him that the time was ripe to develop a pro league with New York as its keystone franchise.

Kase well knew that there had been previous attempts to establish pro basketball in New York. In 1921, a boxing promoter named Tex Rickard arranged several games between two of the city's most elite barnstorming pro teams, the Original Celtics and the Whirlwinds. The contests, played at Madison Square Garden, averaged nearly 10,000 paying customers. Rickard was so encouraged that he took over the Whirlwinds and began arranging games against other outstanding pro teams—such as the Camden Bullets, champions of the Eastern League. But without the attraction of the Celtics, the crowds diminished to the point where the Whirlwinds' games were exiled to various small-time armories scattered throughout the city. After a year of red ink, Rickard disbanded the team.

In the early days of the American Basketball League, the New York Jewels attracted a modicum of both fans and attention, but the flavor didn't last long. The Jewels were succeeded in the ever-faltering ABL by the New York Original Celtics, Yankees, Americans, and Gothams. All of these ventures eventually faded into oblivion.

Even so, Kase was determined to remain faithful to his dream. From his time in Boston (1934–1938), Kase had made the acquaintance of Walter A. Brown, who was president of (among several other enterprises) the Boston Garden. Kase knew that Brown was also an influential member of the Arena Managers Association of America (AMAA), a group that had been tentatively interested in fashioning a professional basketball circuit, mostly as a way of turning on the lights in their buildings when the other regular (ice hockey) and periodic (just about every other attraction) events were not available.

For a pro league in any sport to have even an outside chance of succeeding, it would need to have a strong franchise in New York. Accordingly, Kase's plan was to rent Madison Square Garden and operate this golden franchise himself. But unknown to Kase, the AMAA had an informal "if any, all" agreement stipulating that no one arena could get involved with a pro basketball league without the others participating. Still, Brown was receptive to Kase's arguments, and even interested, but while the war was still raging, nothing came of their meeting.

Not in any way discouraged, Kase continued his periodic discussions with Brown and pressed on. Kase proceeded to work up prospective operating plans for his chimerical league and even entered into negotiation with Nat Holman—who had been the most famous of the Original Celtics and was currently coaching at CCNY—to coach the New York entry in whatever pro league Kase would eventually organize.

Finally, in the spring of 1946, with the war done and won, Brown was ready to make a move.

His father, Walter V. Brown, had been the first president of the Boston Garden Corporation and the first director of athletics at Boston University. Thus, when Walter A. Brown entered the game of life on February 10, 1905 (in Hopkinton, Massachusetts), he was destined to be involved with the local sports scene. After graduating from Boston Latin (1923) and Phillips Exeter Academy (1926), young Walter eagerly joined his father in running the Garden.

Despite his impressive titles, Walter V. was far from being a wealthy man. For sure, there were some stock market investments (that would barely survive the onset of the Depression), but not enough to keep the Browns from working diligently to keep the Garden filled with paying customers. Father and son enjoyed sharing the load, and life was good.

Then, in the summer of 1930, Walter V. suddenly died of heart failure. His twenty-five-year-old son was forced to take over the operation of the Boston Garden.

Nobody was surprised when young Walter showed a remarkable aptitude for the job. With his prematurely receding hairline and his engaging smile, Brown looked like an honest man. And, indeed, honesty was his only policy.

Back then, the Garden's most regular attraction was the Boston Bruins, and it was inevitable that Brown's primary interest was ice hockey. Never a player himself, he nevertheless coached the amateur Boston Olympics to five Eastern Hockey League championships and, in 1933, guided a team (largely composed of Boston-area hockey players) to a gold medal at the Ice Hockey World Championship in Prague, Czechoslovakia. Brown also served as manager of the 1936 U.S. Olympic hockey squad.

If track meets, bicycle races, and rodeos were high-cost ventures that usually operated at a loss, any sport or performance that played on ice seemed to be a surefire moneymaker, so Brown invented the Ice Capades and even had a ski jump erected inside the Garden. Indoor ski jumping proved to be exciting and tremendously profitable, but it had a serious drawback: the jumpers had difficulty landing within the designated area and repeatedly overshot the mark and crashed onto the ice. While the fans loved the action, the oft-injured practitioners quickly lost interest, and the event was short lived.

Throughout the war (Brown was classified 4-F because of his flat feet), the AMAA continued to meet and try to generate more moneymaking attractions that could fill the members' arenas. As with Brown, his partners were heavily invested in ice hockey and ice-borne attractions. Seven of the thirteen members were exclusively associated with the American Hockey League (AHL), the top minor league. These were the following:

Lou Pieri, who ran the Rhode Island Reds and the Providence Arena and was a close personal friend of Brown's

Pete Tyrell, who ran the Philadelphia Arena and the Philadelphia Rockets

John Harris, who headed the Pittsburgh Hornets as well as the Duquesne Garden

Dick Miller, who was in charge of the Indianapolis Capitols and the Indianapolis Coliseum

Al Sutphin, who owned the Cleveland Barons and the Cleveland Arena

James Allinger, overseer of the Buffalo Bisons and the Coliseum

Emory P. Jones, who was in charge of the day-to-day operation of the St. Louis Arena and the St. Louis Flyers

Five members—situated in Chicago, New York, Boston, Detroit, and Toronto—were associated with National Hockey League (NHL) franchises and the venues that housed them. The thirteenth member, Mike Uline, oversaw the fortunes of the Uline Arena, in Washington, D.C., the only building that had no resident professional hockey team.

Because of his successes in promoting college basketball (along with the NHL's New York Rangers) in Madison Square Garden, Ned Irish was a power broker among his peers. When Kase approached Irish to propose a rental agreement, the boy promoter demurred. Not only did Irish refuse to rent MSG to Kase, but also he was reluctant to get his own organization involved in such a huge gamble. After all, in the recent 1945–46 season, the Garden had hosted twenty-one regular-season college doubleheaders, the NIT, the NCAA tournament, and the East-West College All-Star Game. The total attendance had been 527,699, and Irish felt that basketball interest in New York was already on the verge of being saturated.

Irish also informed Kase about the "if one, all" proviso and added that the Garden would necessarily have to own any team that would play there. Kase was crestfallen. All of his dreams and his plans had come to nothing. Eventually, Irish would pay Kase several thousand dollars to compensate the sportswriter for his efforts.

Despite Irish's stature and Brown's enthusiasm, the true founding father of the BAA was Arthur Wirtz, who actually had a hand in both hockey leagues.

The co-owner (with Jim Norris and his progeny) of the Chicago Black Hawks and the Chicago Stadium, as well as the Detroit Olympia and the Detroit Red Wings, Wirtz was also the outright owner of the St. Louis Arena and the AHL St. Louis Flyers. It was Wirtz and the Norrises' attorney, Arthur Morse, who made the important decisions concerning all three teams and all three buildings.

Once Brown spread the word of Max Kase's legitimizing passion and gave his own imprimatur, the genial Al Sutphin simply took over. Sutphin was a multimillionaire whose primary source of income was a factory that produced ink for commercial uses (mostly for newspapers and magazines), and he was eager to bring a new sporting venture into the Cleveland Arena. The Cleveland Rams of the National Football League had just relocated to Los Angeles, a move that Sutphin believed created a seasonal vacuum that would compel the area's rabid sports fans to flock to his building and support a pro basketball team.

Sutphin zeroed in on Arthur Wirtz and his operations in Chicago, Detroit, and St. Louis. Wirtz was instantly amenable, and with Morse's approval, the Norris family quickly agreed that the risks were worth taking. By late spring of 1946, all the other members of the AMAA were likewise in the mix.

The next steps would be to find a commissioner for their as yet unformed and unnamed league and to convene a meeting for the purpose of composing a workable constitution.

4

The Penguin, the Mogul, and the Constitution

A round, pudgy man who exaggerated when he claimed to be five feet tall, Maurice Podoloff was born in 1890, "in a little settlement about seventy-five miles from Kiev," he said. When he was three months old, his parents immigrated from Russia to "the golden land, where the streets were paved with gold." He recalled, "We lived for a year on the east side of New York and then for four years in Setauket, a suburb of Port Jefferson, where my brothers David and Jacob were born. My father worked in a shop making sneakers."

Abraham Podoloff soon tired of working for somebody else and longed to relocate somewhere where he'd eventually be able to start his own business. He also harbored another driving ambition: that his sons would get the best education that their new homeland could offer. After learning about the glories of what was then known as the Yale Academy, the family relocated to New Haven, Connecticut.

They arrived in town via ferry, and Abraham left his family at the waterfront and immediately set out to find a business he could call his own. "The business he found was selling kerosene," said the eldest son, "which was the source of all cooking and illumination at the time. The equipment he acquired included an antiquated horse, a covered wagon containing five gallon cans, and a residence on DeWitt Street."

Gradually, the business prospered to the point where Abraham sold it for a considerable profit. He then began a real estate company that shared a suite of offices with Samuel J. Nathanson, a lawyer. Another of Podoloff's ambitions came to pass when Maurice was accepted into Yale in 1909. Six years later, Maurice graduated from the Yale Law School and was immediately sworn in as a member of the Connecticut State Bar, upon which he was accepted into Nathanson's law firm.

"After some four or five years of practicing law," Maurice said, "I joined my father in the real estate business, moving from one side of the suite to the other. A. Podoloff and Sons, Real Estate and Insurance, was really quite successful. My father was semiretired; my brother Jacob took care of the insurance, and I did a land-office business in the care of twenty-two apartment buildings."

A key to the Podoloffs' success was the brothers' opportunity to act as "beards" for New Haven's Catholic Diocese. When the Church wanted to buy property in and around town without attracting attention, the Podoloffs would undertake the transactions in their own names. The money thusly earned enabled the Podoloffs to gain a controlling interest in the Industrial Bank of New Haven.

Eventually, upon the suicide of one Harry Walker—renowned as the "Ice King"—who couldn't compete with the advent of artificially made ice, the Podoloffs were able to purchase, and then complete, a partially erected building that was blueprinted to contain an ice rink as well as the capacity to store sixty-five tons of naturally cut ice. A significant inducement was that the Yale hockey team had already signed a contract obligating the team to pay $20,000 for a seven-year lease on the ice rink for its practice sessions and intercollegiate games.

With the elimination of the state's notorious blue laws that prohibited the staging of any and all sporting events on Sundays, the New Haven Arena soon became the residence of the New Haven Americans in the Canadian-American League, which was a farm system to the NHL. To turn on the lights on other nights, a portable basketball court (which could be laid atop the ice in thirty-five minutes) was built to host college games.

Because Maurice was the oldest of the four Podoloff brothers (the youngest, Nathan, had been born before the Great War), he became the "governor" of the Americans. Al Sutphin owned and operated the highly successful franchise in Cleveland and was particularly appreciative of Podoloff's business acumen. Podoloff was named secretary-treasurer of the C-A League in 1935, and a year later—almost entirely due to Sutphin's lobbying—he became the league's president. Concurrent with Podoloff's new responsibilities, the C-A League underwent a name change and became the American Hockey League.

To the surprise of none of the businessmen involved, the AHL thrived under Podoloff's guidance. Even so, his round, squat physique and his rolling walk inevitably earned him a nickname that was never uttered in his presence—the Penguin.

Fast-forward to the spring of 1946. Before Arthur Wirtz gave his final approval to join Sutphin's proposed venture into pro basketball, the subject of a league president arose. Sutphin revealed that he had offered the job to Asa Bushnell, who was once the czar of the Olympic Games and was currently the overseer of the Eastern Collegiate Athletic Conference. Wirtz was distressed when told that Bushnell wanted a long-term contract at $25,000 per year.

"What kind of job is Maurice Podoloff doing in the AHL?" Wirtz wanted to know.

"A good job," was Sutphin's response.

"If Podoloff takes the job," Wirtz instantly decided, "then all of my teams and all of my buildings are in."

The very next day, Sutphin and Podoloff met in New York. "Even though I told Al that I knew absolutely nothing about basketball," Podoloff said, "they hired me for eight or nine thousand dollars—I forget exactly."

At the time, Podoloff had personally witnessed only one basketball game. "A Yale game," he said, "that's for certain, but I can't recall who the opponent was. I do remember, however, that Tony Lavelli was the star of the Yale team. He was a hook-shot artist, but I was more impressed by the fact that he was a virtuoso of the accordion. In fact, Lavelli later left the NBA to concentrate on his musical career."

Nor did Podoloff ever issue any apologies about his ignorance of the game. He maintained, "When I became the president of the BAA, everything I knew about basketball wouldn't have filled the bottom of a thimble. And when I retired from the job seventeen years later, I still didn't know anything about the game itself."

Why then was he hired? "I had complete integrity," he said, "and I also had a heart."

With the titular head now in place, the organizational meeting was set for June 16, 1946, at the Hotel Commodore on East Forty-second Street, adjacent to Grand Central Station. Twelve arena owners (or the owner's representative) were present, the most vocal being Sutphin, Wirtz, Ned Irish, and Walter Brown. Podoloff came to the meeting armed with a tentative set of bylaws that was modeled after the AHL's constitution, but its adjustment and adoption would come at an August meeting.

For now, only the most general items were addressed. The new venture would indeed be called the "Basketball Association of America." Also, Podoloff's contract as president was unanimously approved. Some of the partners wanted to identify Podoloff as the league's "commissioner," but he didn't like the idea. "*Commissioner*," he said, "sounded too much like *commissar* and was too suggestive of czarist Russia to suit me." Podoloff was also allowed to continue as president of the AHL.

It was likewise agreed that teams would be named after the cities in which they played, and not after industrial companies (as was the case in the NBL). The entry fee for each franchise was $10,000, with the money earmarked for any expenses incurred by the league office as well as Podoloff's salary.

It was taken for granted that the players would be full-time employees, and the salary limit for each team was set at $40,000 for a ten-man squad (this would later be raised to $55,000). There was no ceiling on what franchises could pay for a coach or a trainer.

Thirteen franchises were awarded. In the Eastern Division were Boston, Buffalo, New York, Philadelphia, Providence, and Washington. The Western Division would comprise Chicago, Cleveland, Detroit, Indianapolis, Pittsburgh, and St. Louis. Because of anticipated transportation complications, the placing of Toronto remained undecided.

Each team would play a forty-five-game schedule (later amended to sixty games). The season would commence play on November 2, 1946.

At the time, the only top-level sport that conducted postseason playoffs to determine a champion was the NHL. In baseball and in the NFL, the top finishers in the two divisions (or leagues) vied for the overall championship. Accordingly, the idea of non-first-place finishers being allowed to compete for a championship was considered to be bush league and had therefore been shunned by the other preceding and contemporaneous pro basketball leagues. Nevertheless, for indoor sports with limited capacities and limited gate receipts, postseason tournaments were absolutely necessary. Playoff prize money was also deemed essential to maintain the players' enthusiasm during the long season.

However, the playoff plan established by the BAA was ludicrous. The two first-place finishers in the Eastern and Western Divisions would meet in a seven-game series, with the winner earning a bye into the championship series. Meanwhile, the second-place and third-place finishers in each division would face off in sets of three-game series, with the ultimate survivor then meeting the winner of the first-place series for the championship. The absurdity of so quickly eliminating one of the season-long divisional winners wasn't considered.

The distribution of gate receipts was also resolved. Ned Irish insisted that, at least during the regular season, the home team would not be obliged to share the gate receipts with the visiting team. Cowed by his reputation as a promotional genius, the others readily concurred. This was the first instance of Irish's using his awareness of the importance of his bellwether franchise, and the expected throngs his team would draw to Madison Square Garden, to impose his will on the majority. The teams agreed that 5 percent of the gate receipts would be sent to the league office to offset any unforeseen expenses.

Another meeting was scheduled for August 19, in which the disbursement of playoff income would be considered and, most important, Podoloff's proposed constitution would be debated and fine-tuned.

Resplendent in a double-breasted blue suit and bright floral necktie that matched his trademark red suspenders, Podoloff called the meeting to order at ten A.M. Most of the franchise owners sent trustworthy representatives, which included lawyers, minority stockholders, and one prospective coach. The list of those present was read aloud by Podoloff:

James Morris, Detroit
Al Sutphin, Cleveland
Ned Irish, New York
Dick Miller, Indianapolis
Walter Brown, Boston
M. J. Uline, Washington
Joseph Fay, Providence
Harold Shannon, Toronto
James Allinger, Buffalo
Eddie Gottlieb, Philadelphia
Emery Jones, St. Louis
Morris Hart, Chicago
James Balmer, Pittsburgh

Of this group, Ned Irish had an excellent working knowledge of basketball promotion and advertising, as did Gottlieb, but the latter was the only participant who also had an Xs-and-Os understanding of the game. For more than twenty-five years, Eddie Gottlieb (no relation to Leo "Ace" Gottlieb) had been well known to the sports public at large as the builder of great basketball teams.

Born in New York City in 1899, Gottlieb grew up with an unbridled enthusiasm for whatever sport happened to be in season. "I was only a little shaver," he recalled, "and I would hitch rides on the back of ice trucks to watch the New York Giants play in the Polo Grounds."

The family moved to Philadelphia when he was nine years old, and in 1913 he entered South Philadelphia High School, where he played varsity football and basketball as well as junior varsity baseball. "There were only two things I couldn't do in baseball," he said, "hit and throw. I was quarterback on the football team only because I was the only guy who could remember the signals." If his athletic prowess lacked distinction, Gottlieb demonstrated a keen mind for numbers and could work out complex mathematical problems without using pencil and paper.

Upon his graduation in 1916, Gottlieb's next stops were the Philadelphia School of Pedagogy (where he once scored 26 points in an intramural basketball game) and then Temple University. With his degrees in hand, Gottlieb taught physical education at a local elementary school for three years before moving on to become a sporting-goods salesman.

Still, he considered these jobs to be only way stations while he pursued his primary ambition—to play and coach basketball. In the process, he played anywhere for any team that would have him. And because he spoke with such confidence about bounce passes, backdoor cuts, and one-footed changes of direction, he was often allowed to coach.

As a hedge against the stark necessities of having to live in the real world, Gottlieb also got involved with promoting as many sporting events in as many venues as possible—wrestling, boxing, and the like—in various armories and dance halls around town. "Because," he said, "that's where the money was."

Gottlieb's dreams began coming true in 1918, when Harry Passon and Hughie Black organized the South Philadelphia Hebrew Association basketball team, nicknamed the Sphas. At their invitation, Gottlieb served as player-coach until 1925, when a hand injury forced him to retire to the bench. "That's also when I quit my job at the sporting-goods store," Gottlieb said, "and devoted myself full-time to coaching the Sphas." Under Gottlieb's passionate guidance, the Sphas quickly became one of the most formidable teams in the East.

In those days, the sport was trying to survive as the prelude to dances. For the Sphas, the scene of these double features was the grand ballroom of the Broadwood Hotel, where the admission was sixty-five cents for men and thirty-five cents for women. The Sphas would play at eight-thirty, and the women would be allowed in at eleven for the dance. Even as he coached the game, Gottlieb would simultaneously count the house.

"Many of the Jewish people wouldn't let their daughters go to an ordinary dance," he said, "except when the Sphas were the opening event. I remember one of my players, Gil Fitch, getting out of his uniform after the third quarter and not having enough time for a shower; he put on a suit, climbed onto the stage, and led his band to kick off the dancing. Kitty Kallen got her start singing with Fitch's band."

Gottlieb was always trying out different ways to draw crowds. One of his brainstorms was to have his publicity man, Dave Zinkoff, compose, print, and distribute a free, numbered program for each game. "There'd be a gossip column," Zinkoff recalled. "Who was dancing with whom. The players were listed, and so was the playlist for that night's dance. The back page featured a big ad for one of Philadelphia's most popular men's clothing stores, and for every game, a lucky number was picked, with the winner getting a free nineteen-dollar suit from the store. One guy was so happy when his number came up that he ran over to me and said that with his new suit, he could now get married."

A lifelong bachelor, Gottlieb began his flirtation with promoting wrestling matches and semipro football and baseball contests in 1928, and he was soon responsible for handling all the bookings and business transactions for the Negro American Baseball League. Through it all, however, he was married to basketball.

Later, Gottlieb also coached various editions of the Sphas in the American Basketball League starting with the 1933–34 season, when they were known as the Philadelphia Hebrews. The Sphas would continue in the ABL, under Gottlieb's ownership but without his day-to-day involvement, until 1949.

By the spring of 1946, Gottlieb was celebrated along the Northeast corridor as "the Mogul." He was rather corpulent, measuring 5'8" and 220 pounds, and he tried to enliven his sad eyes and pasty skin by always wearing a bright red bow tie. Gottlieb was also famous for his sense of humor, his parsimony, and his hatred of referees. "I'm not a referee baiter," he insisted. "I just stand up for my rights. And I've gotta yell to make myself heard above the crowd noise."

So, in large part, it would be Gottlieb's know-how that set the tone for this historical gathering of ambitious millionaires.

Before the question of the constitution could be addressed, however, James Balmer relayed an objection to the very name of the new league. "Harry Keck is the sports editor of all the Hearst newspapers," Balmer said, "and he thinks the name of our organization is off base. He said it sounds like we're a minor league of one of baseball's top minor leagues, the American Association."

Not wanting to risk being ridiculed by the formidable Hearst chain, the attendees put forward other possibilities. Of these, the Major Basketball League of America, the United States Basketball League, and the United States Basketball Association were deemed inappropriate because they failed to give the "proper recognition to Toronto." The North American Basketball League was rejected because the name wouldn't easily fit into newspaper headlines. Reflecting an attempt to emphasize the big-time aspirations of their project, Major Basketball League and Major Basketball Association were also proposed. Eventually, it was agreed to let the original name stand, with a final decision delayed until the convening of another meeting at an unspecified date and location.

Returning to the agenda, in his preliminary remarks concerning the transformation of the AHL's constitution to the BAA's needs, Podoloff read the following excerpt concerning the right of each team to regulate its own affairs: "These powers shall include all questions of intemperance, carelessness, indifference, or other conduct on or off the ice playing surface that may be regarded by the member as prejudicial to its interests. . . ."

For the moment, Podoloff advised those reading along with him to "cross out the word *ice* and leave *playing surface*." Later developments would make this phrase extremely ironic.

Next up was a consideration of the geographical restrictions that would apply to any new franchises that might seek admission into the league in the future. It was proposed that "A franchise shall not be granted or transferred to be operated in a building within a radius of fifty miles of the building of a member of the Association without the consent of such member." Since the distance between Boston and Providence was only forty-one miles, both franchises agreed to their mutual encroachment. Another exception was made for the Knicks, since an application from a group that hoped to establish a team in Brooklyn was expected within two years.

Irish, who was zealous of his domain, was reluctant to agree to this exception. He insisted that he had the right to veto any future franchise in the borough of Queens, or in nearby Jersey City, or Trenton, or wherever. That's when Gottlieb spoke up, saying that Baltimore, for example, was only forty miles from Washington, and how could the league reasonably disallow the establishment of a new franchise in such a large market? And what would happen, Gottlieb queried, if one of the charter franchises happened to relocate? Would the same veto power also be relocated? Gottlieb foresaw the time when new, viable franchises would be prohibited from joining the BAA because of this geographical limitation.

Podoloff objected to all the nitpicking, saying, "We are going too far afield." In any case, Gottlieb's comments created many more questions than answers, so this issue was also tabled.

Only then did the discussion turn to defining Podoloff's presidential powers. In the end, his powers as titular head of the AHL were rubber-stamped. That meant that Podoloff would be the final arbiter of all playing rules. He also had the power to suspend "for a definite or indefinite period" or impose a fine not exceeding $1,000 upon any manager, player, or coach who misbehaved either "in or outside of the playing arena." Individual clubs could face similar fines for being adjudged "guilty of conduct prejudicial or detrimental" to the BAA. The president was also given "extraordinary powers" to cope with undefined "emergency situations."

However, paragraph 31 laid out exactly who ran the league: "The Board shall also have the power to consider any appeal from the decision of the President and shall establish such rules and regulations for the conduct of the appeal as it may consider fair and reasonable, and its judgment shall be final and binding."

Podoloff could oversee discipline, the rules of play, and all the other workaday functions of the league. At any time, though, the owners—that is, the board of governors—could change and override any decision made by Podoloff in order to suit their own purposes.

The board then finalized the procedures by which 5 percent of all gate receipts would be remanded to the league office. It was further proposed that all of the net profits gained from playoff games would be sent to the league, which would then return one-third of the amount to the home teams. After the season, the league would then distribute equal shares of the accrued playoff payoffs to those franchises that failed to qualify for the postseason tournament.

Another concern that resulted in immediate adoption was a fine of $500 for all forfeited games. The sum would go directly to the team (presumably the home team) that had been left waiting at the center circle. No allowances were made for dire weather conditions, and the president also reserved the right to order further compensation and stiffer penalties.

The issue of the eligibility of players roused significant discussion. The AHL's constitution stated: "No person shall be eligible as a player . . . who is a student in any academic institution in which he holds status as an amateur, and is still eligible for intercollegiate athletics, and no player shall be permitted to play . . . until his class has graduated; the foregoing shall mean the class to which the player belonged when he first entered a collegiate institution." The problem here was that the scholastic careers of numerous players had been interrupted, and in many cases terminated, by service in the armed forces. A combat-hardened veteran whose freshman class had long since graduated might choose to play in the BAA even though he still had several years of college eligibility.

The owners were wary of alienating the NCAA and subjecting the BAA to charges that it was raiding the colleges. An opposing concern was the legal aspect of unlawfully depriving an individual of the right to earn a living.

Walter Brown proposed a solution: "When Al [Sutphin] and I went out to see Wirtz in Chicago, I was under the impression that we should not touch boys while they are in college with the exception of boys who were in the service prior to V-J Day. . . . Hell, I don't mind saying I have some of them signed up in my own club right now."

Irish suggested that a player would be eligible four years after he matriculated in college. On this point, it was noted that baseball teams routinely signed prospects to professional contracts upon their graduation from high school. Of what use would Irish's suggestion be if a prospective player had no desire to go to college?

"Could we solve the problem," Brown asked, "if we adopted an age limit?"

Podoloff reminded them that the AHL's constitution already had a sixteen-years-of-age limit. Gottlieb then opined that a boy should not be signed until a year after his high school class had graduated.

However, the Celtics had already signed several players who wouldn't qualify if Gottlieb's stipulation were adopted. A subsequent motion was passed ordering Podoloff to draft a clause that would accept Gottlieb's proposal but would also grandfather any contracts the Celtics had already consummated. Then James Balmer, representing Pittsburgh, asked Brown to specify those players signed by Boston who would gain exemption from the clause-to-be.

"I don't know," Brown confessed. "I don't know enough about basketball. I don't even know the names of my own players. Ned tells me that I have a boy who just got through high school. I know I have two boys who were in service for two years, and they signed with me because they want to take a physical education course at Boston University, and I was able to get them through some of my contacts at BU. They are going to college, and they are also going to play pro basketball. I don't want to be without a team the day before the season starts."

For the time being, the age limit of sixteen was adopted. Further details were tabled pending the drafted clause to be submitted by Podoloff.

It was also unanimously agreed that no black players would be signed. The owners had hopes that the Harlem Globetrotters might be convinced to play preliminaries to regularly scheduled BAA games and did not want to upset Abe Saperstein, the Globbies' owner.

It was decided that teams would have an Active Reserve List comprising their roster players, injured players, and players under contract who were not active because of personal emergencies, military service, attendance in graduate school, or temporary employment in some other field of endeavor. Any player cut from the reserve list would be put on a "waiver list" for an as yet indeterminate period, during which any other team (in an order not yet determined) could make a claim on that player, thereby gaining the rights to him as well as the obligation to pay a waiver fee to the original ball club. What, then, would the waiver fee be?

The forthcoming suggestions ranged from $1,500 to $750, but the matter was tabled pending a meeting of the Executive Committee. The members of this influential group consisted of Podoloff plus the franchise owners who were situated in the BAA's biggest markets—Irish, Wirtz, Brown, Sutphin, and Pete Tyrell.

Next up, it was decided that players could not be loaned from one team to another as was the case in the AHL.

An amateur draft would be conducted in the spring of 1947, with the team having the worst record getting the first pick, and so on. Here, Sutphin issued a warning. "In the NFL," he said, "teams regularly sold their draft choices so they could raise some money to continue operating. The Cleveland Rams always sold their chances in the draft, sometimes for as high as fifteen thousand dollars. This type of thing should be forbidden for us."

Agreed.

Sutphin then suggested that none of the teams be permitted to play exhibition games, not even games played for the benefit of some local charity. "This is what is apt to happen," he argued. "Let's say out in the West, St. Louis or Cleveland might want to pick up some extra money by playing Fort Wayne, the defending champions of the NBL. Let's say they slaughter us. In that case, we wouldn't be a very good drawing card in New York, or Boston, or wherever. So, to protect the whole league against ourselves, it would be a good idea not to permit any exhibition games prior to the season."

This was agreed upon, with an exception made for Toronto to play an undisclosed opponent for the benefit of the local Rotary club.

Each team, it was decided, would keep whatever revenue it could derive from local radio broadcasts of its games. Radio coverage was widely considered a device for earning money as well as luring some fans into the respective arenas. Irish bragged that he'd already sold these rights for $500 per game but warned that franchises in smaller metropolitan areas could expect only a small fraction of this amount. Television, however, was much more dangerous.

"We ought to agree here that no club will do anything with television," said Sutphin. "Televising games only keeps fans away from the games. We can only get involved in a television deal if we do it on a leaguewide basis."

Irish strongly disagreed. "There are currently only six thousand television sets on the entire Eastern Seaboard," he asserted, "and probably by the end of the season, that number might be doubled under the most optimistic forecasts. The extra revenue, if available, would be most helpful, and I don't see any difference between radio and television broadcasting."

Under the current technology, telecasts originating in New York could be relayed only to Schenectady, Washington, and Philadelphia. "What if," said Sutphin, "the people in these places adopted the New York team as their favorite team and stayed away from their local teams' games? Why should they go down to the Uline Arena when they can stay home and see another game without having to pay anything?"

The final decision was that each franchise would make its own radio arrangements, while New York and Chicago would be allowed only two telecasts each.

Podoloff then announced that a preliminary agreement with the Wilson Sporting Goods Company to supply gratis thirty-six or forty-eight balls per team had fallen through. "It was too good to be true," Podoloff said, though he still believed that Wilson would honor the agreement eventually. Irish was doubtful and thought it more likely that the Spaulding Company would improve its initial offer of supplying half the number of balls required. It was agreed to resume negotiations with Spaulding and to give Podoloff and the Executive Committee full power to work out an agreement.

In any case, each team would be required to provide at least two new official "brown" balls for every game. Further, "Each club shall also have for emergency purposes a football timing watch and a gun loaded with blank cartridges, to be used by game officials to announce the closing of the periods."

Agreed.

The size of the numerals on uniform jerseys likewise engendered much debate. It was ultimately determined that the numbers had to be at least ten inches high on the front of the jerseys, and six inches high on the back, so they could be easily seen in the press box and in the upper reaches of the stands. Specific numerals were also proscribed: numbers 1 and 2 were prohibited to prevent any confusion when a referee indicated that a personal foul had resulted in the shooting of either one or two free throws. Only numbers 3 through 15 would be acceptable, although Podoloff supposed that no player would want to wear number 13.

The home team would wear white jerseys; the visitors, colored jerseys. If there was sufficient room, clubs could opt to include their team insignias on the front side only. It was deemed desirable for the name of the city and not the team's nickname to appear on the front of the jerseys, but when Sutphin objected that "Cleveland" or "Philadelphia" wouldn't leave any room for the designated numerals, each team was allowed to make its own decision.

The hour was growing late when Sutphin warned against distributing complimentary tickets to visiting players. "We used to do that in Cleveland," he said, "until we discovered that all of the players on a visiting hockey team sold their tickets at a discounted price to the hotel porter at the Belmont Hotel just across the street from the arena. The porter then turned around and made a tidy profit scalping the tickets right before the game. That's money that was taken right out of my pocket."

Agreed!

The constitution was then subjected to the approval of the membership, with the proviso that it could be altered or amended by a two-thirds vote of the members present at an annual meeting, or at any meeting called for that purpose. It passed unanimously.

Gottlieb was charged with composing a schedule, with the understanding that with thirteen teams, it would not be perfectly balanced. Then Podoloff reported on his efforts to rent an office.

"I am having the devil's own time trying to get any kind of rooms in New York," he moaned. "I was finally offered a suite on Madison Avenue and Forty-first Street, but I wouldn't bring a pig in there."

What about a suite in a hotel?

Podoloff was turned down by the Commodore and the Biltmore, but the BAA was deemed acceptable to the Piccadilly, a notorious haven for high-priced call girls. "I turned the Piccadilly down," Podoloff huffed, "because I think it would lower the dignity of the league."

In conclusion, Dick Miller dropped a bombshell: It was understood that Buffalo had no real plans to field a team, but Miller suddenly announced that the Indianapolis franchise was compelled to fold.

One problem was the presence in the city of the NBL's Indianapolis Kautskys. Another was the threat of Fred Zollner to enlist his Pistons in the NBL in nearby Fort Wayne. Not to mention the NBL's Anderson Packers, which were only thirty-five miles away. The competition would simply be overwhelming.

There was also a tinge of racism in Miller's argument. After all, African Americans would be barred from playing in the BAA, and potential African-American fans were most likely too poor to afford tickets.

"We have four hundred thousand people in Indianapolis," Miller noted, "of which ninety thousand are colored. So, that gives us a prospective fan base of only three hundred thousand. In hockey, we draw ten percent of our fans from Anderson, fans who would be unavailable because of the Packers. All of this puts me behind the eight ball."

Sutphin interjected that the arena in Anderson was twice as large as Miller's building and was equipped with beautiful, up-to-date lighting as well as flawless sight lines from every seat. Also, the owner of the Packers was "a maniac" who was offering ten- to twelve-thousand-dollar contracts and had already signed all-American players from Notre Dame to three-year deals.

"I thought I would be competing in a league where the players would be paid only three thousand dollars," Miller said, "but recognizable players in this area are no longer available at that price. If I persisted in trying to operate, I would only be knocking my own brains out."

There was another problem for Miller, one that centered around the American Legion, which had its national headquarters in Indianapolis.

"Because we don't have a portable basketball court," Miller went on, "we'd have to have one built. Ninety-six feet by fifty feet and one-and-a-quarter-inch thick amounts to quite a lot of wood. The American Legion has already criticized us for diverting wood for our commercial use that should be ear-marked to erect homes for returning GIs. I don't have a Chinaman's chance to win this one either."

As a result, Miller was granted one year to suspend operations for his franchise.

Before he adjourned the meeting, Podoloff said this: "Congratulations, gentlemen, you are now a regularly organized body."

5

The Boston Celtics and the
Clown Prince of the BAA

The start of the season for the newly minted Boston Celtics was a total disaster. Their first game was a 59–53 loss on November 11, to the Steamrollers in Providence. Their home opener, in the Boston Arena versus the Chicago Stags three days later, was even worse, and the culprit was the Celtics' zany 6'7" center, Kevin "Chuck" Connors.

The Boston newspapers had gushed over their city's newest team. The *Boston Globe* claimed that "even before the first paying customer walked through the gate," the eleven BAA franchises had collectively spent more than $1 million. Why, even the new court at the Boston Arena cost $11,000.

What wasn't said was that, with seasoned hardwood in such short supply because of the postwar housing boom, the soon-to-become-famous parquet floor was built by Tony DiNatalie, of Brookline, entirely of scrap wood. That's why the 264 interlocking squares didn't all match.

Another hidden expense was the several thousand dollars that Walter Brown had paid to Jim Furay, manager of the Original Celtics, for the rights to that famous name. Brown had considered other sobriquets—the Whirlwinds, the Olympians, and the Unicorns—before deciding that "Celtics" was the best hook to reel in Boston's large Irish population.

The local sportswriters hoped that even though the opening game fell on Election Day, Boston's sports fans would make it their civic duty to support their Celtics and fill all of the Arena's 7,200 seats. Eventually, 6,000 did show up, and they could barely restrain their enthusiasm as they waited for the opening tip-off. Their wait proved to be much longer than anticipated.

"We were warming up before the game," Connors recalled some thirty-five years later. "Then one of the referees blew his whistle, which was a signal for all the players to hustle over to their benches and get last-minute instructions from their coaches. As I was running over to hear what Honey Russell had to say, I instinctively bent down and picked up a basketball. I was maybe forty feet from the basket, and I threw up a long two-handed heave like it was a last-second, last-gasp shot—a Hail Mary shot. Damned if the ball didn't hit the tip of the front rim, and all hell broke loose. The glass backboard shattered but didn't fall to pieces on the floor, and the whole frame tilted forward about a foot. So, they had to hold up the fucking game and go get another backboard from the Boston Garden."

Other eyewitnesses, including several of Connors's teammates, swore that the damage was done by a dunk shot. "Christ," said Connors, "I could never jump high enough to dunk. My hands weren't large enough to palm the ball, anyway. Nobody could dunk in those days."

The story is also told that when Boston's feisty coach, Honey Russell, cussed out Connors, the big man responded with a resounding "Fuck you!"

Connors swore that this never happened either. "Everybody has their own version of what happened, but most of them are full of shit. I guess nobody likes the way things really went down. The only thing that Honey said was, 'Everything happens to me.'"

The only known replacement was in the Boston Garden, which was way across town and was currently hosting a rodeo. Worse, the space where the Garden's spare backboard was stashed was accessible only by crossing the pen that contained the Brahman bulls. Howie McHugh was the Celtics' director of public relations, and neither he nor any of the Garden's maintenance staff was willing to enter the pen. Eventually, McHugh paid some "drunken cowboys" to do the job. Still, the bulky, top-heavy apparatus was not easily transported, so the game was delayed for two hours.

In the interim, Russell put the players through a series of fancy ballhandling drills—throwing between-the-legs passes and catching them the same way. To further amuse the restless fans, the Celtics competed in a three-on-three tournament for a $100 prize.

"The winners got their money straight out of the cash box at the front gate," said McHugh. "By the time the game finally got under way, about half of the fans had left, and I'm sure they never came back to see us ever again."

Worse still, the Stags won the game, 57–55, on a late basket by Max Zaslofsky.

Back on the road, the hapless Celtics then lost to the Falcons in Detroit (69–46), to the Stags in Chicago (71–61), and to the St. Louis Bombers (64–62). Their record was now 0–5, by far the worst in the league.

There were several reasons why Boston got off to such a terrible start (not to mention middle and end) of its inaugural season, all of them having to do with faulty timing.

Even before the August organizational meeting, most owners had already hired their coaches. Walter Brown was originally counting on enticing Frank Keaney to leave Rhode Island State College (which later changed its name to the University of Rhode Island) and coach the Celtics. Keaney was widely known for teaching a high-scoring, fast-break offense that moved sports-writers to tout his Rhode Island Rams as a "point-a-minute" team. All the publicity coupled with his teams' success understandably puffed up Keaney's ego, and even though he had doubts about the Celtics and the new league, he made the trip into Boston to meet with Brown just to discover how much money might be had. As it happened, Brown was delayed with some other pressing business and was late for the meeting. Offended at being kept cooling his heels, Kearney exited in a huff before Brown finally appeared.

Acting then on the recommendation of John Lockhart, a personal friend who was also in charge of all hockey matters at Madison Square Garden, Brown turned his attention to John "Honey" Russell.

A future Hall of Famer (inducted in 1964), Russell was born in Brooklyn on May 31, 1902, and proved to be an exceptional athlete in several sports. He began his professional career at age sixteen as a cager with the barnstorming Brooklyn Visitations. Two years later, Russell showed sufficient skills as a catcher to quit high school and sign a minor-league contract with the Brooklyn Dodgers. His baseball career was abbreviated, however, when a home-plate collision resulted in a broken arm. For a short time, Russell also played end for the pre-NFL Chicago Bears.

But basketball was his best sport, and he also played for and managed the Bears' basketball team (the Bruins) that barnstormed in the off-season. In his prime, Russell measured 6'1" and weighed 175 pounds and was considered to be the finest defender in the game. He even had a basketball nose: frequently broken, it faked left before going right. His specialty was so much in demand that other touring teams would often hire him to squelch the opposition's most notable scorer.

"There were plenty of Sundays when I played triple-headers for three different teams," he recalled. "For example, I might start off with an early-afternoon game in Scranton; then I'd play in Brooklyn at eight thirty; then wind up in the Bronx for an eleven o'clock game. Hell, I've played games in Harlem at one A.M. and on a stage of a vaudeville theater in Easton at two thirty in the morning. The more I played, the more I got paid."

To keep the money flowing in, Russell also worked as an umpire in high school baseball games, as the athletic director at a Coney Island bathhouse, as the promoter of a bowling league, and as a coach-promoter of his own barnstorming basketball team. "I'd book the other teams," he said, "rent the hall, sell the tickets, hire the band, make the popcorn, coach the team, and afterwards tend bar at the postgame dance."

For one road game, the promoter insisted that Russell spring for the added expense of bringing a sixth player so that the game could continue in case somebody got hurt. Russell agreed, and in addition to the five starters, there was a sixth man in uniform on the bench. After only three minutes of play, Russell pulled a muscle in his calf and couldn't continue. The ref then approached the bench player and ordered him into the action. "I don't know who the hell you are," the sixth man said, "but I'm the taxi driver."

Russell was also a charter member of the Cleveland Rosenblums when the American Basketball League was first organized in 1925. He was named to the league's all-star teams a total of four times—with the Rosenblums, with the Brooklyn–New York Jewels, and with the Rochester Centrals. In 1936, Russell became the basketball coach at Seton Hall while still managing to play a part-time schedule with Rochester in the ABL. When Seton Hall dropped intercollegiate sports during World War II, Russell coached in the Eastern Basketball League (strictly a weekend diversion) and also began managing minor-league baseball teams. He then signed on as varsity basketball coach at Manhattan College for the 1945–46 season.

When he was initially contacted by Brown in late August of 1946, he was managing a baseball team from Rutland, Vermont, in the New England College League. Russell was intrigued by Brown's offer, but he demurred, citing the necessity of finishing the baseball season and then having to find a replacement at Manhattan. Brown was impressed with Russell's integrity and agreed to hire him when his current responsibilities were completed. Besides the money, Russell signed with the Celtics because his current girlfriend lived in Boston.

Since there was no player draft for the upcoming BAA season, each team (usually through some combination of the coach and general manager) had to scramble to locate and sign players who were thought to be capable of playing pro ball. By the time Russell was under contract with the Celtics, virtually all of the elite free agents had already been snatched up. That's why Russell missed out on Ed Sadowski, for example, who had played under him at Seton Hall.

The roster that Russell assembled for the commencement of the Celtics' training camp featured several players he knew from either the Eastern League or the ABL. It was largely a motley crew that included the following athletes:

Virgil Vaughn, 6′4″, 205, from Kentucky Wesleyan. A stylish player lacking in strength, Vaughn played only seventeen games before suffering an injury that eventuated in his left kidney's being surgically removed.

Bill Fenley, 6′3″, 190, from Manhattan College. Russell was initially high on Fenley, who began the season as a starting forward, but Fenley was a loner, and his sour disposition soon alienated his coach and his teammates.

Mel Hirsch, 5′8″, 165, from Brooklyn College.

Art "Speed" Spector, 6′4″, 200, from Villanova.

Michael "Red" Wallace, 6′1″, 185, from Scranton College.

Tony Kappen, 5′10″, 165, who did not attend college. "Kappen was one of the few guys who was serious about playing," said McHugh.

Johnny Simmons, 6′1″, 184, from NYU.

Connie Simmons, 6′8″, 225; no college; Johnny's younger brother.

Al Brightman, 6′2″, 195, ostensibly from Morris Harvey, easily the Celtics' best player. As a senior at Wilson High School, in Long Beach, California, Brightman had once scored 70 points in a game. He was also a hell-raiser who would fight anybody, anywhere, at any time, for any reason.

"I only played at Morris Harvey for one year," Brightman said. "Then I went back to California and got a job with Twentieth Century-Fox as a general laborer. Mostly I worked on making special-effects scenery like miniature airplanes and submarines. I also played on the studio's basketball team, which was a good one."

Universal Pictures was the first movie studio to field a serious basketball team, and because the team won a national AAU tournament in 1936, those players constituted the bulk of the U.S. squad at the Berlin Olympics. Shortly thereafter, a bidding war ensued, and many of Universal's best players jumped to Fox Studios.

"We used to go on tour," said Brightman, "representing the studio at screen clubs in major cities, where people interested in films would meet to watch and discuss the latest releases. We'd show up dressed in tuxedos topped with black satin berets. The major reason why we were on the circuit, though, was to play basketball. We'd play about fifty games every year against the top industrial teams, military teams, and some colleges. In L.A., we played at the Shrine Auditorium and always drew packed houses of about six thousand. Stars like Victor Mature, Henry Fonda, and Tyrone Power never missed a home game."

After serving in the army, Brightman had forsaken basketball and was playing minor-league baseball in Wilkes-Barre, Pennsylvania, when he got a letter from Russell inviting him to Boston for a tryout. "I had no trouble making the team," said Brightman, "and I signed a contract for forty-five hundred. Even so, Russell didn't like me, because I was from California and shot one-handed. He was strictly an old-fashioned guy."

Harold Kottman, 6'8", 220, from Culver-Stockton. When Kottman arrived in Boston, he reported for instructions to Brown's office. Brown's secretary wasn't exactly a sports fan, but she knew a giant when she saw one, so she sent Kottman over to the Manger Hotel, where the circus performers were staying.
Wyndol Gray, 6'1", 175, from Harvard and Bowling Green.

McHugh also remembered a tryout player who had been a POW in Japan: "A sturdy, strong-looking fellow. Maybe he once was a real player, but after his ordeal, he was as weak as a kitten and had absolutely nothing left."

And then there was Chuck Connors, the clown prince of the BAA.

Kevin Joseph Aloysius Connors was born in the Bay Ridge section of Brooklyn on April 10, 1921. Growing up, he had one lesser and one greater ambition: to play professional baseball with the hometown Dodgers, and to be a Hollywood actor. He grew up to be a tall, slick-fielding, power-hitting first baseman whose exploits in numerous sandlot leagues gained him a scholarship to the ritzy Adelphi Academy, situated in downtown Brooklyn. "This happened after my freshman year at Manual Training High School," Connors said. "Part of the deal was that because there were only a dozen or so authentic athletes in the whole school, I also had to play football and basketball. That's how I became acquainted with basketball at the age of sixteen."

Connors was well scouted at Adelphi, and after his graduation, the Dodgers signed him to a minor-league contract and shipped him out to Newport in the Class D Northeast Arkansas League, where he played for most of the summer. "The Dodgers had some kind of in at Seton Hall through Father Lillis [the athletic director]," Connors said, "and they prevailed upon him to give me a baseball scholarship. Father Lillis said that the baseball scholarships were all spoken for but he could get me into the school on a basketball scholarship. What the hell difference did it make to me? I was going to play baseball anyway."

Connors entered Seton Hall in September 1941. Honey Russell was the basketball coach, and he insisted that since Connors had been given one of his valuable scholarships, the big fellow was obliged to come out for basketball. Even then, Connors could run like a guard and rebound like a wolf going after a lamb chop. Shooting and dribbling, however, were skills that he never did master.

"I managed to make the frosh team," he said, "and as a soph, I started the first game of the season. That was the 1942–43 season, and we had the best team in the country. Bob Davies was the star, and I eventually settled into being the sixth or seventh man."

From the start, Connors got along with Russell. "His nickname belied his temperament," Connors said. "With his big hawk face and his hook nose, he would rant and scream about defense, always defense. He wanted to play a slowdown, grind-it-out offense, but he couldn't control Davies, who was nothing less than an offensive genius."

Sometimes Russell would scrimmage with the team. "He couldn't move very well, but he was tougher than rawhide, and he used to beat the shit out of us on a regular basis," said Connors. "If Honey also had a quick temper, his anger was only momentary. Whenever any of us did something good (which I did very rarely), he would also pat us on the back and dish out the praise. He was a no-bullshit guy, and we all liked him."

While still an undergraduate, Connors told a classmate, "Someday I'm going to make the Brooklyn Dodgers, but I'm only going to use that as a

stepping-stone to a career in Hollywood. Ultimately, I'm going to be a director of Oscar-winning films."

Meanwhile, Connors was also a star performer on Seton Hall's baseball
team while simultaneously being carried on the roster of another Dodgers
farm team. Paul Kritchell, the New York Yankees' top scout, realized that
through some clerical error, Connors was eligible to be drafted by another
big-league organization, and Connors soon became property of the Yankees.
Next came stints in the Yankees' farm system, at Binghamton and then
Norfolk.

After being drafted into the army in 1943, Connors continued playing
both sports and was eventually transferred to West Point, ostensibly as an
instructor in tank tactics, but in truth to beef up the resident basketball team.
"We played against everybody and beat them all," he said.

Connors was living the life of Riley, except for a certain Major McBride,
who tried to make his life miserable. "This guy was constantly on my tail,"
Connors said. "He'd make sure I was usually assigned to latrine duty, and
during inspection, my equipment was never in good enough shape for him.
So, I made up my mind that I was going to get this guy to crack."

As a way of training for movie-land stardom, Connors had taught himself
to render dramatic readings of such poetic offerings as "Casey at the Bat,"
selections from "Paradise Lost," and "The Face on the Bar Room Floor,"
as well as various Shakespearean soliloquies. "It happened that I drew KP
one day when this major had a bunch of U.S. senators visiting the Point,"
Connors recounted. "He had arranged for them to eat lunch in this particular
mess hall because the cook there was the best around. Then Major McBride
ordered me to come out of the kitchen and entertain his guests with my
recitation of 'Casey.' I grabbed the biggest ladle that I could find to use as a
baseball bat, and I positioned myself so that every time I swung the ladle, it
came within a half inch of the major's nose. That was my first move."

As a follow-up, Connors would shadow McBride as much as he could. "I'd
just stare at him," Connors said, "from behind a tank, from behind a statue,
from around corners, wherever and whenever—just staring and never saying
a word. What could he do to me for just looking at him? After three weeks,
he asked for a transfer."

Connors was still at West Point when President Roosevelt died on April
12, 1945. His response was to write a poem, "A GI Talks with God," that
lamented FDR's passing. The poem was subsequently published in *Stars and
Stripes*, and Eleanor Roosevelt reportedly wept when she read it.

Whenever he could either get a weekend pass or sneak out of West Point, Connors accepted Honey Russell's invitation to play with the New York–Brooklyn Jewels, the team Russell was coaching in the ABL. It was during a home game against Trenton that Connors developed a sudden reputation as an outstanding defender. "I'd never played basketball for money before," said Connors, "so I was a little nervous. I'm sitting there on the bench when the ref called a jump ball. In those days, a coach could send anybody into the game to do the jumping. Trenton had a big guy named Mike Bloom who did their jump balls, so Honey turns to me and says in his raspy voice, 'Kevin'—he always called me Kevin—'you ain't got no fucking chance to out-jump this guy. You know that, don't cha? I don't want you to jump, Kevin. I want you to just stare at his fucking jaw. Let him jump, and when he comes down, just punch him and knock him on his fucking ass.' So, since I was young and foolhardy, that's what I did: punched his jaw and knocked him on his ass. After that, Bloom was afraid of me. Every time I played against him, he wouldn't even want to shoot the ball. And that's how I got my reputation as a great defensive player."

The Jewels didn't play again until the following weekend, when they faced off against a team whose starting center was Pat Hirlihy. Big and beefy, Hirlihy wasn't much of a player, but his leaping ability made him a valuable center jumper.

Instead of jumping to capture the game's first possession, Connors belted Hirlihy in the jaw, just as he'd done against Mike Bloom. Unlike with Bloom, though, Hirlihy didn't crumple to the floor. Instead, he brutalized Connors throughout the entire first half.

At the intermission, Russell asked Connors, "What in the name of God possessed you to hit Hirlihy?"

"You told me to, Honey."

"For Christ's sake, Kevin. That was last week."

Upon his release from the army in the fall of 1945, Connors played briefly for Rochester in the National Basketball League. After the season, Connors was off to spring training with the Kansas City Blues, the Yankees' Triple-A farm team. He stuck with the Blues for the first three weeks of the season but discovered that hitting AAA curveballs was a tricky business, so he was released, re-signed by Brooklyn, and sent down to Newport News, Virginia, in the Class B Piedmont League.

Wherever Connors played, he couldn't resist being theatrical. He'd do his recitations while holding runners on first base. He'd clout a homer, dash around the bases, and slide across home plate with his hat in his hand. Another trick was to slide into the dugout after he'd scored a run.

At Newport News, Connors batted .310 and swatted 21 home runs. The plan was to invite Connors to the Dodgers' Vero Beach training camp in the spring of 1947. Meanwhile, he got a call from his old coach, Honey Russell, inviting him to be a Celtic.

"Honey offered me five thousand bucks," said Connors. "Holy Christ, that was a lot of dough in those days. Since I was making only three-fifty a month at Newport News, I went to Boston with alacrity."

The Celtics' three-week training camp was another example of poor timing, since it coincided with the preseason workout of the Boston Olympians, the AHL hockey team that Walter Brown owned.

Both teams trained in the Boston Arena, where the ice rink was on the first floor and a basketball court occupied the third floor. The middle floor was furnished with long rows of cots and served as a dormitory for both teams. The players were allowed to sign for their meals at a hotel ten blocks away. "But we couldn't overeat," said Johnny Simmons, "because we knew we had to practice so much."

Russell hired a person McHugh described as "a small, white-haired Irishman named Pops" to try to keep the dormitory fairly clean. It was well known to both the basketball and the hockey players that Pops also served as the coach's spy. To Russell's dismay, Pops also fancied himself a basketball expert and was constantly drawing up plays and making suggestions as to which of the Celtics should be cut, which should be kept, and which should be starters.

Two other staff members were on hand to serve the Celtics. Harvey Cohen, a sprinter on the 1936 U.S. Olympic track team, was supposed to tape ankles and serve as the team's trainer. Unfortunately, Cohen was a heavy drinker and proved to be totally incompetent. As a result, many of the players taped their own ankles, and Cohen was mostly reduced to handling the players' travel bags. His fellow employee was Jock Sepple, a marathon runner whose job was to take the Celtics for a run in the woods near Fenway Park every morning right after breakfast. Once the season began, visiting teams would hire Sepple as their trainer as a means of saving both salary and travel expenses. A die-hard Celtics fan, Sepple would always root for the hometown team even while sitting on the visitors' bench. He was also loud and boisterous in his criticisms of the referees and once went after Jocko Collins in the bathroom during halftime. Collins managed to grab Sepple by the throat and was well on his way to committing murder, when the fracas was broken up by a local sportswriter.

"We were like kids at a summer camp," said Connors. "We'd put dead rats in each other's beds and have pillow fights. And since Brightman and me were ladies' men, the two of us would stuff clothing in our beds so it would look like somebody was sleeping in them. We'd do this to try to fool Pops, who was always on the alert for guys sneaking out. Then me and Brightman would visit the bars, cozy up to the dames, and have as much fun as we could. We thought that by being back at the dorm by midnight, we were restraining ourselves. It really didn't matter, because Honey never gave us a curfew."

Still, when Pops passed the word to Russell that several of his players had come back late, the coach felt compelled to yell at the offenders during the next day's practice session. "Hell," said Connors, "Honey always yelled at me anyway. I'd just say, 'Yes, Honey. Right, Honey. Yes, sir.' After a while, I didn't even know what he was yelling at me for."

The players got even with Pops by fixing the legs of his cot so it would collapse when he climbed into bed. Sometimes they would get hold of Pops's false teeth and put them outside on the window ledge.

A much bigger annoyance to the cagers than their resident tattletale was the hockey players. "They'd come in late all beered up and make a lot of noise," said Brightman. "Meanwhile, we had to be up at seven in the morning to get ready for the first of our three daily practices. We were worn out, and we really needed our sleep. We'd yell at them to shut their Canuck mouths, and they'd yell back. A couple of times, it got so bad that Pops had to call the cops to settle everybody down."

One Saturday night, the Celtics smuggled a keg of beer into the dorm and had themselves a chugalug party. Red Wallace, who was described by McHugh as "a wild-ass guy," got oiled in a hurry, and when the hockey players made their familiar noisy entrance, he started cursing them and challenging them to fisticuffs. Brightman described what happened next: "Somebody shut off the lights, and we just went at each other. We were much bigger than them, so we kicked their asses all over the room and really laid a couple of them out. It was a lot of fun. This time, the cops had to cordon off the building. Walter Brown was pissed, because the hockey team was his biggest moneymaker. He ordered us to keep our mitts off of them, and he had Honey institute a ten-o'clock curfew."

One day, Russell decreed that no fouls would be called in the intrasquad scrimmage. Anything goes. "That was Honey's way of trying to toughen us up," said Johnny Simmons, who was reputed to be a good shooter, a hard worker, and the quietest, most soft-spoken player on the team. According to Simmons, Connors took advantage of Russell's no-holds-barred instruction to pick on a teammate to whom he had taken a severe dislike.

Walter Brown had insisted that Russell keep Wyndol Gray on the team because of his Harvard connection, even though Gray couldn't play dead. "I don't know about Gray and Harvard," said McHugh. "I mean, the guy was barely literate. Maybe he'd once gone to the bathroom in Harvard Square. Anyway, he was a quiet, retiring guy who couldn't do anything right on the court." Connors had no use for Gray.

"Well," Simmons said, "we'd just started when Connors went after Wyndol Gray. I mean, he hit Gray with a cross-body block and knocked him ass-over-teakettle. Russell loved it. After that, every time Gray got the ball, Connors got him again. It was very strange, because there hadn't been, and never was, any hostility between the two of them. I mean, Gray was a very easygoing guy. I guess Connors just went off the deep end that particular day. I was just hoping that no one came after me like that. It was a miracle that we all survived."

Once the season began, the mayhem continued. No single game, and its aftermath, would be as bizarre as the Celtics' 64–62 loss in St. Louis on November 14 (their fifth of five consecutive losses that launched the season).

The St. Louis Arena was a difficult venue for visiting teams because of the inept way the portable court was laid over the ice, causing slick spots on the floorboards and near frigid temperatures by the bench. Many visiting players were also distracted when the organist randomly banged on the keys just as they were shooting their free throws. Even so, before a smallish crowd of 2,070, the Celtics were both focused and on fire.

Behind the unexpected stellar play of Wallace and Gray, Boston forged to a 17-point lead midway through the second quarter. The fact that Harold Kottman had incurred a technical foul when he entered the game without reporting to the official scorer was annoying but not especially harmful. After the halftime break, however, St. Louis began finding the range. Don Putman and Johnny Logan were the hometown heroes as the Bombers slowly began narrowing the gap. Still, the Celtics managed to hang on to their edge, and with only thirty seconds remaining in the fourth quarter, they led by 6 points.

The Celtics were set to inbound the ball under their basket, when Russell called a time-out.

"We've got this one made," he told his players. "All we have to do is this: don't let Kevin touch the ball. They'll only steal it from him, or he'll dribble it off his foot and he'll start fouling everybody in sight. Repeat: don't let Kevin touch the fucking ball."

The players were moving back onto the court, when Russell decided they were so incredibly stupid that they needed another reminder. So, he called another time-out, the team's last one. "Repeat: don't let Kevin touch the ball. And whoever does catch the ball, just stand there and do nothing."

After dismissing the players once again, Russell summoned referee Pat Kennedy over to the bench. Russell and Kennedy were buddies from way back, so the ref didn't blink when the coach said, "I'm out of time-outs, Pat. Do me a favor and tell those dumb bastards not to call another one." Kennedy agreed, and before the players assembled for the inbounds play, he approached each of the Celtics and whispered the warning.

Connors continued the narrative: "There was a bit of a scramble when we came back onto the court, because nobody really knew who was supposed to inbounds the ball. Somehow, I wound up standing out of bounds; the referee handed me the ball, and I had to get it into play. OK, so I threw the ball toward Connie Simmons, but one of the Bombers intercepted it. I was so pissed off that I slammed the guy just as he was shooting. Of course, he made the basket and the free throw. Now there were twenty-eight seconds left, and our lead was down to only three."

In a panic, Speed Spector signaled to Kennedy for a time-out, but the referee ignored him. Disgusted, Russell picked up a wet towel and threw it at Spector but missed.

Once again, the Celtics were obliged to inbound the ball, but this time Connors ran over to the sideline as far away from the passer as he could get. "Guess what?" he continued. "The stupid fucker threw the ball to me. In a heartbeat, one of the Bombers stole the ball right out of my hands and starts dribbling to the basket. Of course, I followed him, then fouled him just as he shot another layup. Count the basket and the free throw, and the game was tied. Naturally, we lost in overtime."

Honey went berserk, screaming and yelling at the players in the dressing room. "What'd I tell ya? Keep the fucking ball away from fucking Kevin! What'd I tell ya?" Then he turned on Connors: "You dumb bastard!"

Connors, who was also upset, responded, "If I'm a dumb bastard, then you must be a dumber bastard, because you're the one who brought me here."

Russell fumed some more and then stormed out of the room.

Boston	Att.	FG	FT	PF	Pts.
Gray, f	13	5	2	4	12
Connors, f	3	2	2	3	6
J. Simmons, f	18	4	1	1	9
C. Simmons, f	11	3	3	2	9
Vaughn, c	3	1	1	1	3
Kottman, c	0	0	0	1	0
Fenley, g	2	1	0	3	2
Kusten, g	2	0	2	0	2
Brightman, g	4	1	0	0	2
Spector, g	5	2	1	2	5
Wallace, g	11	5	2	1	12
Totals	**72**	**24**	**14**	**18**	**62**

St. Louis	Att.	FG	FT	PF	Pts.
Hankins, f	10	3	1	5	7
Logan, f	23	6	2	1	14
Putman, f	19	7	0	3	14
Smith, f	5	0	0	1	0
Davis, f	8	3	0	0	6
Martin, c	8	2	0	1	4
Doll, c	20	2	1	2	5
Barr, f	4	1	0	1	2
Munroe, g	3	0	0	1	0
Roux, g	7	2	2	1	6
Baltimore, g	5	1	0	2	2
Jacobs, g	7	2	0	2	4
Totals	**119**	**29**	**6**	**20**	**64**

SCORE BY QUARTERS	1	2	3	4	OT	Total
Boston	13	28	6	12	3	62
St. Louis	14	12	14	19	5	64

Missed free throws: Boston (12)—Gray 2, J. Simmons 3, C. Simmons 3, Spector 2, Wallace 2. St. Louis (16)—Hankins, Logan 2, Putman, Martin 2, Doll 2, Munroe, Roux 2, Baltimore, Jacobs 4. Officials: Chuck Solodare and Sam Picararo.

The next morning, Connors was sitting in the lobby of the Chase Hotel, whiling away the time until the Celtics were scheduled to leave for the train station. "I wasn't too happy with myself," Connors said. "To calm myself down, I pulled out a volume of Shakespeare's collected plays that I always carried with me and began to read. A few minutes later, Honey comes up behind me. 'What the hell are you reading?' he demanded. When I told him, he blew his top. 'Shakespeare? Christ almighty, you blew a game on me and you're reading Shakespeare?' Then he stormed off again."

Connors never quite understood what connection there was between the game and the Shakespeare in Russell's mind. Perhaps Russell thought he should still have been moaning, weeping, and tearing out his hair. Some three decades later, Connors was still puzzled: "Honey might well have been right. I'm not sure."

When the Celtics arrived at the train station, Russell was nowhere to be seen, but he had left a message for Connors at the ticket window: "You're the only son of a bitch who can figure out how to blow a six-point lead with thirty seconds to go. If you're so smart, you can figure out how to get back to Boston without a ticket."

True to his word, Russell had already left, and the packet of tickets that he'd given to Harvey Cohen, the trainer, was one short. The other players quickly chipped in to buy Connors's ticket, and they were off.

They were scheduled to change trains at Buffalo, but a snowstorm had created an extended delay that left the players stranded there for nearly six hours. No problem. Acting on Red Wallace's suggestion, they simply locked the door to the bar, gave the bartender five bucks to make the joint a private club, and started drinking the hours away.

A statue of a buffalo, a celebrated city monument officially identified as "Stubby the Bison," was perched on the station platform. The players thought it was made of bronze, but it turned out to be a cement-type product coated in copper. "Of course," said Brightman, "Connors had to go outside, climb on its back, and play at being a rodeo rider. He was kind of woozy like the rest of us, and when he started falling off, he grabbed at the tail. Well, sure enough, he pulled the damn thing right off the ass end of the statue. We didn't know what to do, so we went back into the bar to regroup.

"We were definitely a crude bunch," Brightman continued, "and someone mentioned that the broken-off tail looked like Max Zaslofsky's penis. We fished in our pockets for quarters and put them end-to-end to measure the tail, and it came out to the exact amount of quarters that Max was supposed to have hanging on him. So, we decided to wrap it up and send it to Max."

Meanwhile, they kept on knocking back the beer and were totally confounded when the police showed up. "They confiscated the tail," Brightman remembered. "Then they rode on the train with us to the next stop to make sure we calmed down. If they hadn't have done that, I'm positive that we all would've been arrested. As it was, as soon as they left, one of the guys went berserk and ripped all of the clothes hooks from the walls of the train."

The team returned to Boston with still no sign of Russell. By the next morning when they arrived for practice at the gym at Boston University, the "Buffalo Tail Caper" had been emblazoned all over the newspapers. The Celtics were identified as the culprits, and the $600 required to repair the damage was to be paid by Walter Brown.

"Honey was fighting mad," said Brightman. "He sat us down on some benches against a wall and chewed us out: we were losers; we were dumb bastards. But Kottman inadvertently saved us from worse."

Kottman was a small-town boy who had difficulty adjusting to Boston—and also to Russell's hard-nosed attitude. (Russell even referred to his favorite players as "dumb bastards.") The Celtics' tallest player, Kottman was a fairly accurate hook shooter and backed up Connie Simmons at center. He was well liked by most of his teammates, but according to Howie McHugh, he was also "a blubbery kid with a dull personality." When the players congregated after practices or games at the Blue Moon, Kottman would complain to the bartender about what a bad coach Russell was.

Coincidentally, just that morning word had gotten back to Russell that Kottman was cutting his throat behind his back. Russell couldn't understand how Kottman, or anybody else, could think that he was anything less than a genius. So, the Buffalo Tail Caper was momentarily forgotten as Russell began cursing Kottman. "If you get your big ass up off that bench," Russell raged, "I'll pop you in the kisser right here and now." Kottman didn't know what to do, so he just kept his seat. Of course, that only proved to Russell that Kottman was even softer than he thought he was, so the abuse got even worse.

"We felt sorry for poor Kottman," said Brightman. "At the same time, we were happy that he deflected Honey's anger away from the rest of us. Then Honey ran the shit out of us in practice."

The players responded the next evening by beating Toronto, 53–49, in their finest effort of the young season. They then proceeded to duplicate their season-opening five-game losing streak. After an inept, 61–59 show-ing against the Steamrollers in Providence, Boston's record sank to 1–9. The Celtics were still the worst team in the league.

That's when Brightman exploded. "When I first got to training camp," he said, "I was so anxious to make the team that I pulled back on my intensity. For the first ten games, I didn't play much. Mostly I chased the ball around in the waning moments of games that were already lost."

Brightman remained somewhat reluctant to get rough with anybody in the team's practice scrimmages. "Honey used to play along with us sometimes, because we had only ten men and somebody was usually nursing some kind of minor injury. He was in his late forties, but he could still play pretty good. If you turned your head, he'd cut to the basket. He'd also grab hold of our shorts so we couldn't move, and whenever he could catch us, he'd give us a bruise to remember him by. I mean, the guy was tougher than nails. He was all man and a yard wide. I'd tiptoe around him, avoiding him if I could, but with the losses piling up and me wasting away on the bench, I started going out of my way to run him over when he practiced with us. I mean, we went at each other. Finally, after one practice, we sat down and had a talk."

Brightman told his coach that he could guard anybody in the league and demanded to start the next game. What the hell was the difference? The Celtics were in the toilet anyway. Russell liked his feisty attitude and agreed.

Brightman started against the Warriors, but the player he was guarding scored on Philadelphia's first two possessions. Russell called a quick time-out and said to Brightman, "It seems to me we've got a problem here."

"Bullshit," Brightman responded. "I never saw the guy play before, and I didn't know the son of a bitch was left-handed. Watch what happens from here on in."

The lefty didn't score for the rest of the game, but Boston still lost. Even so, for the next several weeks, Brightman spent as much time on the bench as he did on the court.

Nothing changed much as the Celtics' season progressed. They beat Pittsburgh to end their second losing streak and raise their record to 2–10, but the game was still unsatisfying to Russell. This time, the fly in his oint-ment was Connie Simmons.

Under the red-assed guidance of fiery Paul Birch, the Ironmen rated as the roughest outfit in the league. Their defense featured elbows, forearms, and even right crosses. Midway through the game, young Simmons signaled for a time-out, a violation of the precept that only a coach decided when to burn a precious time-out.

"I've got to go to the bathroom," Simmons pleaded as the Celtics approached the bench, but Russell knew that Simmons was just trying to escape from the rough stuff.

"A bunch of pussies," Russell muttered to himself. "That's why we can't win for losing."

There were other reasons as well why the Celtics were unsuccessful—one of the more significant ones being Russell himself. A relic from bygone days, Russell used an ancient offense: a three-man weave with an occasional back-door cut. The weakside forward would also set a cross-pick for the center, thereby enabling Connie Simmons (or Kottman) to settle into the pivot. Any passes into the low post were followed by scissor cuts. Russell did come up with one significant innovation, however—fronting the pivotman on defense.

Russell was also extremely unrealistic in his expectations of the Celtics' capabilities, especially on defense. During training camp, he'd told a reporter that he expected his team to limit opponents to 35 points per game, just as the Original Celtics had done. As it turned out, Boston was the lowest-scoring team in the BAA and still averaged 60.1 ppg.

"Honey had us so focused on defense," said Johnny Simmons, "that we were afraid to shoot. He hated bad shots even more than he hated turnovers. And God forbid that we blew a layup. Honey had a phrase for that: 'While you were out the door, the other team had a five-on-four fast break going the other way.'"

Knowing that he was a harsh taskmaster, Russell frequently tried to lighten up in practice. Before an intrasquad scrimmage, he'd announce that the losing side would have to "asses up." That meant they'd lean forward against a wall, duck their heads, and lift their asses. The winners would stand about twenty-five feet away and fire basketballs at the upraised asses. The baseball players among them included Johnny Simmons (who had played on a Yankees farm team), Brightman (in the Cleveland organization), and Connors, and they always threw the most accurate, and most painful, ass balls.

For one reason or another, Boston's practice sessions were always dramatic. There were other reasons why practices were deemed important. During one intrasquad scrimmage, Kottman was loosely guarding Connors, knowing that his teammate couldn't shoot himself in the foot. Connors became irate. "You're making me look bad, Kottman," he told him. "Guard me, you son of a bitch, or I'll knock every tooth out of your head."

After the Celtics lost to the Stags in Chicago to bring their record to 2–11, Russell was shocked. It couldn't be his fault. Never. "What the fuck did I pick these guys up for?" he asked out loud as the team headed for the dressing room. "They don't know what the fuck they're doing out there." During his postgame comments, Russell asked his players if "the fix was on tonight." As far as the players knew, not even the most pinheaded of bettors would be foolish enough to make a wager on a BAA game.

But Russell had an even bigger headache after the game. Brightman had ripped off his uniform and, instead of shoving it into his gym bag, tossed it on the floor, yelled, "I quit!" and bolted out of the room.

"I was still mad about being chained to the bench for such a long time," Brightman said. "I was playing well, but I felt that I could have been playing all along. I was mixed up, hot-tempered as hell, and a little goony. Anyway, I went and played with the Wilkes-Barre Barons, in the Eastern League. Hell, the deal was that I'd get a hundred bucks a game there, and we'd play three times a week, which came to a hell of a lot more than I was making in Boston. As far as I was concerned, I was through with the Celtics and with the BAA."

To replace Brightman, Russell brought in several hopefuls, including Don Eliason, a 6'2", 210-pound end for the Boston Shamrocks, of the National Football League. Eliason played in one game for the Celtics, registered one shot and a solitary personal foul, and was cut. Still desperately searching for help, Russell signed another member of the Shamrocks, Hal Crisler. A bruising, 6'3" 215-pounder, Crisler wasn't much better than his predecessor, but at least he showed good hands and a ferocious disposition. In the absence of anybody better (or, indeed, anybody else), Russell kept Crisler on the roster for a while.

From Chicago, the Celtics entrained to Pittsburgh. Win, lose, or draw, road trips were always filled with hilarity—and the laugh master was Connors. The self-described ladies' man confessed, "I'd see a pretty girl in a department store or someplace, and I'd go into my routine. 'Glory be to God. And there she is—dawn—on the hills of Ireland.' And she'd be ready to melt in my arms."

Connors also had more persuasive verse to use on women who weren't so easily impressed. He explained, "I'd say, 'Have you ever heard this one, my dear?' Then I'd give them a quote from François Villon. 'If I were king—ah love, if I were king / What tributary nations would I bring to stoop before your scepter and to swear / Allegiance to your lips and eyes and hair. Beneath your feet what treasures would I fling: / The stars should be pearls upon a string, / The world a ruby for your finger ring. / And you should have the sun and moon to wear. / If I were king.' But honey, I haven't got any dough. Let's go to your place."

If mademoiselle was still bashful, Connors would add a few lines of his own composition: "*Ah, Rosalie (or Mary, or Brenda . . .), lips half open like the petals of a rose. God only knows what joy shall be mine tonight . . .* You agree, honey? Let's go."

Connors was always on. He would often approach a stranger in the street or in a train station, some man who stood about 4'10", and say, "Dad, where have you been? I haven't seen you in such a long time."

After a rare win, 46–44, in Pittsburgh, Russell was ecstatic. *That* was the way to play defense. His joy caught in his throat three nights later when the Celtics lost to Detroit at home after suffering several defensive lapses in the stretch. The frustrating loss made Russell realize how much the team missed Brightman's hard-nosed defense, so, on December 6, he sent his AWOL player a telegram: "COME BACK I'LL GIVE YOU $1000 EXTRA"

"A thousand bucks was a fortune in those days," Brightman commented. "Besides, I missed the action in the big cities. So, I jumped on a train early the next morning and headed to Boston, hoping to get there in time to play against the Knicks, but the weather was bad, and the trip took eight hours. I got to the Arena at halftime, and by the time I was dressed and ready to go, the second half had already started. Honey plugged me right into the action. I played about twenty minutes, but I stunk up the court, and we lost by a lot."

The final score was 90–65, and Russell was incensed that any team of his could be so defenseless. *Ninety goddamn points!*

After the game, Russell approached Brightman with a fistful of money. "You missed half the game," said Russell, "plus you played like shit. So, that'll cost you five hundred."

Brightman was unhappy for the rest of the season. In part, he vented his anger during practice sessions, going out of his way to manhandle Harold Kottman, whom he always believed to be both soft and stupid.

After dropping another game in New York, the Celtics went on a minor binge, grinding out a pair of victories against the Detroit Falcons and the Philadelphia Warriors.

Russell had little respect for "modern" ballplayers, even including Philadelphia's Joe Fulks, the league's leading scorer. "Look at that dumb bastard out there," Russell would mutter on the bench every time Fulks scored one of his newfangled jump shots. "In my day, I could play that guy to a dead stop with a piano on my back. He would have had to pay to get into the game."

Connors said he enjoyed playing against Fulks. Before the tip-off, he would amble over to Fulks. "I'd say, 'You cocksucker. I'm a bad player, and you're a good player, so you can't make me look any worse than I am.' Then I'd punch him and bang him around. If he got less than forty points, I figured I'd been successful. I even surprised myself at how well I played against Jumping Joe."

After losing a home-and-home series to St. Louis, Russell decided he needed new and better players. He'd always had his eye on Jack "Dutch" Garfinkel, a six-foot guard from New York, who had played at St. John's and also in various incarnations of the ABL. Celebrated for his intelligent pass work, Garfinkel was then riding the bench for the Rochester Royals, of the NBL.

Before the season, the BAA and the NBL had agreed to a nonaggression pact that forbade player raids. While the negotiations with the Royals continued, the Celtics fell into another painful losing streak: following the home-and-home series with St. Louis, they lost a game at Pittsburgh and another versus the Warriors at home—four consecutive failures.

Walter Brown was so disheartened that he offered Mike Uline $50,000 for four of Washington's starters (Bones McKinney, Fred Scolari, Bob Feerick, and Johnny Norlander). Uline refused.

Russell's despair topped Brown's. He proposed trading his entire roster for the entire roster of the even more inept Pittsburgh Ironmen. Podoloff quickly put a damper on the offer.

By now, the fans began to desert the team in droves. "We tried everything," said McHugh. "One game, we let everybody in for a buck. We gave T-shirts away. We let kids in for half price. We had father-and-son nights, two-for-the-price-of-one nights. We had preliminary games between boys' clubs, little shavers who would play for thirty minutes and end up with a score of two to one. I think our opening-night fiasco, when Connors broke the basket, turned off a lot of casual fans. Also, it's a rare town that will support as bad a team as we were."

Even the local sportswriters were beginning to file cynical stories. "There were eight newspapers in town," McHugh said, "and they rarely sent anybody to cover a game in person. Boston was a hockey town and a Red Sox town. When the Celtics opened for business, there wasn't a single high school team in the city that fielded a basketball team. Honey used to hold clinics for the writers to teach them what a pick was and stuff like that. Only one guy, Jack Barry, from the *Star*, had even an inkling of what was happening in a basketball game. Connors was our biggest draw. A picture of him standing on a chair and sticking his head through the hoop got big coverage. Otherwise, we were lucky to get an inch or two in the back of the sports pages. It got to the point where three thousand was a decent crowd."

Finally, after Podoloff intervened, Brown was able to cut a cash deal (for an undisclosed amount) that made Garfinkel a free agent. Crisler was cut, while Garfinkel made his Celtics debut on Christmas night in Providence. His new teammates weren't used to unselfish play, and Dutch's first three passes hit Art Spector in the head. Despite Garfinkel's extraordinary court awareness, the Celtics lost again, 80–63.

Russell was torn between anger and delight. Every loss was galling, yet here was the playmaker he needed. All he lacked now was some guys who could anticipate being passed to and then catch the damn ball and do something worthwhile with it.

Russell was thrilled to send the troublesome Red Wallace to Toronto for a speedy, hot-shooting guard named Charlie Hoeffer, the only pro player ever to come out of Queens College. In another move, Boston dealt Tony Kappen to Pittsburgh for Moe Becker, a sturdy guard from Duquesne. Becker was also a veteran of the NBL, yet he was destined to be a benchwarmer before being moved along to Detroit.

Connors was likewise moved to bring Hoeffer into the fold. "Charlie was a little guy with a baby face," said Brightman. "He looked like he'd live forever. Well, Connors took care of that in a hurry. Night after night, Connors convinced Charlie to tour the bars, chase the skirts, and stay out late. Charlie gradually wore out and was lucky that he lasted through the rest of the season."

Russell also signed Jerry Kelly, a 6′3″, 172-pound forward from Marshall, who was effective under the basket and also had a nice touch from the perimeter. "Kelly was as silent as the Sphinx," said McHugh. "In his spare time, he was also a hairdresser."

It soon became evident that Garfinkel's best days were behind him. He was destroyed by Fred Scolari as the Washington Capitols downed the Celtics by 70–60 in Boston.

Next up was a game in Toronto on January 4, in which the absurd turned to the ridiculous when it was discovered that the Celtics' trainer, Harvey Cohen, had left the bag containing the uniforms at the check-in counter at Logan Airport. (The bag eventually wound up in Chicago.) For the game, the Celtics were outfitted in black T-shirts that had numbers attached to the backs with white adhesive tape. The numbers kept peeling off and had to be pressed back repeatedly. Finally, by the second quarter, the Celtics removed whatever strands of tape were left and finished the game wearing undifferentiated black jerseys. Even so, they managed to prevail by 58–53.

The rare road victory also proved to be a memorable one for Al Brightman: "The Huskies had a husky little five-eleven guard named Mike McCarron, who hailed from Queens and had played for Honey at Seton Hall. Before the game, Honey told me exactly how he wanted me to play the guy: start off playing him loose; then when he comes through the middle, step up and punch him in the gut. Honey swore that McCarron would be useless after that. So, that's exactly what I did. Wham! I left him doubled up on the floor and clutching his stomach. Two minutes later, I was cutting through the lane, when McCarron unloaded on me, just tore me up. My face was cut. My nose was bleeding. There was even blood coming out of my ears."

During a subsequent time-out, Brightman said to Russell, "That was a hell of an idea. What do I do now?"

"Well," Russell said, "looks like it's going to be a real close contest between you two."

Later, Hoeffer told Brightman about a windowless room in the back of a bar that McCarron frequented back home in Queens. It seemed that McCarron was a notorious brawler, especially after he'd downed a few. He'd get so out of control that he had to be kayoed with a baseball bat and then locked in the back room until he sobered up.

"Mike and I eventually became buddies," Brightman said, thirty-five years after the fact, "yet to this day, I could still kill Honey for his little scouting report."

After a bad outing against Cleveland, the Celtics surprised everybody (except Russell) by embarking on a four-game winning streak that lifted their overall record to 10–21. The undoubted high point of their season was a 47–38 overtime win over the first-place Washington Capitols on January 16. The game was marked by the Caps' unleashing of 91 field goals (making only 14), an incredible number at the time. They also recorded 18 free throws, or, in the parlance of the day, "oakies." Despite the fact that Washington's standout center, Horace "Bones" McKinney, was hobbled by a heavily taped sprained back, Russell was ecstatic—yielding 38 points in fifty-three minutes was in line with his preseason hopes. Perhaps his charges had finally learned their lessons and the Celtics would turn their dismal season around.

Alas, the revival of Russell's dreams was short lived. As the season rounded the clubhouse turn, three two-game winning streaks were interspersed with various losing streaks that ranged from two to four. And the merry-go-round kept spinning.

"Honey wouldn't relent," Connors said. "He got on everybody for everything, especially me. But I was the only one who could make him laugh. He said that I must be a good Catholic, because I was shooting so many Hail Marys. I told him that I had to shoot or else they'd steal the ball away from me."

During one game, after Russell vociferously berated Connors for a particularly egregious turnover, the player's riposte was, "OK, Honey. Now I'm scared. Now what should I do?"

Connors was also on a perpetual mission to make his teammates laugh as well. In addition to delivering his usual shtick, Connors frequently improvised antics that titillated his teammates.

Here's Brightman: "We were flying to St. Louis, and there happened to be a pretty flamenco dancer sitting next to him who didn't understand English too well. That didn't hamper Connors. 'Young lady,' he said, 'there are seven ways to eat pussy. Spoon, flattop . . .' And he goes through all the different ways. Sure enough, he talked her into going up to his hotel room, see? But he had given us advance notice, so we all got there before him. There were guys hiding under the bed, in the bathroom, and guys peeping through the transom. Then Connors says to her, 'This is how deer mate.' So, he goes to the other side of the room, breaks into a run, and jumps on top of her. All of us were laughing so hard that a couple of guys pissed their pants. It was a crazy ball club."

By early February, Wyndol Gray was disgusted by Russell's insistence on keeping him glued to the bench during close games. Gray, who hailed from Toledo, had secretly contacted the Toledo Jeeps, of the NBL, about abandoning the Celtics and signing with them. But the word got out, and the matter was brought to the attention of President Podoloff.

After the Garfinkel transaction, the BAA Executive Committee had reemphasized the illegality of any BAA ball club's making any sort of player deal with a rival league. To circumvent the rule, Boston could simply waive Gray and make him a free agent—but that would allow for another BAA team to claim his rights. Podoloff noted that Boston "needs player strength rather than the amount that might be paid by way of waiver price." Therefore, "In view of Boston's present position in the league standing," he allowed the Celtics to trade Gray to Toledo.

In truth, there was no deal between the two teams. Gray simply jumped from one team to the other, and Podoloff's Bulletin 75 was merely a face-saving gesture. In any case, Gray played only two games for the Jeeps before returning to Boston. The rumor was that he had been able to dribble his first paycheck through the streets of Toledo.

Connors refused to let a season in free fall stop him from enjoying the action. Three days later, the Celtics were playing in Washington. "I knew I wasn't much of a basketball player," Connors readily admitted. "Baseball was my real sport, and basketball was just a way of having fun, staying in shape, and passing time during the off-season. At the same time, I did have a modicum of pride."

The Capitols were easily the class of the league, and even though they stomped the Celtics from the get-go (on their way to a lopsided 83–69 win), the home team continued to play earnest defense late in the concluding period. That included John Mahnken, who wouldn't allow Connors to breathe, prompting Connors to entreat, "Whatever you do, John, please don't foul me, because I'm even a worse free-throw shooter than a field-goal shooter. So, if you foul me, you'll make me look worse than I already look."

Mahnken laughed and backed off.

The Celtics won their final contest, beating Cleveland by 71–66, to conclude their season at 22–33. Seven teams had better records than the Boston Celtics, but none of them had any more fun.

Boston Celtics

	G	FGM	FGA	Pct.	FTM	FTA	Pct.	Asst.	PF	Pts.	Avg.
Connie Simmons	60	246	768	.320	128	189	.677	62	130	620	10.3
Al Brightman	58	223	870	.256	121	193	.627	60	115	567	9.8
Wyndol Gray	55	139	476	.292	72	124	.581	47	105	350	6.4
Art Spector	55	123	460	.267	83	150	.553	46	130	329	6.0
Johnny Simmons	60	120	429	.280	78	127	.614	29	78	318	5.3
Jerry Kelly	43	91	313	.291	74	111	.667	21	128	256	6.0
Chuck Connors	49	94	380	.247	39	84	.464	40	129	227	4.6
Charlie Hoeffer	35	76	316	.241	59	93	.634	24	81	211	6.0
Dutch Garfinkel	40	81	304	.266	17	28	.607	58	62	179	4.5
Harold Kottman	53	59	188	.314	47	101	.465	17	58	165	3.1
Red Wallace	24	55	224	.246	21	48	.438	20	42	131	5.5
Bill Fenley	33	31	138	.225	23	45	.511	16	59	85	2.6
Tony Kappen	18	25	91	.275	24	38	.632	6	24	74	4.1
Virgil Vaughn	17	15	78	.192	15	28	.536	10	18	45	2.6
Mel Hirsch	13	9	45	.200	1	2	.500	10	18	19	1.5
Moe Becker	6	5	22	.227	3	4	.750	1	15	13	2.2
Robert Duffy	6	2	7	.286	4	4	1.000	0	4	8	1.3
Hal Crisler	4	2	6	.333	2	2	1.000	0	6	6	1.5
Dick Murphy	7	1	17	.059	0	4	.000	3	6	2	0.3
Don Eliason	1	0	1	.000	0	0	.000	0	1	0	0.0

Postscript

Connors played in four games for the 1947–48 edition of the Celtics (who were still coached by Honey Russell), averaging only 3.0 points per game. The lesser of Connors's ambitions came true when he was summoned to Brooklyn early in the 1949 season and appeared in one game for the Dodgers. After one fruitless at bat, he was returned to the minor leagues.

The Chicago Cubs then claimed his rights, and he spent 66 games in the bigs during the summer of 1951. His stats included a .239 average, 2 homers, and 18 RBIs in 201 plate appearances.

Toward the end of the 1951 season, the Cubs sold Connors to the Hollywood Stars, of the AAA Pacific Coast League. That's when he was spotted by a scout and signed to a movie contract. He made his film debut playing a police sergeant in *Pat and Mike* (1952). Later, Connors gained fame and fortune starring in a popular TV series, *The Rifleman.*

Here's Connors's last word on his BAA career: "How many points did you say I averaged that first year with the Celtics? Four-point-six per game? Jesus, I was better than I thought."

The Celtics, of course, are one of only two charter franchises that have continued operating in their cities of origin—the other being New York.

The Bottom Line

Average paid attendance	1,682
Net receipts	$57,875
Estimated loss	$200,000

6

The Providence Steamrollers
Hit a Roadblock

The largest city in the smallest state, Providence, Rhode Island, was named by Roger Williams in 1636 in honor of "God's merciful providence." Alas, by the time the Steamrollers appeared, the city had begun a merciless decline that would accelerate for the next fifty years. (The number of residents would dwindle from a population of 253,505 in the 1940 census to 173,618 by the turn of the century.) The decline was blamed on various factors: deteriorating schools, aging housing, rising crime rates, the closing of a naval operating base, and a post–World War II exodus to the suburbs.

Given Providence's small population base and deteriorating economic health, why was Lou Pieri so eager to invest so much of his time and his resources in the Steamrollers?

Even though 990,000 people lived within a thirty-mile radius of the Providence Arena, another geographical factor kept Pieri's American Hockey League team, the Rhode Island Reds, from ever being a significant moneymaker. Providence's proximity to Boston prevented the Reds from competing on equal terms with the winter sports attractions in Bean Town: the NHL's Boston Bruins, the NFL's Boston Yankees, plus dozens of glamorous college basketball games in the Boston Garden. Thus, the Steamrollers (named after Pieri's construction company) represented a last desperate chance to cash in on what was presumed to be the renaissance of professional sports after the war.

"Lou had a great love for basketball," said Joe Fay, the general manager of the Steamrollers. "He had captained the Brown University basketball team back in 1915 and later coached the team." More important, Pieri was a close friend of Walter Brown's, and his pal's enthusiasm and optimism were infectious.

As was the case with Brown, Pieri originally sought to hire Frank Keaney from Rhode Island State but was turned down. Pieri's second choice was Robert Morris, of nearby Pawtucket, one of the most successful high school coaches (and well-respected physics teachers) in the state. Morris was eager for the opportunity and readily agreed to Pieri's terms. However, instead of resigning from his dual positions at Pawtucket High School, Morris hedged his bet by taking a leave of absence.

"Right from the start," said Fay, "we had a tough time attracting established players. No matter how much we offered, they were usually willing to accept less money to play in New York or Boston. We couldn't compete with the lure of the big metropolitan areas. Still, we thought that our only available option was a good one: signing local players who wanted to stay local."

Since Pieri had a cozy hometown feeling about his native Providence, he was more than happy when Morris and Fay set out to sign as many veterans of Keaney's Runnin' Rams as possible. Accordingly, five former Rhode Island State players appeared on the Rollers' ten-man roster at the beginning of the season:

Earl Shannon, a quick-handed, 5'11" guard. "He had great speed," said Dino Martin, one of the Rollers' star players. "A beautiful cutter, Earl filled the wing on our three-on-two fast break with tremendous effectiveness."

George Mearns, a 6'3", 175-pound whippet of a forward. "Despite his slender physique," said Martin, "George was an excellent rebounder who played with a lot of desire."

Armand Cure, a sturdy, 6'0", 198-pound guard who loved to mix it up with the big boys.

Bob Shea, 6'2", 194, who threw an outlet pass as easily and accurately as if he were throwing a baseball. Martin also reported that Shea "never stopped hustling."

Ernie Calverley, a wispy, 5'10", 145-pound guard, renowned for his brilliant passing as well as his scoring heroics.

The other roster spots were given to the following men:

Wilfred "Pop" Goodwin—6'2", 203, no college—a strong-armed guard-forward with a nifty repertoire of shots. Goodwin was also one of the rare Rollers with pro experience, having played all of two games for Sheboygan in the NBL after his discharge from the military.

The aforementioned Dino Martin, 5'8", 160, from Georgetown, a hot shooter and fierce driver. Martin hailed from nearby Newton, Massachusetts, and was mostly known in the area as a tennis player. "I made it as far as the Boston Junior Davis Cup team," Martin said, "but I realized soon enough that there was no money to be made in tennis except as a teaching pro. I did that for a while, but it was too boring, so I went to Georgetown University and concentrated on basketball."

On Providence's original roster until better players were found were Tom Callahan, 6'1", 180, from Rockhurst; Ken Keller, a 6'1", 180, shooter out of St. John's; and Bob "Red" Dehnert, 6'3", 175, from Columbia.

Of these ten, the most significant player by far was Calverley. In the previous spring, he had proved his mettle at Rhode Island State during a first-round game against Bowling Green in the prestigious NIT, then in its ninth incarnation and widely celebrated as an annual athletic event comparable to the World Series. That's when Calverley bagged a dramatic last-second shot from fifty-five feet that tied the contest and sent it into overtime. (The Rams won the game, only to lose by a single point to Kentucky in the championship finale.) Calverley's overall play earned him MVP honors for the tournament.

Calverley's immense popularity in the state was verified when he was named the Best Rhode Island Athlete for 1946 in a survey of the state's sportswriters. His total of 246 votes far surpassed the second-place finisher, a swimmer named Clara Lamore, who tallied 167.

Notwithstanding Calverley's allure, Fay was pragmatic about his team's viability: "The hockey team had a lock on all the Friday night and Sunday afternoon dates at the Arena. That left us with mostly Thursdays and Saturdays. Because we didn't have the prime dates, we didn't expect to draw enough fans to turn the red ink to black. We hoped we'd win enough games, however, to keep the turnstiles clicking enough so we'd at least break even. Making the playoffs would be a huge help."

Before the Steamrollers' season commenced, the team practiced at Hope High School, and local sportswriters predicted a racehorse style of play modeled after Keaney's successful game plan at Rhode Island State. They weren't disappointed.

"I call it Civil War basketball," Morris said. "We shoot and run."

On November 2, the Steamrollers began what they hoped would be their march through the BAA by squeezing past the Celtics, 59–53, before 4,406 hometown fans. (The Providence Arena could accommodate 7,200 for basketball games.) As was the story in most other BAA venues, insulating pads were initially considered to be a wasteful extravagance, and the game was played on a portable court that had been laid directly over the ice rink. Even when the insulating barrier was subsequently installed, visiting players declared the Providence Arena to be the coldest building in the league.

By opening night, the Rollers had already learned to stack towels underfoot and wear caps while they sat on the bench, and to drape more towels around their shoulders. Before long, similar in-game adjustments became de rigueur for visiting teams. This night, however, the Celtics were unaware of the frigid conditions until they made their appearance on the court, and their performance was blighted by cold shooting, bobbled passes, and stiff joints.

Meanwhile, looking sharp in their woolen jerseys and satin shorts—white, with black and red trim—the Rollers thrilled the fans with their madcap pace. Every time Calverley so much as touched the ball, the fans went wild. And as Providence embarked on a late rally that eventually won the game, one enthusiastic onlooker yelled out, "Come on, State!"

The Rollers' home stand continued with a win over Chicago, immediately after which Morris signed an important newcomer: Hank Beenders, a lean, 6'6" forward from Haarlem, Holland. Beenders had been the captain of LIU's 1941 NIT champs. He'd then served a long and courageous stint in the Army Air Corps and now, at the advanced age of thirty, was the team's elder statesman. His presence in the lineup was celebrated by a victory over the Ironmen, but then came a loss to the same sad-sack outfit from Pittsburgh.

After eyeballing three home games, one reporter, Earl Lofquist, wrote that while the Steamrollers' fans were loud by hockey standards, they were also "polite." In fact, the fans' relatively sedate demeanor was a suitable reflection of the rather sober personalities of their hometown heroes.

"We were all business," said Dino Martin, "quiet and well behaved. None of us fooled around much, if at all."

The only oddball behavior was exhibited by Elmore Morganthaler, who soon joined the team after flunking out of Boston College (this, after he'd already flunked out of New Mexico Mines College).

Morganthaler stood 6'9" and weighed 230 but was listed as a seven-footer in hopes that fans would be curious to see such a freak run the court without tripping over the foul lines. That's just about all Morganthaler could manage. The big man was also a bundle of nerves who resorted to chewing gum to calm himself during games. When the action got hot and heavy, he'd extract the gum from his mouth, roll it into a ball, and stick it behind his right ear. As soon as the pace of the game moderated, he'd pop the gum back into his mouth.

The Rollers were 4–3 when Lofquist took another, more subjective look at the ball club. First, he questioned Morris's credentials. How could a high school coach cope with professional players? Added to that was Morris's inability to devise offensive and defensive game plans that could keep up with the brainstorms of more experienced coaches. Lofquist then committed the heresy of claiming that the Rollers had too many wet-behind-the-ears players from Rhode Island State to compete with more seasoned performers. However, Lofquist did concede that the local fans seemed to like the full-court, up-and-down action.

After downing Detroit, Providence lost five of six. Players came, players went, and the team soon settled into mediocrity. The Steamrollers' run-stun-and-have-fun game plan made scoreboards all over the league flash like pinball machines. They ultimately finished third in scoring behind Washington and Chicago with a per-game average of 72.5 points, but their 74.2 ppg allowed made them the worst defensive team in the BAA.

The shrinking audiences at the Arena wondered why such a furiously up-tempo game failed to duplicate the resounding successes that Keaney had achieved at R.I. State.

Honey Russell explained the difference: "Keaney had a six-nine center, big for those days, who did a damn good job of clogging the middle and forcing the other team into bad shots. The big fellow also collected rebounds and could make perfect outlet passes that got them on the run. Keaney's fast break was really a four-man deal. The Steamrollers, on the other hand, had no big men who could do the same things."

Russell went on to particularize Keaney's "brilliant" strategy: "Here's a guy on the opposite team, right? And he sees that he's not being guarded tightly at all. So, he thinks, 'Oh, boy! Gimme the ball and get out of my way! I'm scoring thirty points tonight.' And all of his teammates are thinking the exact same thing. So, while these five guys are fighting amongst themselves for the ball and driving into a clogged-up middle, Keaney just sits back and smiles. He's the greatest defensive genius of his time because he knows the one critical thing that those five hamburgers either forgot or never knew in the first place: *there's only one goddamn basketball.*"

Since the inept Morganthaler was rarely used, the 6'6" Beenders was the Rollers' tallest player. The Dutchman's speed enabled Providence to run a five-man fast break at the cost of inferior board work and undersized interior defense. In their eagerness to run themselves into easy baskets, the Rollers mostly played defense in the starting blocks, always ready to get out and go.

Another reason why Keaney's running game was so overwhelming was that his Rams faced each opponent only once or twice during a season. The bad guys, therefore, were never very comfortable having to play and make decisions at such an accelerated pace. In the BAA, in contrast, the Rollers encountered each opponent six times in the course of the season, so the surprise element was trumped.

Other factors as well doomed Morris's adaptation of Keaney's philosophy. To be consistently effective, a running team required all of the following: good defense, big men who could rebound and make quick and precise outlet passes, a deep bench, outstanding physical conditioning, team-oriented players, and several good ball handlers who could make savvy decisions while moving at full speed.

Determination was more important than flat-out foot speed. A fast-break offense resembled a marathon race with a relay team.

The advantages of track-meet basketball were considerable:

- Every offensive player could run himself into easy shots, thereby boosting the team's overall morale.
- Players at every level of the game loved to run downhill on the break and hated to run uphill on defense.
- Lots of points could be scored in a hurry.
- Having to deal with a relentlessly running team tested an opponent's will to win.
- The opponent's defense never got a chance to get set.

- Opponents could be overly cautious when they had the ball, knowing that the slightest mistake would lead to an easy score on the other end of the court.
- Two good passes could produce a high-percentage shot, whereas the normal, station-to-station offenses required seven or eight passes, which increased the chances of steals, mishandlings, and zig passes to players who had already zagged.

The theory and practice of scoot-and-shoot likewise had a significant downside. Careless up-tempo play could lead to an inordinate number of turnovers (a statistic that was not recorded at the time). The rapid pace meant that the on-court time of a team's best players had to be somewhat limited; conversely, a team's lesser players would get more playing time than normal. A running team that had a flat game could easily get blown out.

The traditional slowdown offenses usually kept the score close and enabled teams to win games they might ordinarily have lost. At the same time, deliberate offenses also kept weaker opponents in the game.

As expected, the Steamrollers were involved in many more lopsided games than any other team except the Washington Capitols (who were by far the most outstanding ball club during the regular season). A blowout in those days was considered to be any game that ended with a minimum 10-point margin. Of these, the Rollers were 11–14. (The Caps were an amazing 34–2.)

Providence competed in only nine games in which the differential was 3 points or less. The team's record here was 4–5.

Moreover, while the Rollers topped the 90-point mark on three occasions, they yielded 90-plus six times (including a pair of 100-plus outbursts by Chicago and Philadelphia). Primarily because the Steamrollers lacked the requisite defense and deep bench, Morris's game plan was doomed to fail.

The Steamrollers' defeat of the Chicago Stags, 81–77, in Providence on December 19 was at once a highlight and a lowlight of their season. The Stags were already considered to be one of the best outfits in the league (second only to the Washington Caps and somewhat better than the St. Louis Bombers), so the win seemed to augur glorious possibilities for the home team. At the same time, the game was marred by fifty-three personal and three technical fouls being called. Five players were disqualified when they committed their fifth foul. To ice that cake, mild-mannered Calverley was assessed a technical foul when he was tooted for a traveling violation and innocently tossed the ball to the referee; the trouble was that the ref had turned his back. Judging that Calverley had acted with malicious intent, the ref nailed him with a tech. The loyal fans were on the verge of rioting, until their hero patted down their mounting anger.

The BAA's board of governors so valued Calverley's passing skills—and his potential to be boffo at the box office   that the league introduced a new statistic: assists, which comprised any pass that led directly to a basket by a teammate. Neither the colleges nor any of the other pro leagues had bothered to record and tabulate this aspect of the game. (The same neglect was given to rebounds, steals, blocked shots, and turnovers.) It was said that if the NCAA had tracked assists, Calverley would have averaged 15 or more during his tenure at Rhode Island State.

True to form, Calverley wound up comfortably leading the BAA in this new category. His per-game average of 3.4 assists was 1.2 better than the runner-up, Kenny Sailors, of Cleveland.

As the season progressed, many BAA watchers were caught off guard when Dino Martin evolved into a dynamic scorer as well. The release on his two-handed set shot was so quick that it often seemed as if he'd catch a pass, and the ball would bounce off his hands and start its journey to the hoop. He also drove to the basket with all the speed and power of a bowling ball. On January 9, 1947, the Steamrollers subdued the visiting Cleveland Rebels by 91–68 in what observers likened to a prolonged layup drill. Even better, Martin registered a league-record 40 points. Unfortunately, the record lasted for only five days, at which time Joe Fulks notched 41 against Toronto.

To celebrate Martin's feat, the city of Newport sponsored Dino Martin Night at the Arena on February 21. A boys' club presented the "mighty mite" with a radio, a group of politicians gave him a "purse" filled with an undisclosed amount of cash, and the Steamrollers' management handed him an engraved gold watch.

"By that point in the season," Martin said, "I was exhausted. Not only was I supposed to score, I was also assigned to guard the other team's best offensive player—guys like Freddie Scolari and Frankie Baumholtz. The only times when I got a break from that duty was when the other guy was too big for me to handle, like Joe Fulks or Bones McKinney. I guess all of those presents seemed to energize me."

Martin showed his appreciation by scoring 25 points, but in the Steamrollers' next game, the Capitols refused to cooperate and won by 82–74.

Washington	FG	FT	Pts.
McKinney, f	12	1	25
Norlander, f	4	4	12
Passaglia, f	2	0	4
Mahnken, c	2	1	5
Scolari, g	2	1	5
Torgoff, g	2	2	6
Feerick, g	10	3	23
O'Grady, g	0	2	2
Totals	34	14	82

Providence	FG	FT	Pts.
Calverley, f	4	2	10
Goodwin, f	4	1	9
Martin, f	12	1	25
Grimshaw, f	0	0	0
Shannon, c	4	1	9
Pastushok, c	1	0	2
Beenders, g	3	4	10
Morganthaler, g	0	0	0
Mearns, g	2	0	4
Rosenstein, g	1	3	5
Totals	31	12	74

(Note that the 5'10" Calverley was listed as a forward, while the supposed seven-footer Morganthaler was identified as a guard. Apparently, either true positions were ignored or the stat men had little understanding of the game and couldn't tell who played where.)

Besides Martin's point making, the most noteworthy event of the contest occurred when Pop Goodwin netted a long shot just before the first half ended. After a tape measure revealed the distance to have been fifty feet, the Steamrollers claimed that Goodwin's feat constituted an official record for distance. The league office, however, had no time for such trivialities.

As the season drew to a merciful conclusion, the Rollers suffered what Morris deemed to be their most aggravating loss of the entire campaign. The backboards in Washington's Uline Arena were supported by several sets of guide wires that extended out of bounds past the baselines, but also over all four corners of the court itself. The Rollers were embroiled in an overtime period of a fast-paced battle with the Caps, and with the home team ahead by 96–95, Providence had the ball as the clock was on the verge of expiring. That's when Earl Shannon uncorked a midrange flipper from the right corner. The shot felt good coming out of his hands; the arc and the rotation were likewise picture perfect. Rising from the bench, Morris was positive that the shot would fall and the Rollers would win. Still on its upward path, the ball glanced slightly off one of the wires, but the shot was so true that the deflection failed to prevent the ball from making the net dance.

The celebrations of Morris and his minions quickly turned to grief when both refs tooted their tooters. By rule, any shot that made contact with any of the wires was a dead ball. The shot was therefore nullified, and the Capitols were declared the victors.

Morris voiced his beef to the press afterward but was surprisingly calm: "Take the wires off the court. They don't belong there in bounds. At other courts, the wires run out to the side. I have no other kick. Everything else was fine, and a good team beat us."

The season ended on an up note when the Rollers flattened the Stags in Providence, 83–79. After the final buzzer, the fans rose to give the team a standing ovation.

Although Morris had chosen the wrong strategies for his too short and defensively challenged ball club, most experts agreed that he'd done a fine job given the players at his disposal. The 28–32 record ranked the team in fourth place in the Eastern Division, 21 games behind first-place Washington. Providence was also 5 games behind third-place New York and therefore failed to qualify for the playoffs.

The Steamrollers and their fans were inadequately consoled by several statistical honors garnered by their players:

- Calverley led the BAA in assists, with 3.4 per game, with Shannon's average of 1.5 placing him seventh among the league playmakers.
- The top scorers were ranked according to total points, and four Rollers finished in the top sixteen: Calverley was the league's sixth-best scorer (14.3);

Martin ranked eleventh (12.2); Beenders finished thirteenth (12.3); and Shannon was sixteenth (12.1).

- George Mearns was the ninth-most-accurate free-throw shooter (.720).
- Shannon had the third-best field-goal percentage (.339).

Lou Pieri, for one, was sufficiently encouraged and vowed to bring the Steamrollers back for the 1947–48 season.

Providence Steamrollers

	G	FGM	FGA	Pct.	FTM	FTA	Pct.	Asst.	PF	Pts.	Avg.
Ernie Calverley	59	323	1,102	.293	199	283	.703	202	191	845	14.3
Dino Martin	60	311	1,022	.304	111	168	.661	59	98	733	12.2
Hank Beenders	58	266	1,016	.262	181	257	.704	37	196	713	12.3
Earl Shannon	57	245	722	.339	197	348	.566	84	169	687	12.1
George Mearns	57	128	478	.268	126	175	.720	35	137	382	6.7
Pop Goodwin	55	98	348	.262	60	75	.800	15	94	256	4.7
Hank Rosenstein	29	81	245	.331	87	130	.669	17	101	249	8.6
Jake Weber	39	52	178	.292	49	71	.690	3	91	153	3.9
George Pastushok	39	48	181	.262	25	46	.543	15	42	121	3.1
Bob Shea	43	37	153	.242	19	33	.576	6	42	93	2.2
Woodie Grimshaw	21	20	56	.357	21	44	.477	1	25	61	2.9
Tom Callahan	13	6	29	.207	5	12	.417	4	9	17	1.3
Elmore Morganthaler	11	4	13	.308	7	12	.583	3	3	15	1.4
Red Dehnert	10	6	15	.400	2	6	.333	0	8	14	1.4
Armand Cure	12	4	15	.267	2	3	.667	0	5	10	0.8
Lou Spicer	4	0	7	.000	1	2	.500	0	3	1	0.3
Ken Keller	3	0	0	—	0	1	.000	0	1	0	0.0

Postscript

Robert Morris returned to his teaching position, and the second edition of the Steamrollers was coached by Albert Soar and then Nat Hickey and set the standard for futility, sporting a record of 6–42 in the relatively short 1947–48 season. This was the lowest win total in the history of the BAA-cum-NBA. In the team's third and last year of existence, the Steamrollers were led by Ken Loeffler and finished at 12–48.

Pieri had lost enough money by then and folded his franchise. Still, the lure of pro basketball continued to enchant him. In the summer of 1949, Walter Brown allowed Pieri to purchase 50 percent of the Boston Celtics.

In 1980, a Providence rock-music promoter, Robert "Skip" Chernov, filed a lawsuit against the National Basketball Association. Chernov, who sported shoulder-length hair, favored red velvet jackets, and bore a striking resemblance to Tiny Tim, sought to reactivate the Steamrollers' franchise, but a local judge dismissed the action as being frivolous.

The Bottom Line

Average paid attendance	2,596
Net receipts	$117,740
Estimated loss	$140,000

Paul Birch Fires Up the Pittsburgh Ironmen

Paul Birch knew the difference between winners and losers. The former always played with all their might; win or lose, they were totally drained physically and emotionally once the final buzzer sounded. Wins instantly replenished their chops, but losses left them empty and needing extra time to recover, time to brood, time to apportion—and accept—blame, time to reconstitute their depleted psyches. What fueled their recovery was anger and frustration, along with the desire for revenge, to kick the stuffing out of the next team on the schedule.

On the other hand, losers always kept their sense of self intact by never making an all-out effort during games. The very idea of risking even a temporary psychological annihilation was too frightening to even consider. After losses, their anger and frustration was bogus, and they couldn't wait to go out and party.

Winners did not suffer losers gladly. And Paul Birch knew that he was a winner.

Born in Homestead, Pennsylvania, on January 14, 1910, Birch went on to become an outstanding player at Duquesne University under legendary coach Chick Davies. Most observers believed Birch to be the best ever to play for the Dukes. After he graduated in 1933, he was invited to join, and barnstorm with, the Original Celtics, the highest possible commendation. Fifty years later, he still loved to wax nostalgic about those days.

"We were gypsies," he said. "We played about a hundred fifty games each year, traveling by car to every tank town in the country. Playing three games a day was normal for us. We had an agent named Tom Humphries, who worked out of Chattanooga. He'd book us for the whole year and get a ten percent cut of our earnings. Usually we'd get a one-hundred-and-fifty-dollar guarantee, with the option of claiming anywhere from thirty to thirty-five percent of the gate."

Traveling with only six players and no supporting staff, the Celtics were often swindled out of their rightful shares. "Promoters would simply run away with the box-office money before the game was finished," he said. "One promoter said that thousands of fans had jumped over a fence and had gotten in to see the game for nothing. We had no way of checking these things out, although Dutch Dehnert sometimes tried using a hand clicker to check the house. Lots of times, though, we'd draw upwards of ten thousand fans in places like Cleveland and Indianapolis and wind up with a couple of hundred each. Our attitude was, 'Let's get the hell out of there and go on to the next town.'"

The Celtics were billed as "The World's Champions" and prided themselves on their passing and their defense, which featured lots of bodychecking and outright holding. If a ref was a homer, two Celtics would sandwich him and give him a quick but definitive going over. Sometimes confrontations with the refs and the fans got "a little bloody," but the Celtics would form themselves into a circle and take on all comers. "We were the ultimate team," Birch said proudly, "the first to concentrate exclusively on team play. We never paid any attention to personal statistics. We had to stay in great shape, so we ate well, got our rest, and only occasionally chased the broads."

To make a few extra bucks, the Celtics were not above placing bets and controlling the outcome. "The older guys handled the betting," said Birch, "and we'd do things like making sure a game ended in a tie by claiming we had a train to catch; then we'd play the same team a few days later, raise the bets, and beat them by twenty. But we did OK. I mean, we made a nice living out of it. And, man alive, were we tough."

Birch quit the circuit in 1937 to coach a high school team in his hometown. "We won the state championship in 1938; then I went back to the Celtics for a year. In 1940, I started playing with the Fort Wayne Zollner Pistons, in the old National League."

Fred Zollner was a wealthy Fort Wayne businessman and sports enthusiast, who recruited basketball and baseball players to work in his factory and compete under his banner. "Zollner made heavy-duty pistons," said Birch, "and had about fifteen hundred employees. My job was to arrange the transportation of the pistons and, once the war started, to dole out gas coupons."

All of Zollner's workers and players were exempted from the military draft because piston making was deemed an essential war industry. But the ball games never stopped.

"The company would pay all of our expenses, and the players would then split the profits at the end of the season. The first seven guys on the team had a full share; the others got one-seventh of a share. By the time the war broke out, I was in my early thirties, and my best playing days were a fading memory, so I'd make about fifteen thousand every year. Our best player was Bobby McDermott, the best clutch shooter I ever saw, and he'd take home about twenty thousand. The team was great advertising for the company."

The rules in the NBL were different from those in the BAA. The older league played four ten-minute quarters, and games were mostly supervised by a single referee. "The games were much more physical, too," said Birch. "Hell, they were even more physical than the ones the old Celtics played. It's a wonder that a single ref managed to keep things from getting too crazy. Pat Kennedy worked the NBL. So did a guy named Nat Messenger, who was rumored to be running with a bad crowd and was involved with drugs, or something." There would be even worse rumors about Messenger during the BAA playoffs.

As Birch's playing career faded, he naturally moved into coaching. "I wound up coaching the Youngstown Bears in the NBL," he said. "I actually liked working in a smaller city where my team played the only game in town." In the smaller gyms, Birch was sometimes able to stick a foot onto the court and trip opposing players as they sped by. When he was caught, he'd blame the tripee for being too close to the bench.

His exploits at Duquesne were still legendary, so John Harris was eager to make Birch the coach of his new team—the Pittsburgh Ironmen. Birch agreed, but with the proviso that he could bring in his old college coach, Chick Davies, as an adviser. Harris readily concurred.

However, Birch was still under contract to Youngstown, so, as with Honey Russell in Boston, he got a late start in signing players. "I had about four weeks before the season started to get a team together," he said. "Pittsburgh was not a very appealing place for guys to play basketball, because baseball and football had a lock on the sports public. I brought in some guys I had been coaching in Youngstown and added some locals who had played at Duquesne or at Pitt."

The most notable of these were the following:

Press Maravich, 6′0″, 185, out of Duquesne and Youngstown. Maravich was born in a Serbian ghetto in Aliquippa, Pennsylvania, where virtually everybody worked in the Jones & Laughlin steel mill, and where his first "basketball" was a tin can covered in black tape. He learned his basketball fundamentals in a local church before starring at Duquesne under Davies. After some rigorous combat duty in the Pacific, Maravich was sent to Pensacola, Florida, to serve as a flight instructor. "I had enough points to get out," he said, "but I was more interested in flying, so I stayed where I was. When Chick Davies found out I was back in the States, he told me that Birch was coaching in Youngstown and suggested I go join him. I totally respected Davies, but when I was a kid, Birch was playing at Duquesne, and he was my idol. I used to comb my hair like he did—parted down the middle. I used to walk like him. I even had his pictures from the newspapers all over my room; no matter where I turned, I could see Paul Birch, shooting, passing, and so on. So, off I went to Youngstown. Birch was good to play for back then. Sure, he'd get to ranting and raving when things weren't going our way, but once the game was over, he'd be angelic."

Overall, Maravich enjoyed his first taste of pro basketball. "The NBL was great fun," he said. "The games were exciting, and the fans were enthusiastic. Some were too enthusiastic, especially in Sheboygan, where they shot us in the face with peashooters when we went in for layups."

Birch added, "Press was a hell of a good kid, but he was very sensitive, so I couldn't say too much to him. He always worked hard, though, especially on defense."

Stan Noszka, 6′1″, 185, another veteran of Duquesne and Youngstown. "I got out of the service in January of 1945," Noszka relayed, "and I was working for the city of Pittsburgh doing title searches when Birch called and asked me to join him in Youngstown. By the time I could get away, the season was nearly over, so I only played in a couple of games. I was lucky to get my municipal job back, and then Birch called me again about possibly playing for the Ironmen. This time, I agreed to participate in a tryout camp in a small gym on the second floor of the Duquesne Garden. I was thrilled just to make the team."

Noszka and Maravich were happy to resume a friendship that had started at Duquesne and developed on the South Side playgrounds in Pittsburgh. "That's where all the poor kids used to play," Noszka said. "Both of us so admired Chick Davies that we got into the habit of chewing tobacco just like he did." (Once the season started, Maravich and Noszka would play cards during the long train trips. To avoid soiling railroad property, they placed newspapers on the floor.)

"Another nice kid," said Birch, who also recalled that even though Noszka had "developed some kind of nervous condition in the army," he always worked hard. "His two-handed set was the best part of his game."

Moe Becker, 6'1", 185, still another graduate of Duquesne and Youngstown. "I was supposed to sign with the Chicago Stags," said Becker, "until Davies and Birch took me out to dinner and convinced me to stay home and play for the Ironmen. Little did I know that Birch had changed his tune. Where he used to be easy to get along with in Youngstown, he turned into a monster in Pittsburgh. The two of us had trouble right from the start."

Perhaps it was Becker's good-natured view of the world that initially riled Birch. "Moe's constant chatter kept all of us loose," said Maravich. "Everything was a joke to Moe, and he was never serious enough about basketball to suit Birch."

After praising Becker's shooting, Birch offered this perspective: "We'd been on good terms in Youngstown, but for a variety of reasons, me and Moe didn't hit it off too well in Pittsburgh. Like Press, Moe was another very sensitive guy."

John "Brooms" Abramovic, 6'3", 195. Born in nearby Etna, Pennsylvania, Abramovic emigrated to Salem College, in North Carolina, where he averaged 29.9 points per game in his senior season. "I once scored fifty-seven in a game," he said, "and I was the first college player to reach two thousand career points, but Salem was not exactly a collegiate power-house, so not too many basketball people took notice of me."

Birch did. "He called me when I was still in the service and left a message," said Abramovic, "so I returned the call as soon as I was discharged. Being a local kid, I wasn't even aware of any of the other teams in the BAA. Playing for anybody else was out of the question."

His nickname? "My dad owned and operated a company that manufac-tured brooms and mops. I was called Brooms as a kid and took it for granted. When I grew up, I rarely answered to John anymore."

The scouting report on Abramovic noted that he could shoot both one-handed push shots and two-handed sets, was constantly on the move, had quick hands and a knack for the ball, was agile in the lane, and played aggres-sively at both ends of the court. By midseason, Abramovic emerged as the Ironmen's second-leading scorer.

Ed Milkovich, 5′9″, 170, from Duquesne, the oldest player on the team. "I'd played a little with Birch with the Original Celtics before the war," said Milkovich. "I was a typical guard for those days. I moved the ball, cut through the middle, and could defend guys who were five or six inches taller than me. When I got out of the air force, Birch recruited me to play for the Ironmen. I signed for sixty-four hundred, which was the highest salary on the team."

Milkovich, who later changed his last name to Melvin, was also a buddy of Maravich's. "We'd played together for Birch at Duquesne," said Milkovich, "and also in the annual Serbian basketball tournaments."

Milkovich had also been one of the legendary "Iron Dukes," so named when Davies used only five players in a game at Madison Square Garden. "Moe was one of the other Iron Dukes," said Milkovich, "and we became part of the local basketball mythology in Pittsburgh. The use of 'Ironmen' was an attempt to cash in on that."

Abramovic had this to say about Milkovich: "He was a few years older than the rest of us and held himself a little aloof. He had a lot of confidence in himself and tried to run the show, but we did play well with him."

Walter Miller, 6′2″, 190, who had also come to the Ironmen by way of Duquesne and Youngstown. "Walt was one of the greatest pivot passers

I ever played with," Becker attested. "He never shot. All he did was pass. One guy would cut, and everybody else wanted to cut off the cutter's tail, because they knew that Walt would eventually pass to whichever cutter was open. But Walt also had a full-time teaching job that he was committed to, so he didn't last long with us. Too bad."

Hank Zeller, 6'4", 210. Zeller had gone to Pitt before transferring to Washington and Jefferson. The tallest man on the squad as the season began, Zeller was another top-notch passer, but he was also a premed student and had to miss several games.

Joe Fabel, 6'1", 190, from Pitt. Fabel had played one game for the NBL's Pittsburgh Pirates in 1938. "He was the team wise guy," said Abramovic. "He was also a ladies' man, who would go out with stewardesses in whatever city we happened to be in. Then Joe would brag about all the highfalutin people he knew. Ed Milkovich had a brother in Chicago who would take him out on the town whenever we played there. But except for Milkovich and Fabel, the rest of us were clean-cut guys."

Mike Bytzura, 6'1", 170, who had transferred from Duquesne to LIU when he was offered a more lucrative scholarship. Having played for two seasons with the Cleveland Almen Transfers, of the NBL, Bytzura was the team's most experienced pro. "He was a good ball handler and set shooter," said Abramovic. "Also on the quiet side."

The season opener—a 56–51 loss at St. Louis—was a portent of trouble to come. "The court was put right on top of the ice," said Milkovich, "and there was no footing at all. Guys were slipping and sliding all over the place. We couldn't cut sharply or stop short. During halftime, nobody wanted to go back out and play, because it was just too dangerous, and we were afraid of getting hurt. But Chick Davies was traveling with us, and he told us how bad it would look if we forfeited our very first game, how we would endanger our entire season and probably find ourselves without jobs. So, we went out and skated around for another twenty-four minutes."

The next game was even worse: a home loss to Washington, 71–56. "We had the worst court in the league," Birch moaned. "It wasn't compact, and when the underlying ice started to melt, the water seeped through the spaces between the floorboards. There were also lots of dead spots where the ball wouldn't come up on a dribble. After a while, we learned just where those dead spots were and took advantage of them by going for steals whenever an opponent dribbled there."

After only two games, the players discovered to their distress that Birch was impossible to play for. "He cursed everybody for every mistake," said Abramovic, "especially for committing turnovers. We quickly developed a passive dislike for Birch, but we kept everything to ourselves."

"He had a really bad temper," said Milkovich, "and he used his outbursts to try and jack us up, but his act grew old in a hurry."

"Chick used to give you hell if you pulled a bonehead play," said Becker, "but ten seconds later, all was forgotten. Birch tried to be like Chick but didn't have the compassion for his players that Chick had. Birch just kept yapping at us and never stopped. Every mistake we made was like a personal insult. He got on Press the most and almost drove the poor guy crazy. The more Birch yelled at him, the worse Press played."

All that Maravich would say is, "Birch had a bad temper. He also had the best basketball brain in the world. He was a perfectionist, so he was a tough taskmaster."

Stop number three on the road show was Philadelphia—a hard-fought 81–76 loss—and things went from bad to worse.

Early in the game, Becker tossed up, and missed, a couple of long-distance two-handers before the team had a chance to set up its offense. Birch was more than irritated and let Becker know about it. This was the first overt incident that eventually led to the showdown between the two.

More trouble followed. "Birch put me into the game with about five minutes left in the first half," said Noszka, "and I pulled a couple of boo-boos. He just about went nuts back in the locker room. He picked up a folding chair, and I swear he threw it at me, but it smashed up against the wall. Uh-oh—this guy was totally out of control."

Becker had settled down after those two ill-advised set shots. "I actually wound up playing a good game," said Becker. "Birch was still hot after throwing the chair, so he began ripping me for having fouled out. That's when I decided I'd had enough of him."

Becker traveled with the ball club to Providence the next morning and then sought out Joe McGrevey, the general manager, who had accompanied the team on the road trip. "I wanted out," said Becker, "but McGrevey talked me into staying."

By now, Birch was so far gone that Chick Davies wanted nothing more to do with the Ironmen and returned to a teaching position at Duquesne.

After losing in Providence, 76–66, the Ironmen finally copped their first win, an 84–71 victory over the Steamrollers in Pittsburgh. Even the victory turned out to be somewhat of a curse, though, when Abramovic broke his right hand. "Birch wouldn't hear about a fracture," said Abramovic. "He said it was nothing more than a sprain and that the old Celtics used to play with broken arms. So, I played for three games with a broken hand."

After an x-ray finally revealed the true extent of the injury, Birch was desperate to find a replacement. He made calls to everybody he could think of, until Bob Drum, a Pittsburgh sportswriter, recommended a player he'd once seen in New York. And that's how Coulby Gunther became an Ironman.

Before Gunther arrived, Pittsburgh suffered a painful, 64–62 defeat at the hands of the Knicks in New York—and more trouble. Sid Borgia, one of the BAA's finest referees, told the tale: "The Knicks were hosting the Ironmen at the Sixty-ninth Regiment Armory, and this was the first pro game I'd ever worked in New York. My partner was Chuck Solodare, a veteran official. Well, the Knicks won a close one, 64–62, and Paul Birch had been on my case the whole game. At the end of the game, Birch came after me, but Chuck was my protector, so he got in the way. Then Birch said to Chuck, 'Get out of the way, or I'll knock you on your ass.' So, Chuck and I get back to the dressing room. Next thing I know, Chuck is wrapping the knuckles on both hands in his hankies, and he's on his way over to Pittsburgh's dressing room to have it out with Birch. I chased after Chuck, and after some shouting and threats, the players broke it up. Birch, like many of the coaches in the league, had no fear of the refs. We were an unnecessary evil and were treated accordingly."

Birch's threat, however, prompted Podoloff to levy a $25 fine. (Several BAA insiders believed that Podoloff was eager to fine coaches and players, because the monies collected went to pay his salary.)

After Pittsburgh bested Toronto and Detroit, Gunther arrived on the scene with the Ironmen sporting a 3–5 record. "That's when the ball club really went downhill," said Abramovic.

Gunther was 6'4", 190, and had played his undergraduate ball at Boston College. "He had a great hook shot," said Abramovic, "and that's all he was interested in doing—no passing, no defense, nothing else. Before Gunther, we played an old-fashioned offense—pick-and-roll, pick away, handoffs for set shots—all at a very deliberate pace, with unselfishness as our general rule. With Gunther, Birch put in mostly pivot plays. We pass the ball inside and then make all kinds of cuts, but he never gave up the ball. It also took us longer to set up our plays, because we had to wait for Gunther to settle into the low post. None of us were happy about the way he played. What made us even more unhappy was that as soon as Gunther showed up, Birch cut Walt Miller. Besides, Gunther was a loner who didn't have much to do with the rest of us."

The Ironmen lost in Gunther's debut—62–60 in Cleveland—and Birch earned another fine from the league office. "The Rebels had a player named Mel Riebe, who was killing us," said Maravich. "Everybody was on edge, and there were some fisticuffs between the players—nothing really out of hand, just some harmless swings and a lot of bitching. But then Birch goes out onto the court and socks Riebe a good one, and suddenly the fans go nuts. They came out of the stands and were headed toward Birch. He got scared and asked us to come help him out. No, sir. Not us. God almighty, we could've gotten killed with the crowd all angry like they were. So, we just hugged the sidelines until the cops came and calmed things down. Anyways, I guess Birch got a clue of what we all thought of him."

A clenched fist seemed to be Birch's answer to every defeat. While he paced back and forth in the dressing rooms and delivered his accusatory postmortems, he would sometimes throw a punch at the players. "We had to watch out for both his right and his left," said Maravich. "To protect ourselves, whenever he came close, we'd interlace our fingers and form catcher's masks with our hands."

Whenever a player made any kind of mistake in practice, Birch would curse at him and then throw a ball at his head. No wonder the players were tight, afraid to take even the mildest risk, and thus were unable to play with the looseness and spontaneity that characterized winning teams.

Since Becker had enjoyed a good relationship with Birch in Youngstown and could put his personal grievances aside for the sake of the team, he went up to his coach's room after a road game. "I told him how the team was falling apart," Becker said, "how we all resented Gunther's unwillingness to share the ball. I also advised Birch to get close to the players—have a couple of postgame beers with us, anything to show that he was really a nice guy at heart. He wasn't very comfortable listening to what I had to say, but when we got back to Pittsburgh, he had a little shindig and treated us all to dinner. That helped some, until he went off again."

As the losses kept mounting, Birch became even pettier in his dealings with his players. "We were responsible for keeping our uniforms in reasonably good shape," said Becker. "On the road, that usually meant washing our jerseys, shorts, socks, and jocks in the sink and then draping them over a radiator to let them dry overnight. But sometimes we didn't even have time enough to do that. We could easily deal with the smell, because a few trips up and down the court, and we'd be sweating anyway. But the jerseys were made of a coarse woolen weave, and even when they were clean, they'd rub up against your nipples and cause a painful rash. Back in Youngstown, we solved the problem by wearing T-shirts under our jerseys, and Birch had no problem with that. In Pittsburgh, though, he wanted to fine me a hundred bucks for doing the same thing. I had to use Band-Aids, but they'd always come off during the game, so I'd wind up with a rash anyway."

The discord that was brewing between Becker and Birch finally came to a violent boil on November 30, when the Ironmen were in Washington. The game was extremely physical, with a total of forty personal fouls being called.

Here's Becker's version of what happened: "Irv Torgoff was with the Caps, and he was having a field day. Nobody could guard him, including me. Birch was always riding opposing players, and he called Torgoff a 'kike.' I resented this, and I cursed at Birch from my seat on the bench."

Birch kept after Torgoff, and their argument escalated to the point that they swapped a few punches in the waning moments of the game. The refs quickly banished both of them.

"Birch was already there when the players came into the dressing room after the game," Becker said. "I was so mad that I was ready to attack him, but Zeller and Mills [John Mills, a latecomer to the team] grabbed me, lifted me up, and put me in the shower to cool off. When I came out, Stan Noszka started to tell me that Birch didn't mean what he'd said to Torgoff as an anti-Semitic remark. By then, I was totally crazy. I thought that Noszka was siding with Birch, so I squared off against him. The other guys pleaded with Birch to break us up and not let us start throwing punches. Birch just sat back and said, 'Let the Jew take care of himself.'"

Red Auerbach was the coach of the Capitols, and he later buttonholed Becker in the hallway. "I was so mad," said Becker, "that I was crying. Red told me that if Birch released me, he'd find a spot on his roster for me."

When the Ironmen got back to Pittsburgh, Becker sought out Davies at Duquesne. "Chick was like a father to me," said Becker. But all Davies could do was to join in Becker's outrage at Birch's bench-side manner.

Two weeks later, Becker was indeed released, and his rights were claimed by the team with the worst record in the league—the Boston Celtics. Rather than just surrendering Becker for the waiver fee, Birch demanded a player in return. So, the obliging Celtics sent Tony Kappen off to Pittsburgh.

Here's Birch's rendition of the name-calling incident: "It was all a case of misunderstanding. All of the coaches were accomplished bench jockeys. To call a guy a kike or a Polack or a wop was common practice—anything to get under an opposing player's skin. Some of the other players came to Becker and asked why he was getting so upset. He was just a very sensitive guy. I was never prejudiced in my life. Hell, I used to play a lot of ball at the Pittsburgh YMHA."

Birch also downplayed the significance of the chair-throwing incident: "That's something that coaches do. There's nothing exceptional about it. My coaches did the same thing when I played. It's just a way to show the players that you're really pissed."

And the screaming, cursing, and temper tantrums? "I'd lose my temper, but only up to a point. Being a coach means you also have to be a ham actor to try and get the most out of your players. Sometimes it worked, sometimes not. I've always had a great admiration for all of my players. Look, most of the guys on that Pittsburgh team had never been in a pro league before. I knew more than they did about what the competition was like. All I was ever trying to do was to toughen them up."

Birch did admit to a strong sense of frustration. "I knew what the team was capable of doing and what it was incapable of doing. I also knew what the other clubs had, and that we had to get good in a big hurry. Besides, after playing so long with the Original Celtics, I was used to winning, and there we were, losing game after game. It took a lot out of me to lose so often—at least a day or two to get over each loss."

Birch was likewise proud of what he brought to his job, noting, "My greatest asset was my ability to concentrate. That's why I never fraternized with the players. It would be too much of a distraction. You know something? When players lose, they're always looking for excuses, and their coach is an easy target. I guess my most glaring shortcoming was a lack of patience. That was something that I developed later in my coaching career."

Birch was also proud of the fact that even if his players disagreed with his methods, they always said that he was a good coach: "To the last man, they always made no bones about learning a lot from me."

Another accomplishment that Birch liked to emphasize was that, with all the losing and the aggravation, he never developed an ulcer. He added, "My wife used to say that I gave them to other people."

An additional mitigating circumstance could at least partially justify Birch's sadistic treatment of his players. Among many old-time cagers, it was considered acceptable, and even desirable, for a coach to inspire his players' hatred. The players would then be highly motivated to perform at their best just to show their son-of-a-bitch coach that they were better than he claimed they were. This was also deemed an acceptable way to unite the players in a common goal and thereby establish teamwork and unselfishness on the court. Birch, then, saw himself as a martyr who was sacrificing his popularity at the altar of winning.

Following the debacle in Washington, the Ironmen suffered an overtime 46–44 loss at home against the lowly Celtics, and Birch was on the warpath once more.

"I was soaping up in the shower after the game," said Maravich. "I hadn't played badly, but Birch was mad that we had lost. And he always took it out on me, because I never talked back to him. Anyway, I had all this soap on me, and he told me if I came out of the shower, or even rinsed off, it was gonna cost me a hundred bucks. And one of the guys came over and said, 'Come on, Coach. Let him go.' But Birch said, 'He comes out, it's a hundred-dollar fine.' So, I just stood there and waited in the shower. When he left about an hour and a half later, I finished up my shower."

Some of the Ironmen's losses were especially humiliating. A 66–55 drubbing in St. Louis on December 5 was Pittsburgh's fifth consecutive downfall. During the mess, five "Irons" fouled out, and with Abramovic still incapacitated, in the closing moments of the game the visitors were able to put only four players on the court. Their record had dipped to 4–12.

Through it all, Birch refused to give up. He and McGrevey kept searching for players who could rescue the season, and the revolving door started spinning faster and faster. The new hopefuls included these names:

The Jorgensen brothers, from the Pittsburgh area. Noble was 6'9", 228, and Roger was 6'5", 200.

Nat Frankel, 6'0", 195, from Brooklyn College. Frankel had played briefly in the NBL prior to the war.

Red Mihalik, 6'0", 180, no college, another local lad.

The most exotic newcomer, also born and raised within hailing distance of Pittsburgh: Gorham Getchell. The robust, 6'4" 205-pounder was destined to have more of an impact as a two-way end for the Baltimore Colts in the transitory All-American Football Conference.

Even with the new blood, nothing and nobody could stop the Ironmen from losing.

Birch tried to compensate for his undersized and undertalented players by forgoing a man-to-man defense and relying exclusively on zones. A subsequent 53–46 loss in Philadelphia on December 26 proved to be so slow and boring that the board of governors began debating the outlawing of zone defenses altogether.

John Harris tried to elevate the spirits of his players by hosting a Christmas dinner and presenting them with portable radios. Unfortunately, another of Harris's employees was inadvertently contributing to the Ironmen's failures.

Ray Downey was the official scorer at the Pittsburgh Arena, and either his vision was compromised or he had difficulty with simple arithmetic. Downey's incompetence was initially manifested when the Philadelphia Warriors visited Pittsburgh on December 26.

The Ironmen were clinging to a 40–37 lead midway through the third quarter when the Warriors' Art Hillhouse was awarded two free throws after he was fouled in the act of shooting. According to all of those present (except Downey), Hillhouse converted only one of the ensuing freebies, but Downey credited him with making both. Instead of Pittsburgh's lead being 40–38, which was initially posted on the scoreboard, the official book had the score at 40–39.

The later stages of the game were extremely competitive, but the Ironmen always seemed to be a point short and had to resort to intentional fouling in the endgame. As a result, three Ironmen were disqualified because of personal fouls. At the final buzzer, Philadelphia had prevailed, 62–60.

There was no doubt that the Ironmen would have played out the game differently had the correct score been known. After the discrepancy was discovered, Podoloff refused to honor Pittsburgh's appeal, claiming that the home team was responsible for the error. In any case, the "phantom foul" became infamous.

On January 8, 1947, the Ironmen's victory over the visiting Warriors took place before a slim crowd of 897, the team's lowest turnout of the season so far. Harris couldn't understand why the city wasn't supporting his team. After all, Pittsburgh was putting on a bright new face under the umbrella of "Renaissance I," a municipal program that was cleaning up the rivers and controlling the pollution from the steel mills. And weren't new buildings springing up all over the place? Weren't Harris's movie theaters attracting thousands of folks every week? Weren't the ice shows and hockey games drawing SRO crowds? Wasn't almost everybody sharing in the postwar boom?

What the hell was going on? Nobody had any answers.

On January 11, the BAA's board of governors officially outlawed the use of "stationary zone defenses." Eddie Gottlieb had been lobbying for this restriction even before the season began. "Zone defenses have no place in pro basketball," Gottlieb pontificated. "All they do is ruin the game for the spectators."

No reason was given in Podoloff's announcement, but it was understood that he sought to speed up the game and to increase scoring. Still, the ruling didn't make clear exactly what a "stationary" zone was, nor how it differed from a switching man-to-man defense. And was there such a thing as a "shifting" zone? And if there was, or if one of the coaches could concoct one, would it be legal?

According to the original ruling, no fines would be levied if a team persisted in employing a zone. Podoloff believed that a gentlemen's agreement would suffice.

Everybody involved knew that Pittsburgh, Detroit, and St. Louis had been the main practitioners of zone defenses, yet Birch felt the ruling was aimed directly at him: he was being punished for trying to win the only possible way he could with a team of runts. The day after the decree, Birch showed his defiance by ordering the Ironmen into a zone during the third quarter of a game in St. Louis. The Bombers' coach, Ken Loeffler, was also a staunch advocate of zones, and since he didn't complain to the refs, Pittsburgh was not penalized.

The Ironmen still came up short, 72–59, bringing their record to 8–20.

Birch remained determined to defy Podoloff. Pittsburgh employed a zone at home on January 15, again incurring no penalties as the team surprised Providence and won 65–53. The losing coach, Robert Morris, complained to the press that because of the ban, his team wasn't prepared to play against the outlawed defense.

The sportswriters reported that Birch was still "red-headed" over the prohibition and would not yield. For Birch, zones were as much a part of the game as dribbling, setting screens, and taking set shots. His was a righteous anger, and he refused to be dissuaded.

On January 20, the Ironmen grounded the Detroit Falcons in Pittsburgh. Throughout the contest, Birch's verbal abuse of the visiting players and the officials was more flagrant than ever. Also, after several close calls went against the home team, Birch turned to the stands and raised his hands in protest, thereby inciting the fans to shower the court with coins, beer cans, newspapers, candy wrappers, and whatever else they could lay their hands on.

Pittsburgh	FG	FT	Pts.
Gunther, f	2	5	9
Noszka, f	9	7	25
Maravich, f	0	0	0
Zeller, c	1	2	4
Mills, c	0	1	1
Kappen, g	4	9	17
Bytzura, g	2	0	4
Milkovich, g	1	0	2
Totals	19	24	62

Detroit	FG	FT	Pts.
King, f	2	0	4
G. Pearcy, f	3	1	5
Brown, f	3	4	10
McCarty, f	0	0	0
Dille, f	0	0	0
Aubuchon, f	0	1	1
Miasek, c	3	2	8
Lewis, c	1	0	2
Maughan, g	4	0	8
H. Pearcy, g	2	1	5
Janisch, g	7	0	14
Totals	24	9	57

SCORE BY QUARTERS	1	2	3	4	Total
Pittsburgh	16	14	18	14	62
Detroit	10	17	10	20	57

Now it was Podoloff's turn to be irate. He fined Birch $100 for "unsports-manlike conduct," while noting that Pittsburgh's irascible coach had been fined $25 on similar charges many times before. Birch's habitual behavior was given as one reason for the increased penalty; another was that he "acted in such a manner as to incite disorderly action by the spectators." Podoloff warned that any further repetitions would result in "an indefinite suspension."

The fine did the trick. On January 27, the Ironmen once again hosted the Steamrollers, and Birch once again began the game with a zone defense. After three minutes, referee Pat Kennedy approached Birch and simply ordered him to play man-to-man defense. Birch submitted without a word of protest, and the Ironmen won, 71–63.

Pittsburgh's record now stood at 11–23, tying the Ironmen with Boston as the worst team in the entire league.

Five games later, Ray Downey struck again. Toronto was in town, and with five minutes remaining in the game, the Huskies' center, Leo Mogus, was tagged with his fifth personal foul. At least, that's the number arrived at by everybody in the second-floor press box. According to Downey's official record, however, the infringement was only Mogus's fourth, so he was allowed to stay on the court.

Shaking their heads, all the sportswriters checked and rechecked both their own and each other's notes and unanimously agreed that Mogus had five fouls and should therefore be banished to the bench. No dice: Downey's haywire account was gospel.

Mogus proceeded to toss in a critical basket that greatly contributed to Toronto's stirring 58–55 victory. Even Birch's feisty spirit was finally broken.

The Ironmen played out the season with little enthusiasm. Playing for Birch was little more than a job. The only highlight of their last few weeks was provided after another loss on the road when Press Maravich finally stood up to Birch's constant abuse. "Goddamn it," Maravich shouted at his erst-while idol, "I'll fight you right now!" The other players quickly intervened, and no punches were thrown.

A miserable end of a miserable season. Brooms Abramovic spoke for his teammates in saying, "The whole thing was like a bad dream."

Pittsburgh Ironmen

	G	FGM	FGA	Pct.	FTM	FTA	Pct.	Asst.	PF	Pts.	Avg.
Coulby Gunther	52	254	756	.336	226	351	.644	32	117	734	14.1
Brooms Abramovic	47	202	834	.242	123	178	.691	35	161	527	11.2
Stan Noszka	58	199	693	.287	109	157	.694	39	163	507	8.7
Hank Zeller	48	120	342	.314	122	177	.689	31	177	362	7.5
Tony Kappen	41	103	448	.231	104	123	.846	22	61	310	7.6
Ed Melvin/Milkovich	59	99	376	.263	83	127	.654	37	150	281	4.9
Press Maravich	51	102	375	.272	30	58	.517	8	102	234	4.6
Mike Bytzura	60	87	356	.244	36	72	.500	31	108	210	3.5
John Mills	47	55	187	.294	71	129	.550	9	94	181	3.9
Moe Becker	17	46	229	.201	16	30	.553	14	50	108	6.4
Noble Jorgensen	15	25	112	.223	16	25	.640	4	40	66	4.4
Joe Fabel	30	25	96	.260	13	26	.500	2	64	63	2.1
Roger Jorgensen	28	14	54	.259	13	19	.684	1	36	41	1.5
Walt Miller	12	7	21	.333	9	18	.500	6	18	23	1.9
Nat Frankel	6	4	27	.148	8	12	.667	3	6	16	2.7
Red Mihalik	7	3	9	.333	0	0	—	0	10	6	0.9
Gorham Getchell	12	0	8	.000	5	5	1.000	0	5	5	0.3

Postscript

Shortly after selecting Clifton McNeeley from Texas Western (who never played pro ball) in the BAA's first college draft, John Harris folded the team.

Paul Birch couldn't get another coaching job for four years. Then in 1951, he was rehired by his old boss and resurfaced at the helm of the Fort Wayne Zollner Pistons. Birch was only marginally more subdued, but he did manage to avoid any major incidents. During his three-year tenure in Fort Wayne, Birch improved the team year by year, gradually raising the number of wins from 29 to 40. During each of those seasons, the Pistons qualified for the playoffs, but Birch soon developed what he called "a little ticker trouble" and was compelled to resign.

Press Maravich had his fill of pro basketball and never dribbled a ball in anger again. He turned to coaching in high school and soon worked his way up to the college game, eventually landing at Louisiana State University in 1967.

Oh, yes: ten weeks after that first BAA season ended, Press and his wife celebrated the arrival of their firstborn—Peter Press Maravich—who'd become better known as "Pistol Pete."

The Bottom Line

Average paid attendance	1,363
Net receipts	$56,005
Estimated loss	$200,000

8

Of Money, Time, and Justice

The season was barely under way when several apparently unsolvable problems began piling up on President Podoloff's desk, the most important one being that except for New York and Philadelphia, attendance was hugely disappointing all around the league. The Executive Committee was in constant touch with Podoloff and with the BAA's newest hire, press agent Walter Kennedy, to try to figure out what remedies, if any, were available.

The lack of ready cash was particularly embarrassing for the league office, whose only official income was its 5 percent cut of each team's gate receipts. Since Podoloff readily granted deferments to franchises that needed all of their game-related income to pay their own day-to-day expenses, the BAA office was always desperately short of funds. When Jim Hefferman, of the *Philadelphia Bulletin*, called to arrange an interview of Kennedy for a feature story, Podoloff was ecstatic. Here was an incredible opportunity to garner some free publicity in the league's second-biggest market, so Kennedy quickly agreed to meet Hefferman and even extended an invitation to "lunch." Then, because of Kennedy's limited expense allowance, he and Hefferman wound up sitting on counter stools and eating sandwiches at a local luncheonette. Not exactly a big-league image.

Several solutions to the attendance problem were suggested by the Executive Committee. Earlier, during the summer, it had been decided to adopt a forty-eight-minute game—eight minutes longer than what the colleges, the ABL, and the NBL played. The idea was to give the customers the same return for their entertainment dollar as they would get from a Broadway play, a movie, or a baseball game. Arthur Wirtz, owner of the Chicago Stags, now proposed making BAA contests even more appealing by extending the games to sixty minutes. Podoloff canvassed the owners and "secured the consent of more than a majority of them to the immediate trial of sixty-minute games to be played by the only teams willing to do so, Chicago and Detroit." Left unstated was Podoloff's fear that the players and the referees would object to the extra workload and might demand some kind of salary modification.

Unfortunately, the longer games proved to be prolonged exercises in tedium. Podoloff witnessed the first experiment, which paired the Stags and the Falcons in Chicago, and observed that the game would have been boring even if it had lasted only forty minutes. Indeed, for the three sixty-minute games that were played, the attendance was even lower than usual.

Several franchises had also attempted to boost attendance by scheduling preliminary games that matched teams representing life insurance companies, department stores, banks, boys' clubs, city league and YMCA champs, social clubs, and any other reputable organizations that could field a team and hopefully bring their own rooters through the turnstiles. Other attractive preliminary foes were basketball teams that featured football players from the New York Giants and the Philadelphia Eagles, but this particular appeal was strictly localized.

In Bulletin 58, Podoloff noted that when the Philadelphia Sphas played the Harlem Renaissance ("a colored team") as a preliminary to a Capitols-Warriors game in Philadelphia, the gate receipts totaled $10,000. "This was double the receipts at a game of the week previous when New York, definitely one of the 'hottest' teams in the Eastern Division, was the opponent. To those who have the thought that a large negro attendance swelled the receipts, I wish to advise that the negro attendance, which was carefully checked, was very little in excess of 400, and so far as I am able to ascertain, not for the more expensive seats."

This brought up several intriguing possibilities, the most obvious being that doubleheaders involving four BAA teams "might be the solution." Some of the owners believed that this measure could not be implemented for the current season, but Podoloff suggested that doubleheaders could work if the games were reduced to forty minutes. Eddie Gottlieb, Podoloff added, could easily revise the regular-season schedule.

Podoloff also suggested that the teams could reduce their rosters from twelve to ten and then use the "extra" players to form a subsidiary league. The absurdity of having the BAA, whose very existence was precarious, form a subsidiary league was not considered. This was a measure of just how desperate the situation was.

The popularity of the Rens and the Harlem Globetrotters was another topic that required investigation. The NBL had included several black players in the 1942–43 season, but it had none during the rest of the war years. Currently, however, several blacks were active in the NBL: Dolly King, of the Rochester Royals; Pop Gates, with the Tri-Cities Blackhawks; Willie King, with the Detroit Gems; and Bill Farrow, with the Youngstown Bears. Since there was nothing in the BAA's constitution that prohibited the signing of black players, perhaps the league could follow suit.

But would black players help or harm the gate? They certainly wouldn't be welcomed to play either in St. Louis or in Washington. And where would any prospective black players be found: by raiding either the NBL, the Rens, or the Globetrotters? This would necessarily involve asking players to abrogate previously existing contracts and would eventuate in expensive litigation.

Also, since major-league baseball was still lily white, a league in any other sport that broke the color line just might be seen as a bush-league circuit. It would be best to wait and see what happened when the Brooklyn Dodgers promoted Jackie Robinson from their minor-league affiliate in Montreal to the big-league roster come spring.

Podoloff fully appreciated the necessity of standardizing as many aspects of their product as possible. To that end, in Bulletin 48, he ordered that corrective measures be taken to avert a repeat of Chuck Connors's shattering of the backboard prior to the Celtics' opening home game. "The hoop brackets should be fastened to the frame, not the backboard glass itself." In addition, "Each team should provide itself with at least one spare backboard, completely equipped with hoop, which can be readily attached to the standard with a minimum delay." Podoloff further decreed that whereas some of the hoops in certain cities had been painted black, they should all be painted gold, for a "better contrast."

In lieu of paying exorbitant prices for the design and construction of twelve-minute clocks, all of the arenas were using their preexisting hockey clocks. Since hockey periods lasted for twenty minutes, there was a great diversity as to how these clocks were used for the basketball games. Podoloff cited Madison Square Garden's procedure as being the one that should be adopted everywhere:

> The first two minutes of the first quarter were taken care of by stop watch, the clock being started at the beginning of the third minute in each quarter, so that when the clock showed ten minutes, the first quarter was over, and when twenty minutes was showing, the second quarter was over. The same performance, of course, was repeated during the second half of the game.

Podoloff was also distressed by some of the media reaction to the BAA. Arthur Daley, venerated sportswriter of the *New York Times*, said that the BAA was proof that "roundball" was being taken over by "giants" and "galloping goons."

Phog Allen, who coached at Kansas after learning the game from Dr. James Naismith, chimed in that the damage was too far gone to be rectified. Allen cited an experimental game played with a twelve-foot basket, in which 6'9" Elmore Morganthaler had scored twelve field goals.

Equally as disturbing was an attack made on the BAA by Osborne Cowles, the varsity basketball coach at the University of Michigan. According to Cowles, the top college teams would beat the top BAA teams three out of every four games they played against each other. Cowles argued that the college players had better stamina, were more eager to learn, had better discipline, and played much better defense. Hearing this, Podoloff ordered Walter Kennedy to put together a counterattack.

Kennedy dutifully ascertained that while BAA teams averaged 2.7 points per minute, college teams averaged 2.5. Prompted by Kennedy, Eddie Gottlieb offered this explanation: "We score more because we have better scorers. And we're certainly in better shape than the college players, because our games are longer and there are more of them."

Ken Loeffler offered to make his St. Louis Bombers available to play Cowles's Wolverines "any time, any place."

Don Martin, of the Providence Steamrollers, pointed out that each BAA team had at least five truly outstanding players, compared with two of the same on college squads; therefore, it was much more difficult to find any weaknesses to exploit among the pros. Also, whereas the average college team played at least five cream-puff opponents per month, BAA teams never played cripples. Joe Fulks unwittingly offered the incriminating argument that BAA teams emphasized offense just to please the fans.

All of the defendants that Kennedy rounded up also emphasized that BAA action was more difficult to officiate. This was another problem with which Podoloff and the board of governors had to wrestle all season long. How should the BAA games be officiated, and who should do the officiating?

Late in October, the BAA had organized "clinics" for potential referees in New York and Chicago under the supervision of Pat Kennedy. Kennedy then prepared a list of some three dozen officials whom he judged to be acceptable. Since they would be paid only by the game, on a sliding scale from $30 to $50, all of these men had full-time jobs. Sid Borgia, for example, worked in the New York City school system in the Office of Continuing Education. Lou Eisenstein was in the sports-uniform business. Others were car salesman, real estate brokers, and golf pros. Kennedy usually worked six games per week. The others averaged two or three.

"From the start," said Borgia, "the owners didn't care if the players beat the shit out of each other. They were delighted if there was a fight every night, because they thought that would get a few more people in the stands for the next game. It was the survival of the fittest out there. But ball games often got out of hand."

Since blatant holding, elbowing, and even punching went unpunished, the players played with blood in their eyes, and every whistle ignited passionate contentions. "The refs were lunch meat," said Borgia. "The players and the coaches would curse us from one end of the game to the other. They'd spit at us, challenge us to fights. If we booted too many guys, then Podoloff would complain. So, all we could do was beg Podoloff to hit them with paltry twenty-five-dollar fines."

The first BAA game that Borgia ever worked was a sign of things to come: "Washington was playing in Philly, and fortunately, I was working with Pat Kennedy, who was my idol. Anyway, I simply froze out there. I mean, I was awful. The players were raging at me the whole game, and it got so bad that Pat had to call two technicals that I should have called. He could have fired me right on the spot, but he bailed me out."

As abusive as the players were, Washington's coach was worse. "Red Auerbach had some very uncouth mannerisms on the bench," said Borgia, "and he was understandably incensed with the poor job I was doing. After the game, Red barged into our dressing room and cursed me from head to toe. 'Gutless son of a bitch' was the nicest thing he said. Now, I had just returned from serving in the army for five years, which included forty-eight months' worth of battle campaigns in the South Pacific. So, I wasn't going to take that kind of stuff from a guy like Auerbach. I got up out of my chair and started to go after him, but Kennedy intervened and chased Red out of there. That was the beginning of a true love story. Red was my nemesis for the next twenty years."

Borgia noted that several of the more veteran coaches—such as Russell, Gottlieb, and Loeffler—could persuade Podoloff to blackball certain refs. "That's why," said Borgia, "I didn't work any games in Washington for quite a while."

Here's Auerbach's rebuttal: "One of the plays that got my Irish up was when the other guy had the ball, and my man pushed him so hard that the other guy took an extra step. So, Borgia says that it's a 'forced walk' and gives them the ball out of bounds. A forced walk? What the hell is that? Either my man fouled him, or the guy walked. Borgia comes back with my guy didn't hit him hard enough for him to call a foul, and the other guy didn't walk on his own. It was a cop-out call, so I started out having little respect for Borgia. But I will say this about Borgia: he eventually became a good guy to have on the road, because he'd fight the crowd and not be intimidated. On the other hand, if you had him at home, you knew he was going to lean a little to the visiting team. I'd much rather have a guy like Pat Kennedy, because even with all his flamboyance, Pat always gave you an honest job. You could also talk to Pat without him being quick on the trigger with his techs. As for the rest of them? The more you cursed them, the more breaks you got."

Auerbach certainly wasn't the only abusive coach. Borgia ran down the list: "Honey Russell was on the refs even before the tip-off. Before a game against the Knicks up in Boston, he came over to me and said, 'I understand you're from New York. For Christ's sake, just remember that you're not in New York now.'"

Ken Loeffler was another problem. "People in the Midwest hated anything to do with New York," said Borgia, "and Loeffler made sure they made a big production of it whenever I worked in St. Louis. He was a hard man, a wild man. He'd have the public address announcer introduce the players and then the refs. 'And from New York . . .' Then the announcer would pause so all the fans could start working themselves up. 'Sid-*ney* . . .' Another hesitation. '*Bor*-gia.' And the fans would go nuts. They'd boo every time I made a call against the Bombers, and Loeffler would shout out, 'Goddamned Easterner.' It was always quite a night when the Knicks played in St. Louis."

Borgia praised Eddie Gottlieb for being a subtler bench jockey. "One time, Gotty had been on me pretty good the whole game. Then he called a time-out, stood up, and said, 'Hey, SB. Come here!' What? The guy was calling me a son of a bitch? I was ready to T him, when Gotty got this pained expression on his face. 'I didn't call you a son of a bitch,' he said. 'Those are your initials.'"

Borgia cited Dutch Dehnert, in Cleveland, and Robert Morris, in Providence, as being well behaved on the bench. He described Neil Cohalan, of the Knicks, as an "introvert who never said a word." As for the rest, "The other guys would do or say anything to get an edge. They didn't care how they won."

Many refs were appalled by the constant insults and threats and decried the lack of control they had over the in-game violence. "Not only were we abused during games," said Borgia, but also "whenever the home team lost a close game, the refs would be crucified in the local newspapers. Lots of guys worked one game and then quit. They wanted nothing to do with the BAA. It got so bad that the league had to advertise for referees in the newspapers. But the owners didn't care about us one bit. In Philly and New York, the fans would wait for us as we left the court and spit at us and kick us as we passed. We had no protection whatsoever. We just protected our faces as we ran the gauntlet. If the fans were unusually rowdy, we'd make a weapon by taking off our belts and wrapping them around our hands so that the buckle stuck out. Listen, the teams were lucky to have enough cash to pay the players, so they certainly had no money to spend on security for us. We were strictly on our own."

Sometimes the refs also vied with each other. The prestige venues, such as Madison Square Garden, the Chicago Stadium, and the Philadelphia Arena, often had alternate refs sitting at the scorer's table in case of an emergency. The emergency ref at the Garden would routinely work his rosary beads during a game, praying that one of the on-court refs would pull a hamstring or sprain an ankle so he'd have a chance to earn a few extra bucks.

Because of the numerous defections, the BAA was forced to bring in refs who had only college experience, and who therefore tended to call more fouls than refs who had worked in the ABL, NBL, or any of the other past and present pro leagues. The tighter restrictions only served to further inflame the players and the coaches. Sportswriters in cities where pro basketball was a novelty also criticized the new refs.

Newspapers in St. Louis and Toronto were especially insistent that the BAA's refs "throw away their whistles." Furthermore, the *Toronto Star* railed against a player's being disqualified after picking up his fifth personal foul. Instead of fouling out, it was suggested that severe fouls be punished by putting the fouler in a penalty box for two minutes and forcing his team to play shorthanded.

The players did have reasonable gripes against the refs. Borgia was thought to give defenders more liberty to hack, push, and shove than other refs did. Most players also felt that his gyrations after making calls were both insulting and obnoxious.

"As part of our pregame preparations," Auerbach said, "we used to scout the referees. When Borgia had the whistle, we told our guys to be real tough under the boards and not get pushed around, because he liked to let the big guys play extra rough. We had a big team, so that was OK with us."

Kennedy, also, was considered to be too much of a showboat. After blowing his whistle, instead of making the call, he'd point to the player who'd committed the infraction and shout, "Oh, what you did!" Then there was the time when Kennedy called a charge on what Bud Palmer, of the Knicks, believed to have been a blocking foul. Still on his knees, Palmer pressed his palms together as he implored Kennedy to change the call. Kennedy didn't respond immediately to Palmer's theatrics but went over to the scorer's table and assessed Palmer a personal foul for blocking and a technical foul for, as he put it, "praying."

The BAA's tight budgetary conditions extended to the referees' expense accounts. "We were allowed seven bucks for hotel and meals," said Borgia. "We were expected to stay overnight in our hotel, then take the train the next morning. But our standard practice was to check out before leaving for the game, then take a sleeper to the next city. This way, we'd make a three-dollar profit. Sometimes we got caught doing this, and sometimes not. I remember one ref who included ten cents he'd spent for a newspaper on his itemized expenses, and Podoloff wouldn't allow it. The BAA was definitely a nickel-and-dime league."

According to veteran referee Doc Miller, some of his compatriots sought more nefarious means to enhance their earning power. "Gamblers were all over the place," said Miller, "especially in New York. I'd see an old friend at a game and say, 'How're you doing?' and his answer would be, 'I have the Knicks minus four points.' It was no surprise that a couple of BAA refs were betting on the games that they were working. I know of one ref who got five hundred bucks a game for calling fouls that never happened. But that was only a couple of guys. A whole bunch of them were betting on games that they weren't working. Did that mean that they knew one of the refs working that game was turning tricks? Who knows?"

With all of the troubles that the BAA faced day after day, Podoloff thought that everybody concerned would be extremely fortunate if the league stayed afloat long enough to finish out the season.

9

There's No "D" in Chicago Stags

Chicago lived up to its second-city status by being the second-best sports city in the country. While it couldn't match New York's three major-league baseball teams, the Cubs and the White Sox were beloved institutions in Chicago. George Halas's Bears were also golden, and the Blackhawks were silver.

Professional basketball in Chicago dated back to Halas's Chicago Bruins, which played in the American Basketball League from 1925 to 1931 and ultimately became a charter member of the National Basketball League in 1939. Other Chicago entries in the NBL were the Studebaker Flyers (1942–43), and the American Gears, which had operated during the 1944–45 season before folding. After signing George Mikan, who had starred locally at DePaul, the Gears were resurrected just in time to compete with the Stags.

Mikan had a lucrative piecework deal with Maurice White, the owner and operator of the American Gear and Manufacturing Company. The big fellow's base pay was $7,000 for the season, plus $5 for every field goal he scored and $2 per free throw. Since Mikan was also attending law school, he could earn another $50 for every appearance he made in the company's legal department. This arrangement illustrated the advantages that a company-owned team had over BAA ball clubs.

Despite Mikan's enormous popularity, Arthur Wirtz figured that if Chicago could support both the Cubs and the White Sox, then the Stags and the Gears could at least coexist, and at most succeed. To oversee the fortunes of the Stags, Wirtz hired Harold "Ole" Olsen, the longtime coach at Ohio State.

Born on May 10, 1895, in Rice Lake, Wisconsin, Olsen was a heavyset, jowly man and a lifelong basketball enthusiast. He earned all-conference honors twice at the University of Wisconsin, and immediately after graduating, he served his coaching apprenticeship at Ripon College (1919–21). After moving on to Ohio State, Olsen quickly established his credentials as an out-standing motivator and tactician. It was Olsen, in fact, who was credited with originating the ten-second rule that forced a team to bring the ball across midcourt in a timely fashion. Under his calm and resourceful guidance, the Buckeyes won five Western Conference (later, Big Ten) titles. Olsen reached the apex of his career in 1939, when Ohio State appeared in the finals of the first-ever NCAA postseason tournament (losing to Oregon, 46–33).

After twenty-four years on the job, Olsen was ready for a new challenge. Wirtz and Olsen agreed that the Stags would play a college-style game. Quickness and finesse would be emphasized instead of brute force. An up-tempo game plan was preferable to a grind-it-out pace. Fresh faces and young legs were valued more than stubborn and jaded veterans.

As Olsen recruited his players, he also sought to sprinkle his roster with local players who were already well known to the Stags' projected fan base:

Mickey Rottner, 5'10", 180, had played at Loyola in Chicago and, after completing his military service, had returned home in time to play five games for Sheboygan in the NBL.

Wilbert Kautz, 5'11", 180, was likewise from Loyola and backed up Rottner.

Don "Swede" Carlson, 6'0", 175, and Tony Jaros, 6'3", 185, were both from Minnesota, and both had solid guard skills. Jaros was the best all-around athlete on the Stags and had enjoyed several successful seasons playing in baseball's high minor leagues.

After hearing about the excellent play of a trio of West Coast players on military teams, Olsen signed them as well:

Jim Seminoff, 6'2", 190, was an excellent passer and driver from the University of Southern California.

From California came Chet Carlisle, at 6'5" and 195 pounds.

Chuck Gilmur, 6'4", 225, from Washington, was a defensive specialist known for his smarts and his toughness. Gilmur was commonly called "the bad man of basketball" because of his penchant for committing overly aggressive fouls.

Also joining the team were Bill Davis, 6'3", 215, from Notre Dame, and Doyle Parrack, 6'0", 165, who had quarterbacked Oklahoma A&M to an NCAA championship in 1945.

The two jewels of Olsen's player search were Chuck Halbert, 6'9", 225, out of West Texas State Teachers College, and Max Zaslofsky, 6'2", 170, from St. John's.

Though Halbert had been impressive on the several occasions that West Texas (billed as "the tallest team in the world") had played in Madison Square Garden, he was still seen as somewhat clumsy and unformed. However, after he served a short stint in the service, additional seasoning with the Boeing Aircraft Company team and then the Phillips 66ers had turned him into a polished passer, rebounder, and scorer.

"I was down in Bartlesville, Oklahoma, where Phillips had their offices," said Halbert, "and Arthur Morse, the Stags' business manager, came down from Chicago to talk to some of us who played for the company team. This was early in the summer of 1946, and when I was offered seven grand, I was out of there. I was the only one of the 66ers who took a chance and signed with the Stags. It was a decision that I've never regretted."

A native of Brooklyn, Zaslofsky was drafted into the military directly upon his graduation from Jefferson High School, where he had played in the long shadows cast by Hy Gotkin and Sid Tannenbaum. He spent two years in the navy before getting married and then entering St. John's. During his only season with the Redmen, Zaslofsky started at guard and was the team's third-leading scorer (7.8 points per game). Zaslofsky understood there was no way he could support his family if he continued at St. John's and wondered if he was good enough to play for pay.

He consulted with his high school coach, Sammy Schoenfeld, who told him, "If you do a lot of practicing over the summer, I think you can make good with the pros." Zaslofsky took this advice to heart and played every day in the most competitive schoolyards and playgrounds all over the city.

Olsen signed Zaslofsky on the recommendation of a friend who had seen Max score a bundle of points for a hotel team in the Catskills. "Ever since I was a kid growing up in the Brownsville section of Brooklyn," Zaslofsky said, "I dreamt of playing pro ball, and part of that dream was to get a bonus for signing. I remember telling that, very naively, to the front-office people during our talks in Chicago. I asked them would they mind giving me some kind of bonus. So, the Stags gave me a five-thousand-dollar make-good salary and a five-hundred-dollar bonus."

It took only a few intrasquad scrimmages during training camp for Olsen to see that Zaslofsky had the goods and that the Stags had a bargain. At twenty-one, Zaslofsky became the youngest player in the league. Before long, his soft-spinning shots earned him a nickname—"the Touch."

"Max turned out to be our best player," said Halbert. "He was a terrific set shooter, and if he wasn't lightning fast from baseline to baseline, he was very quick and tricky with his dribble. What also stood out about Max was how much he enjoyed playing the game and how much heart he had. I thought he was a fine young man. It helped that Max hadn't been around long enough to be set in his ways, so he fit in perfectly with Olsen's concept."

On offense, Olsen wanted his players to run at every opportunity. When they were compelled to play half-court basketball, he favored guard hand-offs as well as cuts and screens centered around Halbert in the pivot. Good defense was valued, but offense was emphasized.

"Olsen was a real gentleman," said Halbert. "He was always fair and respectful in his dealings with the players, and he expected the same from us. Olsen was also low key on the bench, no matter how heated a game might get. That was a model for us, so we rarely lost our composure."

It was no secret that several other teams in the league had better talent than the Stags. The consensus was that Detroit and St. Louis would be the elite teams in the Western Conference. "But through Olsen's leadership," said Halbert, "we played extremely well as a unit. We executed our plays to perfection, and nobody cared who got the most shots or the most points, because we were totally dedicated to winning. I never played with a team that was as cohesive as the Stags were. For most of us, this was our first experience with pro ball, and Olsen made sure that we learned to take what we did for a living very seriously."

When things got too serious, the team's trainer, Joe Dollar, could easily lighten everybody's mood. "He was always joking around," said Halbert, "and he had a million one-liners for all occasions. I give Joe a lot of credit for keeping all of us so calm through all the tight games, the bad calls by the refs, and the long road trips."

The ball club's front office also helped create a first-class environment. "We stayed in good hotels," said Halbert, "ate well, and our travel arrangements were also the best they could be."

(Visiting teams weren't treated quite as well. The only practice site made available to them was a court on an otherwise abandoned Navy Pier, which jutted out into Lake Michigan. To cut costs, the heat was never switched on, and the players' breath visibly vaporized in the frigid air.)

Add up all the factors, and the Stags had a tight, harmonious group of players, excellent leadership, a solid work ethic, and the ability to relax when that was appropriate.

As a by-product, they never thought of doing or saying anything that could possibly embarrass themselves, the coach, or the organization. They spent their free hours and their travel time playing cards for minimal stakes, gossiping about the happenings all over the BAA, and playing basketball geography: Remember that player? That coach? Referee? That gymnasium with the coal stove adjacent to the sideline? This game? That call?

They'd all served in the military—Olsen called his players "veteran rookies"—yet they studiously avoided talking about their respective combat experiences. It was sufficient to identify the theaters in which they saw action. They had no desire to re-remember so many years' worth of bloody battles, liberated concentration camps, and blasted body parts.

They'd survived with their physical well-being intact and were being paid handsomely for traveling the country and playing basketball. The Chicago Stags were heaven on earth. The Stags opened their season at home on November 2, with a 63–47 trouncing of the Knicks. In a scenario that was the norm throughout the league, the ice beneath the floorboards was a significant problem.

"After the people started coming in and the temperature got a little higher," said Nat Militzok, of the Knicks, "the ice melted, and there were puddles all over the court. When the referee threw the first ball up for the center jump, eight players fell down."

The visitors also complained about the fog created when the ice water gradually warmed. "Even with the fog, the puddles, and the ice-cold floor," said Militzok, "having to spend any time sitting and freezing on the bench was even worse. Guys wanted to play all forty-eight minutes just to keep warm."

A close-fought 57–55 win in Boston followed. Then came a loss in Providence before the Stags stampeded to consecutive wins at home against Toronto, in New York, and again in the Chicago Stadium against the hapless Celtics.

On November 16, the Stags hosted the Washington Capitols, the team that would prove to be their primary nemesis throughout the season. The visitors cruised to a 73–65 win that wasn't nearly as close as the final score indicated.

The Stags' 5–1 start had puffed up their confidence, but the easy way in which they were handled by the Caps was deflating. They won only four of their next seven games, beating Boston, Providence, Pittsburgh, and Cleveland. Except for the Rebels, the other ball clubs would prove to be among the dregs of the league.

Even so, Olsen remained optimistic. Because the Stags' offense depended so much on timing, they'd need some practice to get synchronized. Meanwhile, Zaslofsky had developed into a big-time scorer, Halbert proved to be a dominating man in the middle, and Rottner was more than just a reliable passer; he was the epitome of the savvy, trustworthy point guard and became what Olsen called his "coach on the court." Olsen would even confer with Rottner before composing the Stags' starting lineup and then submitting it to the official scorer. And Carlson did yeoman's work on the boards.

The offense would come, but Olsen couldn't help fretting over the team's porous defense. Was this failing his fault? The guys certainly looked as if they were hustling. Perhaps they simply didn't have the proper skills. Anyway, at least high-scoring teams provided more crowd-pleasing excitement than dull, defensive-oriented ball clubs.

The Stags were 9–7 when a rousing, 86–78 win over the visiting Rebels marked the turning point of their season. On December 11, the Stags had a repeat performance against the same Rebels—this time the score was 88–79, and, following another failed experiment, the game time was increased to sixty minutes. To compensate for the additional clock time, the individual foul limit was extended from five to six.

"We were in pretty good shape," said Halbert, "so, although we were exhausted afterwards, the extra twelve minutes really didn't hurt us. Still, it was like playing an extra quarter, and the whole game did have a different feel to it—more like a marathon than a sprint. But none of us had any objections, because we understood that we were playing for money and that we needed to draw fans and please those who showed up. Our livelihood depended on it."

From then on, the Stags became a scoring machine, ripping off seven wins in their next eight games. Discounting the team's 81–77 loss in Providence, Chicago scored an average of 87 points per game during this streak. The critical factor was the rapid development of Zaslofsky, who had become one of the BAA's premier outside shooters. During halftime of their home games, the Stags began to stage shooting contests to spur the fans' interest, and Zaslofsky always won.

The team was erratic in January, alternating wins with losses over the course of ten games, before embarking on an eight-game winning streak. On February 6, the Stags set a league scoring record when they dismantled the Ironmen in Chicago, 109–85.

Pittsburgh	FG	FT	Pts.
Abramovic, f	5	5	15
Gunther, f	2	8	12
Fabel, f	2	0	4
N. Jorgensen, c	1	1	3
Mills, c	3	2	8
Kappen, g	3	1	7
Noszka, g	2	4	8
Milkovich, g	1	2	4
Maravich, g	9	0	18
Bytzura, g	3	0	6
Totals	**31**	**23**	**85**

Chicago	FG	FT	Pts.
Zaslofsky, f	8	1	17
Carlson, f	4	2	10
Carlisle, f	4	5	13
Jaros, f	4	1	9
Parrack, f	5	1	11
Halbert, c	5	2	12
Gilmur, c	4	1	9
Davis, f	1	0	2
Rottner, g	8	0	16
Seminoff, g	5	0	10
Kautz, g	0	0	0
Totals	**48**	**13**	**109**

SCORE BY QUARTERS	1	2	3	4	Total
Pittsburgh	15	24	17	29	85
Chicago	28	28	27	26	109

Missed free throws: Pittsburgh (5)—Gunther 3, Fabel, Noszka. Chicago (10)—Carlson 2, Jaros, Parrack 3, Halbert 3, Gilmur. Personal fouls: Pittsburgh 17—Abramovic 2, Gunther 3, Fabel 2, N. Jorgensen 3, Mills, Maravich 5, Bytzura. Chicago (28)— Zaslofsky 3, Carlson 2, Carlisle 3, Jaros 4, Parrack 2, Halbert, Gilmur 5, Davis 4, Seminoff 4.

From February 23 to March 3, the Stags reeled off a record of 15–2—overall, they stood at 35–16 and were clearly the outstanding team in the Western Division. Only the Capitols had a better record.

On March 8, the Stags clobbered the visiting Steamrollers and challenged their own scoring record, winning by 107–81. During the game, Pat Kennedy, the league's "umpire in chief," twisted a knee and had to be removed from the court on a stretcher. Kennedy was replaced by Tom Kouzmanoff, a registered referee who doubled as a sportswriter for the *Chicago Herald-American*. The Steamrollers weren't exactly thrilled by what they perceived to be Kouzmanoff's home cooking, but given Kennedy's misfortune, they kept their objections to themselves.

Then, on March 26, the Stags suffered another dispiriting loss in Washington. The game was a runaway, and by the fourth quarter, the only question to be answered was whether the Caps would surpass the Stags' one-game scoring record. To prevent this from happening, the visitors resorted to a freeze, with Rottner dribbling the time away above the key and the rest of the Stags in a spread formation. The tactic succeeded in rescuing the small consolation of "holding" the Caps to 105 points (while registering only 77 themselves).

The Stags concluded their season by dropping three of four, finalizing their record at 39–22 (the odd-numbered 11-team format led to St. Louis and Chicago playing one more game than the others) and, as the best team in their division, setting up a playoff series with the Capitols.

The Stags had overwhelmed the BAA's lesser teams, sweeping their twelve contests versus Pittsburgh and Boston and taking four of their six-game regular-season's series with Toronto. They'd also split with New York, Providence, Detroit, and St. Louis and had won five of six from Philadelphia and Cleveland. The only opponent that owned an edge over the Stags was the Caps, who'd prevailed five times.

Also, at least half of Olsen's early-season wishes came true when the Stags completed the regular season as the BAA's highest-scoring team (77.0 points per game) and best-shooting squad (29.8 percent). The fact that they'd finished as the second-worst defensive outfit (yielding 73.3) was a severe disappointment.

Looking back, it seems almost inconceivable that the Stags' meager field-goal percentage was sufficient to lead the league. How could the best players in the world be successful on less than 30 percent of their shots?

There were several reasons:

- The players favored Converse (the Chuck Taylor All-Stars model), Spaulding Double-S, or (rarely) Kinney sneakers. It was stylish to use extra-long laces and wrap them around the top of each sneaker and then tie them with a double bow at the back of the ankles. Whereas today's NBA players get their footwear gratis and use each pair only once, the original BAA players wore their sneakers as long as possible, sometimes even until the soles were smooth. The lack of consistent traction prevented the sharp cuts and one-footed changes of direction that have become standard in the modern game.
- The uniforms were trim, but the woolen jerseys soaked up perspiration to the point where they'd weigh as much as two pounds by the end of a game. The added weight and the discomfort significantly inhibited the players' freedom of movement.
- Because there was either no or minimal insulation separating the ice underneath from the court above, players' hands were cold and unable to properly grip the ball. Also, because of the oftentimes chaotic traveling caused by bad weather, teams frequently arrived for games with only a few minutes to warm up.
- The combination of fog and cigarette smog at virtually all of the arenas dimmed the players' vision.
- Set shots were routinely taken from twenty-five to thirty-five feet out.
- Defenders routinely held, pushed, shoved, hacked, elbowed, shouldered, and occasionally landed a punch in close quarters; if the referees hadn't permitted that kind of rough defensive play, there would have been upwards of one hundred free throws taken in every game.
- The biggest factor was the ball itself. The exterior pebbling was minimal, and the nonpebbled grooves were far apart, making the ball much more difficult to handle than later models.

The interior seams on the balls that connected the combination leather-latex strips were hand sewn and then glued. A rubber bladder was inserted through a six-inch opening, which was then closed with latex-covered leather laces.

As a result, no two balls were exactly alike, and they only approximated roundness. The rubber bladder and the glue also increased the weight, and the protruding laces made the ball unbalanced. Moreover, after being used for a game or two, the balls tended to become increasingly lopsided. Accordingly, airborne shots tended to wobble, and dribbles and bounce passes frequently went askew if the laces hit the floor at certain angles.

In any case, Olsen knew that the Stags had to outscore the Caps in order to advance to the playoffs.

Chicago Stags

	G	FGM	FGA	Pct.	FTM	FTA	Pct.	Asst.	PF	Pts.	Avg.
Max Zaslofsky	61	336	1,020	.329	205	278	.737	40	121	877	14.4
Chuck Halbert	61	280	915	.306	213	356	.598	46	161	773	12.7
Don Carlson	59	272	845	.322	86	159	.541	59	182	630	10.7
Tony Jaros	59	177	613	.289	128	181	.707	28	156	482	8.2
Jim Seminoff	60	184	586	.314	71	130	.546	63	155	439	7.3
Mickey Rottner	56	190	655	.290	43	79	.544	93	109	423	7.6
Doyle Parrack	58	110	413	.286	52	80	.650	20	77	272	4.7
Chet Carlisle	51	100	373	.268	56	92	.609	17	136	256	5.0
Wilbert Kautz	50	107	420	.255	39	73	.534	37	114	253	5.1
Chuck Gilmur	51	76	253	.300	26	66	.394	21	139	178	3.5
Bill Davis	47	35	146	.240	14	41	.341	11	92	84	1.8
Buck Snyder	15	5	26	.192	5	10	.500	0	6	15	1.0
Garland O'Shields	9	2	11	.182	0	2	.000	1	8	4	0.4
Robert Rensberger	3	0	7	.000	0	0	—	0	4	0	0.0
Norm Baker	4	0	1	.000	0	0	—	0	0	0	0.0

Postscript

Arthur Wirtz kept the Stags alive for three more seasons before disbanding the team and devoting more of his attention to the Red Wings.

Harold Olsen coached the Stags until the last days of the 1948–49 season, when ill health forced him to leave the team. After a brief recovery, he returned to the college ranks, coaching Northwestern for one season (1950–51) until his health faltered once more.

Max Zaslofsky remained with the Stags throughout their existence. Whereas he'd been easygoing and committed to team play as a rookie, his attitude underwent a major alteration after the 1947–48 campaign, in which he led the BAA in scoring with 21.0 ppg. By the time Zaslofsky joined the Knicks in 1950 (via a dispersal draft after the Stags folded), he had become interested only in his own accomplishments.

According to Joe Lapchick, the venerated coach of the Knicks, "We'd win a game by twenty, but if Max only got seven points, he'd be pouting in the corner. The next night, we'd lose a close one, but when Max filled it up for twenty-three points, he was at the mirror, combing his hair and whistling a happy tune."

The Bottom Line

Average paid attendance	2,346
Net receipts	$93,951
Estimated loss	$160,000

Ed Sadowski, player-coach for the Toronto Huskies (and eventually, center for the Boston Celtics) played in the inaugural BAA game against the New York Knickerbockers.

Leo Gottlieb of the New York Knicks

The St. Louis Bombers
angle for a rebound,
1948.

The St. Louis Bombers,
lined up during
practice, 1947

Max Zaslofsky, forward for the Chicago Stags (in this photo for the Knicks) and the youngest player in the league at twenty-one

Grady Lewis, guard for the Detroit Falcons

Bob Cluggish, center for the New York Knicks

Joe Fulks, forward for the Philadelphia Warriors, eventually became the BAA's first superstar.

George Senesky, guard for
the Philadelphia Warriors

Fred Scolari, guard for the
Washington Capitols

Red Auerbach and the Washington Capitols, 1946

The Washington Capitols, lined up during practice, 1946

John Mahnken, center
for the Washington
Capitols and eventually
the Boston Celtics

Bob Ferrick, guard for the
Washington Capitols

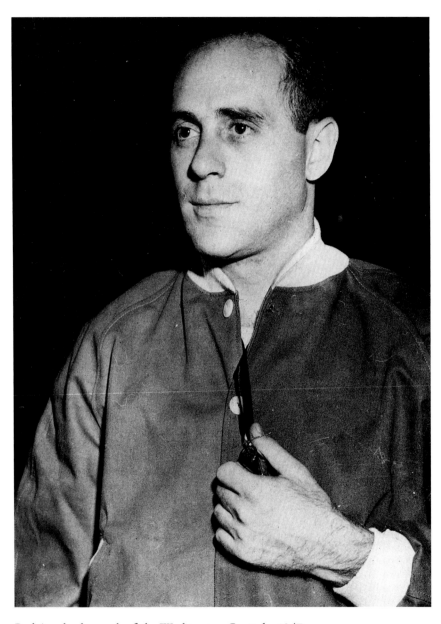

Red Auerbach, coach of the Washington Capitols, 1947

10

Big Ed Drives the Toronto Huskies to Ruin

Ed Sadowski sure liked the size of his salary—$10,000, the highest in the league. But he didn't like everything that he had to do to earn it. Oh, the playing was fine. Hadn't he starred under Honey Russell at Seton Hall in the late 1930s? And wasn't he a monster in the middle during his seven-year stint in the NBL with Indianapolis, Detroit, Sheboygan, Toledo, and Fort Wayne?

Absolutely. His hook shot was always unstoppable, and he could still make a scoreboard flash like a pinball machine. Hell, if he didn't turn out to be the best player in the BAA, it would be the biggest surprise since Pearl Harbor. Hadn't Honey said that Big Ed could kick George Mikan's ass? That he could pick up Mikan and toss him into the third row?

That's the kind of player Big Ed was.

Being a player-coach, however, was more than he'd bargained for. Big Ed's idea of practice was to make certain that the cigar stub he clenched between his teeth while he rehearsed his dreadnought hook shot was unlit.

Besides, he hadn't planned to play this far from home in the first place. Although he'd lived for much of his teenage years in the almost ritzy Elmhurst section of Queens, home these days was a modest wood-frame house in Bloomfield, New Jersey, just a long set shot away from the pleasures and perils of New York City.

Sadowski's brief stint in the army had worn him out some, and he'd also had enough of the kind of up-tempo basketball they played in the Midwest. Hell, on virtually every ball club in the NBL for which he'd played, his team-mates would often hoist up a shot before he even crossed the midcourt line.

What Sadowski really wanted to do was play in this latest cockamamy league for the New York franchise, but Neil Cohalan was more interested in signing younger guys. Too bad. Sadowski would make sure to kick their asses extra hard whenever the Huskies played the Knicks.

Second choice would have been the Boston Celtics, if only because Honey was coaching there. In fact, Sadowski had waited by his telephone for several weeks after hearing that Honey got the job. But Honey was too busy coaching some baseball team somewhere, so the right call never came. Too bad.

When the Huskies called and started talking about big money, Sadowski jumped at the chance. What the hell. He figured that coaching would be a snap. All he had to do was make substitutions, tell everybody to pass him the ball, and chew their asses out whenever they lost.

Recruiting players? That was another snap. Lew Heyman was the Huskies' business director and was happy to do Sadowski's bidding.

It was easy as pie for him to sign a bunch of Seton Hall graduates who'd been his neighbors in Elmhurst, guys he knew and on whom he could depend, guys who had aimed to reunite with Honey and were also frustrated when the summons never came.

One such guy was Mike McCarron, 5'11", 180, who specialized in passing the ball and throwing punches. Along with McCarron, there was Dick Fitzgerald, 6'2", 175, a rough-tough boardman, and Dick's older brother, Bob, 6'5, 190. Another was Charlie Hoeffer, 5'9", 158, who was from Queens College and was quick as a wish.

McCarron, the Fitz brothers, and Hoeffer all went to Newtown High School, in Elmhurst, and Sadowski had played either with them or against them in thousands of schoolyard courts, money tournaments, and exhibition games. Hey, that was a starting five right there!

Every team needed a big stiff to slop up Sadowski's leftover playing time, and George Nostrand seemed to fit the bill.

Harry Miller, 6'4", 230, from North Carolina, had patterned his game after Sadowski's. So, how bad could the guy be?

He also rounded up Frank Fucarino, 6'2", 175, from LIU, and Ray Wertis, 5'11", 175, from St. John's. In addition, Sadowski had played with Roy Hurley in Indianapolis. At 6'2" and 170 pounds, Hurley was a tough cookie and a good guy to pal around with.

All he had to do now was add a couple of Canucks to sit on the bench and make the yokels happy, and that was that.

Six Canadians were invited to try out for the Huskies, with the understanding that the two best would make the team. Under the pressure of the local sportswriters, however, two more Canadians were added to the list of hopefuls. Eventually, Gino Sovran and Hank Biasatti made the final cut.

Sovran, 6'2", 175, was a native of Windsor, Ontario, who had played sparingly at the University of Detroit. Biasatti, 5'11", 175, was born in Beano, Italy, and had been the star player at Assumption University, in Ontario.

"We'll have two Canadians on the team," Big Ed told the American players, "but don't worry, because neither of them will play."

Despite Sadowski's casual confidence, his discontent started to simmer before the season began. He subscribed to the old-fashioned game, with five players touching the ball three times each before a shot was taken. He also favored weaves and sturdy screens, long-distance set shots and cuts off the single pivot, plus the good ol' give-and-go. Not that he himself was much interested in passing.

Nor did Sadowski want to be bothered with drills and complicated strategies. Players could learn how to play with each other only by playing with each other. What could be more self-evident? That's why Sadowski's practices consisted mostly of scrimmaging and then some shooting practice. All of the other stuff was too dull, eh?

The Huskies were scheduled to conduct their training camp at the Galt Armory, in Galt (now Cambridge), Ontario, but when they arrived for their first practice session, they discovered that the baskets lacked backboards. Managing director Lew Heyman saved the day by piling the players into three taxis and speeding the fifteen miles over to St. Jerome's College, in Kitchner. For the next two weeks, the players continued to taxi from their hotel in Galt to the court at St. Jerome's. This helter-skelter arrangement irked Sadowski, since it made his insistence on holding twice-daily practices extremely inconvenient.

Sadowski was pleased, however, when, during an October 22 practice session, Hoeffer and Biasatti came to blows. The word was that Hoeffer became frustrated by Biasatti's aggressive defense, which prevented the American from getting a shot off. Big Ed thought that the fisticuffs proved that the guys were feisty, competitive, and ready for the season to commence.

The Huskies played three preseason games against colleges in the upstate New York–Ontario region and won them all with minimum exertion. They then practiced at the Central YMCA in downtown Toronto on the two days prior to the official opening of their season. Heyman also arranged for referee Pat Kennedy to be there to explain the rules to the local sportswriters.

Their last practice at the YMCA was abbreviated when Sadowski noticed a scout from the Knicks in the audience. The scheduled scrimmage was abandoned, and the Huskies concentrated solely on their shooting.

On the eve of the season, Sadowski made his complaints public. Two weeks of preseason rehearsals was insufficient, he maintained, as was the level of competition during their exhibition schedule.

Following the Huskies' opening 68–66 loss to the Knicks, Toronto traveled to Cleveland, where the team suffered another disheartening defeat, 71–60. After the return to Toronto, Sadowski filled a five-day open stretch in the team's schedule with grueling twice-daily practices. He'd get this damn ball club in shape even if it killed them.

The Huskies' third game was the charm, a 73–71 victory over the Falcons in Maple Leaf Gardens. Unfortunately, the Huskies would win as many as two consecutive games only three times during the entire season. After downing the Falcons, they lost eight of their next ten and fell to a 3–10 record.

The most noteworthy event in this disastrous stretch came on November 22, when Gino Sovran scored a pair of critical hoops in the overtime period as the Huskies scratched out a gritty 83–82 win against the Celtics that thrilled the hometown Toronto fans. Afterward, Sadowski told the local sportswriters that Sovran would definitely "get more work" when the Huskies played at Washington three days hence. He also dismissed reports that he had injured his shoulder and swore that he would also take the court against the Capitols. (His teammates told each other that Big Ed's shoulder was sore because he took too many shots.)

As it turned out, Sovran went scoreless in just a few garbage-time minutes, and Sadowski never got off the bench as the Caps drubbed the Huskies by 74–50. Sadowski coached the game in civvies and was utterly disgusted at how easily his players surrendered. Despite the mounting deficit, only Mike McCarron kept playing all-out, eventually leading the Huskies' diminutive point parade with 14.

Besides making a mark with his rough-tough board work, McCarron was one of the most hostile players in the league (as Al Brightman already knew).

Early in the third quarter, McCarron took offense to a hard foul committed on his person by Horace "Bones" McKinney. McCarron's reaction was to square off and punch Bones in the chops so hard that the Caps' 6′6″ forward landed in the first row of the courtside seats. After McKinney climbed to his feet, McCarron went over to him and said, "Bones, I'm sorry that I knocked you into the first row. I should have knocked you into the second row." While the referees continued to silently suck on their whistles, that's exactly what McCarron then proceeded to do. And that's exactly why McCarron was Sadowski's favorite player.

As the season slowly unwound, Sadowki's frustrations increased. He didn't like too may of his players. And he didn't like the hassles that the Canadian winters created.

For example, on November 29, the Huskies hosted the Rebels, losing 87–72, and were scheduled to play the following night in Providence. During the game, a blizzard hit Toronto, and the Huskies had to jump into four taxis and hasten to Buffalo, ninety miles away, to make a train connection to Providence. The bad weather delayed them en route, and their train was gone when they finally arrived in Buffalo. To avoid a forfeit fee, the only option was to stay in the taxis and drive five hundred more miles to Providence, which is what they did. Sadowski wasn't at all surprised when the Huskies were skinned again, 79–65.

That was the clincher. After the game, all of the Huskies checked back into their motel on the outskirts of Providence—all, that is, except for Sadowski. For the next two days, Sadowski was as hard to find as Judge Crater. There were rumors that Big Ed was seen in attendance at the Grey Cup football game in Toronto, that he was rejoining the Fort Wayne Zollner Pistons in the NBL, and that he had checked into a Toronto hospital. Lew Heyman investigated all of the rumors and found them false. He tried calling both Sadowski's apartment in Toronto and his home in New Jersey, with no results.

Finally, on December 2, Sadowski called President Podoloff, and a meeting was arranged in New York. During the ninety-minute conference, Sadowski complained that his dual role was too much for him and stated that he wanted out. He also implied that he'd like to be traded to a winning team. The Huskies responded by suspending Sadowski, entertaining trade offers, naming Dick Fitzgerald as interim coach, and beginning the search for a new coach. Podoloff desperately wanted Sadowski dealt to Boston (a big-market franchise that dearly needed a drawing card), but Heyman insisted on waiting for the best possible offer.

While all this was going on, the remaining Huskies were glad to be rid of Sadowski and responded by besting Chicago, 65–61, and Providence, 62–52, on a brief road trip. After a home loss to Philadelphia, Heyman took over the coaching duties, and the Huskies lost again, this time to Pittsburgh.

Every team in the BAA made a bid for Sadowski, but when the Huskies offered their high scorer to Washington for either Bones McKinney or John Mahnken, Red Auerbach refused. Meanwhile, on December 5, Toronto did pull the trigger on the league's very first trade—sending George Nostrand to Cleveland for Clarence "Kleggie" Hermsen, a 6'9" 225-pounder from the University of Minnesota, who had briefly played in Sheboygan both before and after his military service. Hermsen was averaging only 3.9 points per game with the Rebels, to Nostrand's 8.9 ppg, but the former was considered to be much tougher and had greater potential as a force in the paint.

Also on December 5, the Huskies released Hank Biasatti, leaving Sovran as the only surviving Canadian on the roster. Biasatti announced his plans to attend spring training with the Philadelphia Athletics in March. He wound up playing twenty-one games at first base for the A's in the 1949 season (going 2–24, for a batting average of .083).

After more conferences with Podoloff, Heyman found his new coach. Robert "Red" Rolfe, best known as a hard-hitting third baseman for the New York Yankees from 1931 until illness forced his retirement in 1942. (With the Yankees, Rolfe had sported a lifetime batting average of .289, which included a career high of .329 in 1939, when he led the American League in hits, runs, and doubles.)

In addition to demonstrating his prowess on the diamond, Rolfe had been a star basketball player at Dartmouth and, during the war, had coached basketball (to a record of 49–28) and baseball at Yale. He was a soft-spoken yet forceful man, who told his new players during their initial meeting that, for the duration of the season, they were forbidden to smoke cigarettes or cigars and to drink alcoholic beverages of any kind. Rolfe's on-court game plan was much more organized and up to date than Sadowski's had been. "I like bucket play," Rolfe said, "and the one-hand shots from outside."

Rolfe's debut came at home on December 14, when the Huskies were edged 62–52 by Pittsburgh. Despite the loss, local observers were impressed by the team's newfound toughness, enthusiasm, unselfishness, and discipline. The Huskies alternated wins and losses in their subsequent eight games as Rolfe evaluated his players.

Finally, a deal was struck on December 17 that sent Sadowski and Ray Wertis to Cleveland for Leo Mogus (a high-scoring, 6'4", 190-pound pivotman from Youngstown) and Dick Schultz (a 6'2", 192-pound veteran from Wisconsin), plus an "undisclosed amount of cash." On the very next day, the Rebels defeated the Huskies in Cleveland, 78–62, with Sadowski scoring 18 points, Wertis 2, Schultz 5, and Mogus 8.

Still on a seesaw, the Huskies notched an inspiring victory on New Year's Eve, clawing the Chicago Stags, 87–76, in Toronto. The start of the contest was delayed when it was discovered that the game ball had been left in the Huskies' overheated dressing room and was totally misshapen. The crowd of less than a thousand fidgeted for thirty minutes until a new ball was located in a basement storeroom and then properly inflated.

The celebratory mood among the faithful was somewhat diminished when it was discovered that the next morning the Huskies had given Gino Sovran his unconditional release. Sovran was bitter, and he complained that the Huskies simply didn't want any Canadian players on the squad. The anti-Canadian bias was not restricted to Toronto, Sovran claimed. He declared that the Chicago Stags had announced the release of Norm Baker, another Canadian, early in December, but the truth was that Baker had left on his own initiative because he was disgusted with "the whole setup."

"I'm certainly not prejudiced against Canadians," Rolfe insisted. "I'd be glad to have one or more of them on the team if they were good enough, because they'd bring in the crowds. Unfortunately, Sovran lacked toughness and didn't move very well."

Three days later, Rolfe announced more changes: Chuck Hoeffer was sent to Boston in exchange for Red Wallace.

The Huskies responded to all the comings and goings by beating the Falcons at home, 76–61, bringing their record to 10–15. The Toronto fans, however, were confused by the changes and insulted by Sovran's release. They showed their displeasure by staying away in droves. For the January 6 win over Detroit, only 650 spectators were on hand.

Lew Heyman tried every trick he knew to attract fans:

- Free booklets explaining the rules of the game were distributed all around town.
- There were quiz competitions after games, with the prizes including coal, tires, radios, Stetson hats, bags of groceries, and bicycles.

- High school games were booked as preliminaries.
- "Booster seats" were sold for sixty cents, but only for games against the BAA's lesser teams.
- A huge newspaper ad announced that the first one hundred ladies in attendance would each get a pair of nylon stockings. The giveaway was squashed, however, when the Ontario Provincial Government declared that war-rationing restrictions were still in effect and the distribution of the nylons was illegal.

Heyman also undertook a massive advertising campaign in the local newspapers, but he made some serious mistakes. In one ad, he encouraged the public to come see "America's Most Thrilling Sport!" While this may have been true, it was not the best-received message north of the border. And before a late-season game against the Stags, Heyman publicly said in all seriousness, "We can only seat the first fifteen thousand fans. The rest will have to stand." When a mere three thousand showed up, the only standees were the extra ushers Heyman had hired.

The Huskies' cause was not aided any further by comments from Gordon White, assistant director of physical education and health for the province of Ontario. White said that since the Huskies played thirty home games at the Maple Leaf Gardens, amateur hockey in the Toronto area lost one night per week in practice time. With the bashes balancing the boosts, a late-season game against Providence drew 500 fans.

Rolfe, however, was more interested in what was happening on the court. On January 21, with the Huskies showing a dismal record of 12–19, Bob Fitzgerald was moved to New York for Bob Mullens (a 6'1" and 175-pound tricky ball handler out of Fordham) and cash. By now, the BAA's previously established trade deadline of January 1 was routinely ignored, gone and forgotten.

With the latest deal, only four Huskies who had played on opening night were still on the roster: Mike McCarron, Harry Miller, Roy Hurley, and Dick Fitzgerald.

The latest (and last) revision of the ball club seemed to be the best. On January 31, the Huskies achieved their biggest win of the entire season when they upset the league's most potent team at home. Even though Red Wallace had to sit out most of the third quarter after being tagged with three fouls, he had the game of his life.

Washington	FG	FT	PF	Pts.
Feerick, f.	4	7	1	15
Gantt, f	0	0	5	0
Keller, f	0	0	0	0
Mahnken, c	6	0	2	12
McKinney, g	5	3	2	13
Norlander, g	2	1	0	5
O'Grady, g	0	1	0	1
Passaglia, g	1	1	1	3
Scolari, g	6	4	1	16
Torgoff, g	4	1	2	9
Totals	**28**	**18**	**14**	**74**

Toronto	FG	FT	PF	Pts.
Fitzgerald, f	1	2	0	4
Hermsen, f	1	0	0	2
Hurley, f	3	1	0	7
McCarron, c	3	0	0	6
Miller, g	0	0	1	0
Mogus, g	4	5	3	13
Mullens, g	3	1	1	7
Schultz, g	2	2	3	6
Wallace, g	16	6	2	38
Totals	**33**	**17**	**10**	**83**

At this time, the Huskies were still only 13–22, but Rolfe felt that his team was coming together. He was positive that a late-season spurt would send Toronto into the playoffs. Then, a mere three days later, the ball club's fragile equilibrium was disturbed when Hermsen, after receiving his January paycheck, informed Rolfe that he had to "temporarily" leave the team to go home to Minneapolis and await the imminent birth of his first child.

Even though Hermsen's play had been erratic, he showed signs of someday becoming an impact player in the pivot. And because he was also regarded as a solid citizen, neither Rolfe nor Heyman had any objections to his being absent with leave.

It turned out, however, that after the baby was delivered, Hermsen signed a contract (at twice the salary he was getting from Toronto) to play for the

Baltimore Bullets in the ABL. Jake Embry, president of the Bullets, smugly announced that his team did not recognize BAA contracts and would therefore retain the services of Hermsen. Podoloff countered by barring Hermsen from ever again playing in the BAA. (When Baltimore joined the BAA for the 1947–48 season, Podoloff's ban was lifted.)

Despite Rolfe's optimism, the Huskies played .500 ball for the next several weeks. This, of course, was an improvement, but solid mediocrity didn't satisfy Rolfe. He finally came to a pair of discouraging conclusions: The players and neighborhood chums that Sadowski had originally recruited simply weren't good enough to compete on equal teams with the rest of the league. In addition, all of the wheelings and dealings that Rolfe had instigated were necessary, but they created so much instability and confusion that the new players didn't have sufficient time together to develop a consistent synchronicity. Then the team ran off a ministreak that teased Rolfe's expectations once more.

It began on February 21, with a rousing home-court win over the hapless Celtics. A sidelight to that game was the fact that one of the referees was Bugg Horton, the athletic director at the University of Toronto. This marked the first time that a Canadian referee had worked a professional basketball game.

A loss in Detroit was followed by victories over Providence and Philadelphia at the Gardens. Suddenly the 19–28 Huskies were only two and a half games behind New York, and gaining a spot in the playoffs was no longer a fantasy. The Huskies forthwith went into another tailspin, losing four of five and falling out of contention for good.

On March 11, a victory at home against St. Louis was tainted by the fact that the two referees assigned by the league office never arrived. Heyman reconnoitered the slim crowd and spotted Bob Mockford and Alex Campbell, a pair of referees who regularly worked in one of Toronto's amateur leagues. Even though the Bombers' coach, Ken Loeffler, was incensed, there seemed to be no other choice except to let Mockford and Campbell take over the game.

The players were on their best behavior for the first half, but by the middle of the third quarter, the game became a brawl. Elbows were blatantly brandished, punches were thrown, and bodies thumped to the floor, with no reaction from the overwhelmed refs. The only technical foul resulted when a disgruntled player punched the ball into the stands. Sportswriters concurred that the home team had gotten the benefit of every marginal call, and nobody was surprised when the final score favored the Huskies by 79–71. Afterward, Loeffler seriously considered filing an official protest, but since the Bombers were already locked into the playoffs, he backed down.

The Huskies considered themselves lucky to have beaten a far superior team, and most of them were eager for the confounding, helter-skelter season to be over. While Toronto was a nice enough city, and business was business, they longed to return to their familiar lives and haunts back in the States.

After losing six of their last seven games, the Huskies finished their one and only season at 22–38.

Toronto Huskies

	G	FGM	FGA	Pct.	FTM	FTA	Pct.	Asst.	PF	Pts.	Avg.
Mike McCarron	60	236	838	.282	177	288	.615	59	184	649	10.8
Leo Mogus	41	186	653	.285	172	237	.726	56	126	544	13.3
Red Wallace	37	170	585	.291	85	148	.574	30	125	425	11.5
Dick Fitzgerald	60	118	495	.238	41	60	.683	40	89	277	4.6
Kleggie Hermsen	21	95	327	.291	64	97	.660	15	54	254	12.1
Dick Schultz	41	87	372	.234	74	107	.692	39	94	248	6.0
Roy Hurley	46	100	447	.224	39	64	.609	34	85	239	5.2
Bob Mullens	28	98	341	.287	42	68	.618	36	62	238	8.5
Ed Sadowski	10	73	209	.349	45	66	.682	8	42	191	19.1
Harry Miller	53	58	260	.223	36	82	.439	42	119	152	2.9
Charlie Hoeffer	23	54	198	.273	32	46	.696	9	61	140	6.1
Frank Fucarino	28	53	198	.268	34	60	.567	7	38	140	5.0
Bob Fitzgerald	31	47	241	.195	45	70	.643	26	86	139	4.5
George Nostrand	13	46	136	.338	24	61	.393	10	22	116	8.9
Nat Militzok	21	38	129	.295	24	39	.615	14	29	100	4.8
Ray Wertis	18	38	171	.222	23	37	.622	18	29	99	5.5
Ralph Siewert	14	5	31	.161	6	10	.600	4	10	16	1.1
Edward Kasid	8	6	21	.286	0	6	.000	6	8	12	1.5
Gino Sovran	6	5	15	.333	1	2	.500	1	5	11	1.8
Hank Biasatti	6	2	5	.400	2	4	.500	0	3	6	1.0

Postscript

Rolfe's frustrating experience with the Huskies (his record at the helm was 17–27, compared with Sadowski's 3–9) sent him back to baseball. He managed the Detroit Tigers from 1949 to 1952; then, from 1954 until his retirement in 1967, Rolfe served as the athletic director at Dartmouth, his alma mater.

Postseason rumors that the Huskies were moving to Montreal were squelched by the front office. In fact, the owners' spokesman, Harold Shannon, said that they were far from being discouraged by the team's poor attendance. They assured Rolfe that he would be retained as coach for the next two seasons. Notwithstanding, on July 27, 1947, during a meeting of the BAA's board of governors, Shannon announced that the Huskies were folding.

Most Torontonians were blindsided by the news, and the media immediately began to conduct a postmortem. Of course, Sadowski's lackluster recruiting received the major share of the blame. It was also suggested that Toronto was simply not ready for a pro basketball team, because college and amateur basketball had not been developed in the area.

Economic reasons were also put forth. The average weekly salary in the city as of November 1946 was $33.47. The price of tickets ranged from seventy-five cents to $2.50, which meant that if a father took his two sons to a Huskies game and bought three tickets at $1.25, his initial outlay would be $3.75. Add the cost of parking and perhaps a soft drink, and the total cost would be about $5—much too large a percentage of the average weekly wage.

The other regular tenants of Maple Leaf Gardens were likewise cited as contributing factors. In addition to the Maple Leafs, these included the Toronto Marlboroughs and St. Michael Pats, both of the Ontario Hockey Association. All three hockey teams routinely played to SRO crowds, which accounted for most of the leisure-time money spent by local sports fans. Toronto was such a hockey town that high school skaters drew more attention than did the Huskies.

In other words, the Huskies never really had a chance to succeed.

Bottom Line

Average paid attendance	2,103
Net receipts	$43,590
Estimated loss	$215,000

The Evolution and Extinction of the Cleveland Rebels

Roy Clifford had been on the job for only a few months, yet he already understood how demanding his new boss was. "Al Sutphin got into the office at eight A.M. and worked until midnight," said Clifford, "and he expected his employees to do the same. My job title was basketball director of the Cleveland Arena, and my duties included scheduling the college basketball doubleheaders, plus hiring a coach for the Rebels and then putting a new team together."

Clifford's qualifications included an insider's knowledge of the game from both the bench and behind a desk. From 1929 to 1943, Clifford had coached Western Reserve University, in Cleveland, and succeeded in transforming a mediocre basketball program into a regional powerhouse. During the war, Clifford coached the Hawaii team into the finals of the Pacific Army Olympics. Upon his return to Western Reserve, he decided he'd had his fill of the stresses and frustrations of coaching. When the school's athletic director was forced to resign because of ill health, Clifford was delighted to accept an appointment as acting AD.

Part of his job at the school was to chair the Intercollegiate Hockey League, and that's when he got to know Sutphin. "The so-called Big Four all had popular hockey teams," Clifford said. "That included Western Reserve, Baldwin-Wallace, John Carroll, and Case. But all of the schools had money troubles. So, Sutphin stepped in and paid for the uniforms and the equipment for everybody. I was so impressed by him that when he offered me a job with the Rebels, I couldn't turn him down."

Even before Clifford began evaluating prospective coaches and players, Sutphin's latest business venture got off to a bad start. "Al announced that there would be a contest among the local newspapermen to determine the name of the team," said Clifford, "with the winner to get a custom-made suit. But all along, Al had his mind set on 'Rebels,' so when a sportswriter came up with the same name, Al said that we were going to use the name anyway and refused to buy the guy a suit. Naturally, that got all of the media teed off."

Nobody except Sutphin liked the name. In the *Cleveland Press*, Whitey Lewis wrote, "Rebels — Ugh! Ugh!" Lewis was so influential in the area that many of his readers actually thought that the team was to be called the Cleveland Ugh.

"From the start," said Clifford, "we couldn't catch a break in the local papers. Lewis always hated basketball. He derisively called it 'roundball,' and all of the other writers were quick to say negative things about us even before the season got going."

As his efforts to mollify the not-so-gentle men of the fourth estate remained fruitless, Clifford turned his attention to cobbling together a ball club. "There was some talk about my coaching the team," Clifford said, "but I already had my hands full, and besides, Dutch Dehnert was an easy hire."

No other coach in the BAA had as impressive a résumé as Henry "Dutch" Dehnert. Born in New York on April 5, 1889, Dehnert began playing for petty cash in 1906 with ragtag outfits in and around the metropolitan area. During the next thirty-three years, his journey through the early backwaters of professional basketball would include stops with the Danbury Hatters, Jersey City Skeeters, Norwalk Company K, Nanticoke Nats, Wilkes-Barre Barons, Bridgeport Blue Ribbons, Thompsonville Big Harts, Utica Utes, Scranton Miners, Cleveland Rosenblums, Toledo Red Men Tobaccos, and New Britain Jackaways. The broad-beamed, 6'1", 215-pound Dehnert earned his most noteworthy bona fides during his various stints playing for the Original Celtics (1918–19, 1921–28, 1931–33, 1935–39).

In fact, it was while Dehnert was toiling for the Celtics that he was credited with inventing pivot play. The Celtics were struggling against a strong local team in Chattanooga in the winter of 1925 when Dehnert came up with the radical strategy. "I volunteered to stay in front of the standing guard with my back to the basket," Dehnert said, "so that he couldn't break up our passes. We tried this a few times, and it worked. My teammates would pass to me, and I would give it right back to them. Then, on one sequence, before I had a chance to make a pass, the standing guard moved around to my right side and tried to bat the ball out of my hand. All I had to do was turn to my left, take one step, and lay the ball in. Of course, we didn't know it at the time, but this was the first pivot play."

Dehnert's penchant for playing belligerent, chest-to-chest defense and for eagerly seeking contact in the battle of the boards led some of his Celtic teammates to insist that too many collisions had addled his brain. Honey Russell loved to tell about the time the Celtics were waiting for a train at a subway station in New York. "Dutch wasn't paying too much attention to where he was walking," said Russell, "and he unexpectedly bumped into a pillar. Dutch reacted by jumping back and hollering, 'Switch!'"

More important, Dehnert's credentials also included a highly successful tenure as coach of the Detroit Eagles, in the NBL, that was capped with consecutive World Pro championships in 1940 and 1941. In addition, Dehnert had coached Harrisburg, Trenton, and Sheboygan in the ABL (1942–46). For Roy Clifford, though, the clincher was Dehnert's tour of duty with the Rosenblums (1928–31).

Unfortunately, the squad assembled by Dehnert and Clifford was a dysfunctional mixture of contrasting styles. "The players I brought in were recent college all-Americans," said Clifford, "guys who liked to run and keep the ball popping. Dutch picked old, slow guys who were used to handling the ball a lot."

Clifford's signees included Kenny Sailors, 5'10", 175, from Wyoming, who could pass and score on the run as well as anybody. In his senior year (1943), he had led Wyoming to an NCAA championship and been named MVP of the tournament. A unanimous all-American, Sailors was widely considered to be the best guard in the college ranks. His basketball career was interrupted by a two-year stretch in the marines, where he gained the rank of captain.

"After the war," Sailors said, "I went into the dude-ranching business up in Alaska, but I did participate in the first East-West College All-Star Game in 1946. After that, I was invited to make an all-expenses-paid visit to the Rochester Royals, who were playing in the NBL, and to hear their pitch. Otto Graham had played football at Northwestern, and he was currently playing for the Royals. For some reason, he took a liking to me and said that I should sign with Cleveland instead of Rochester. A few months later, Graham signed with the Cleveland Browns, so I guess that's what was behind his recommendation."

Clifford had a close personal connection with Ed Shelton, the coach at Wyoming, and was able to arrange a telephone conversation with Sailors.

"Kenny said he was interested in playing with the Rebels," said Clifford, "so I flew him into Cleveland and put him up at my house overnight. It didn't take much convincing for him to sign a nine-thousand-dollar contract, but Kenny was very anxious to hurry back home, so I put him on a plane and didn't announce his signing until he was gone. Since he was obviously unavailable for interviews, the newspapers now had another reason to be pissed."

Clifford was also responsible for signing Mel Riebe, 5'11", 180, who'd never attended college. "Mel went to Euclid High School, in a suburb of Cleveland," said Clifford, "and I knew him from there. He was a nice fellow, always courteous, but he felt inferior to guys who had played college ball." Riebe was also guaranteed to be a local favorite, since he was born and bred in Cleveland.

"Riebe had a freaky little shot," said Kenny Sailors, "that he let go from his right hip while on the dead run. The ball would hit the backboard with a lot of English and spin through the hoop. It was a great shot, but he could only shoot it from the right side of the court."

Several years previous, Clifford had tried to recruit another Cleveland native, Frankie Baumholtz, 5'10", 170, to Western Reserve, but Baumholtz chose Ohio University, because it was a few miles closer to his home. In the same mold as Sailors, Baumholtz was an up-tempo player with a sure shot and quick feet. After gaining MVP honors in the 1941 NIT, he'd further established himself as a top-notch scorer with the Youngstown Bears (1945–46) after his discharge from the service. However, Baumholtz's commitment to basketball was compromised and overshadowed by his phenomenal skills on the baseball field. In the summer of 1946, Baumholtz had led the Sally League with a .343 batting average and was considered a shoo-in to start in center field for the Cincinnati Reds once the next baseball season commenced.

"I looked at playing with the Rebels as a great way to stay in shape and also have a good time during the off-season," said Baumholtz. "The fact that I was also living in Cleveland at the time made signing with them an easy choice."

Baumholtz soon became popular with his new teammates for his ever ready smile. While Dehnert wasn't overly fond of Baumholtz's giddyap style of play, he did appreciate the player's military-style obedience, replete with "yes, sir"s and "no, sir"s.

Bob Faught, 6'5", 185, an all-American center from Notre Dame, was a hardworking boardman who likewise thrived in a quick-paced game. As was Riebe, Faught was a native Clevelander.

George Nostrand was 6′8″ and 198 pounds and was signed on Sailors's recommendation after being cut by Toronto. "George was a big ol' beanpole," said Sailors. "He wasn't very strong, and the only plus besides his height was his hook shot. We'd been teammates at Wyoming, but he didn't play much."

Whenever Sailors saw or thought about Nostrand, he was reminded of a game Wyoming had played in Madison Square Garden. "I came down with an offensive rebound," said Sailors, "and then I jumped off the floor. George anticipated that I was going to shoot, so he turned for the rebound, but I passed to him instead. The ball hit him on top of his head, bounced high in the air, and came down right through the middle of the basket. After much confusion, George was credited with the basket."

Dehnert's recruits consisted of Nick Shaback, 5′11″, 180, from the Bronx, who'd joined the army straight out of high school and had not attended college. Shaback was a devotee of the throwback game, which featured a maximum of dribbling, along with setting screens and taking two-handed sets. Another was Ben Scharnus, 6′2″, 173, from Seton Hall.

Leo Mogus and Kleggie Hermsen were both lead-footed pivotmen who were perfectly suited to Dehnert's philosophy. However, one of Clifford's duties was to negotiate players' contracts. The first players he contacted were happy to sign for $3,500, but as the competition to assemble competitive teams increased, Clifford was forced to raise the ante. Accordingly, many of the lesser players wound up with $6,000 contracts. Mogus, for one, was especially bitter about the differential—and his constant bitching convinced Clifford that eventually he'd have to trade him.

Even as Sailors warmed up prior to the first day of training camp, he had reason to question his decision to play in Cleveland. When Dehnert saw his most expensive player practicing jump shots, the old coach was aghast.

"Where'd you get that leapin' one-hander?"

Sailors shrugged. "I don't know, Coach. I've been shooting this way for a long time."

Sailors had originally developed the shot in his one-on-one games against his 6′5″ older brother. It had been born of the desperate need to prevent his every shot from being blocked.

"Well," mused Dehnert, "you'll never make it as a pro with that kind of shot. You've got to get you a good two-handed set shot."

"Coach, I don't know if I can shoot a two-handed set shot or not."

Turned out that he couldn't and didn't want to.

Despite the Rebels' unworkable roster, the word around the BAA was that Cleveland would be one of the league's elite teams. The Rebels did nothing to refute this view when they opened the season by blasting Toronto, 71–60, at home. However, the court in the Cleveland Arena had the same problems with ice as most of the other courts around the BAA. Moreover, sections of the newly constructed court came apart as the game progressed, sending Ben Scharnus sliding on the ice.

For Kenny Sailors, the distressing playing surface wasn't nearly as devastating as the halftime happenings in the Rebels' dressing room: "My coach at Wyoming was very strict about training—no smoking or drinking. And the first night of the season, I went into the dressing room at the half and saw two or three of the old-timers just sitting around playing blackjack and smoking cigars, all this while Dutch was up there at the blackboard telling us what we should do in the second half. These old pros kept up their card playing and smoking without paying any attention to what Dutch was saying. It was quite a shock to me."

According to Sailors, here was the gist of Dehnert's halftime spiel: "If you forget about the goils in the crowd and the erl on the floor and get some pernts like we useta in She-bergen, then we'd win this game."

Afterward, the newspapers were happy to ridicule the Rebels' opening. The game was referred to as "The Wood Capades," a takeoff on the Ice Capades. With this, Sutphin popped his cork.

"He had every right to go off," said Clifford. "Trying to run on that court was like Eliza crossing the ice in *Uncle Tom's Cabin*. Al called me at four in the morning, screaming that we were having a meeting in four hours. So, I had to wake up all the arena staff and let them know. At the meeting, Al simply scorched us, one and all."

On November 10, the Rebels blasted the highly regarded Washington Capitols at home by 92–68. A series of insulating pads inserted under the floor solved the condensation situation, but another problem arose when the Caps' Gene Gillette suffered a dislocation of his left knee in the third quarter, and it was discovered that there was no doctor in attendance. A lengthy delay occurred while a stretcher was located and Gillette was carried to the visitors' dressing room to await an ambulance.

From then on, Clifford made sure that there was always a doctor in the house.

Washington	FG	FT	Pts.
Norlander, lf	7	7	21
McKinney, rf	3	1	7
Mahnken, c	7	3	17
Scolari, lf	3	2	8
Torgoff, rg	0	2	2
Negratti, rf	2	1	5
Gillette, lf	1	2	4
O'Grady, lg	1	2	4
Totals	**24**	**20**	**68**

Cleveland	FG	FT	Pts.
Sailors, lf	0	0	0
Baumholtz, rf	9	1	19
Rothenberg, c	4	0	8
Riebe, lg	8	0	16
Mogus, rg	6	2	14
Scharnus, lg	0	1	1
Shaback, lf	1	1	3
Faught, rg	6	3	15
Hermsen, c	4	0	8
Endress, lf	0	0	0
Schultz, rg	4	0	8
Totals	**42**	**8**	**92**

Missed free throws: Washington (13)—Mahnken 2, Norlander 2, McKinney 4, Negratti, Gillette, 2, O'Grady 2. Cleveland (11)— Sailors 2, Baumholtz 2, Mogus 2, Faught 2, Schultz.

The team's promising beginning gave Sutphin the wrong idea. "He'd made a considerable part of his fortune with the hockey team," said Clifford, "and he knew nothing about basketball. After those two wins, Al half-believed that we just might go through the season undefeated. He learned the ropes in a hurry, though. Still, as long as things appeared to be going well, Al was incredibly generous. Both Dutch and I started out with unlimited expense accounts, and at Christmas, Al handed out new suits like they were candy canes."

After beating the Caps, the Rebels' schizophrenic roster lost all sense of coherence, and the team dropped sixteen of its next twenty-six games. "The old guys didn't worry about what happened in the games," Sailors said. "They led a royal life and got paid well. To them, the games were just part of their job, and their lack of intensity infuriated me."

Despite the mounting losses, Dehnert stuck with the old-timers. "Joe Fulks had a two-handed jumper," said Sailors, "and Joe Lapchick always gave me the credit for being the first to shoot jumpers the way I did, but Dutch couldn't deal with anything so new and so radical. He had trouble dealing with the younger guys anyway, so I spent much more time sitting than playing."

In addition to Dehnert's resistance to change, his players were astounded by his routine forgetfulness. "Dutch wore thick glasses," said Sailors, "and he used to push them up on his forehead, forget they were there, and start looking around for them. Along the same lines, Dutch could never remember our names. He called us by our numbers: 'Number five. Go in there for number three.' He was a great guy, truly friendly and good-natured, but it was clear that the game had passed him by."

Baumholtz was too good for even Dehnert to bench, but he was also the frequent victim of Dehnert's mental lapses. "I scored twenty-five in an early-season game at Toronto," said Baumholtz. "The next game, I got nineteen at home against Detroit, and we won both games. But then I didn't get off the bench for the next three games. Dutch simply forgot about me. I had to go to him and say that I was the kind of player he had to put in there and let me go; yanking me in and out wouldn't do me or the team any good. After that, Dutch kept me out there until I was so tired that my tongue was hanging out."

Baumholtz also recalled another game in which he was playing extremely well: "Dutch took me out for a short breather, then forgot that I wasn't on the court. After a while, he came over to me and told me that Baumholtz was stinking up the court and that I should go in for him."

Playing too much was certainly preferable to hardly playing, and Sailors and Scharnus became increasingly frustrated by playing only in the tail end of lopsided games. One day, Scharnus told Sailors, "If we continue to sit on the bench for the rest of the season, then our careers are done. What we should do is go talk to Roy Clifford and tell him we want to be traded."

Sailors agreed, and the two malcontents voiced their complaints to Clifford. "Sit tight for a little bit," Clifford advised. "There's going to be some changes."

The first change was to trade for Ed Sadowski, who wholeheartedly endorsed Dehnert's slowdown precepts. "I never liked Sadowski, because I thought he was a bully," said Clifford, "but Dutch knew him from the ABL and insisted on making the trade. I mean, we had to get rid of Mogus anyway, so I pulled the trigger. Dealing Hermsen was a tough pill to swallow, though, because I thought he had the makings of a star."

What Clifford disliked most about Sadowski was the big man's refusal to run under any circumstances. "After he scored a basket," said Clifford, "he'd pull up his pants and walk downcourt while his man ran. I supposed this was a holdover from the days of the center jump. Anyway, our guards had to cover for Sadowski and pick up the guy he was supposed to be guarding. That meant little guys had to guard big guys. As a result, the guards got banged around and also got tagged with too many unnecessary fouls."

Right off the bat, Sadowski's refusal to move fast became a source of disharmony for a team that wasn't especially copacetic to begin with. Whenever his new teammates got too frisky, Sadowski would call a time-out and lay out the options: "If you want to win this game and make some money in the playoffs, you've got to wait for me to set up in the pivot. If you want to get your names in the newspapers, then go ahead and shoot it before I get there."

After a few games, the young players decided it was easier to keep the ball away from Sadowski than it was to stand around and watch him shoot. Sadowski finally got the message and went to Baumholtz complaining that he was being ignored in the pivot. "Let's you and me make a deal," Baumholtz told him. "For every three times I pass you the ball, you'll pass it back to me once." He reported, "Sadowski was agreeable, and we had no trouble for the rest of the season." Mel Riebe, however, refused to enter into a similar bargain and continued freezing Sadowski out of the offense.

Without having to worry about coaching, Sadowski was much more aggressive on the court than he had been in Toronto. On January 23, in the latter stages of an 83–78 loss in Philadelphia, Big Ed had tallied only 7 points, to Joe Fulks's 28. Sadowski decided the only way to slow Jumpin' Joe down was to knock him out. Fortunately, Sadowski's roundhouse punch missed. After referee Johnny Nucatola banished Sadowski from the game, the still furious Big Ed had to be escorted through the hostile crowd by a bevy of policemen.

Even though Sadowski was rambunctious on and off the court, the Rebels were not very rebellious. "Most of us were happy to play pinochle on the trains or in the hotels," said Baumholtz. "Once in a while, a guy would get a hair up his ass and want to spend some time at a bar or a nightclub, but that was unusual. We were usually too tired to be out on the town."

Finally, on February 10, after a loss to Detroit had the Rebels languishing with a 17–20 record, Clifford reluctantly replaced Dehnert. Because Dutch was still a popular personage in Cleveland, rather than being fired outright, he was assigned scouting duties. Even so, Dehnert went out of his way to blast the younger players in the newspapers, claiming that Sailors, Faught, and Riebe refused to work with him.

"Coaching wasn't something that I wanted to get back into," said Clifford, "but I had to take one for the team."

Right away, Clifford instituted drastic changes. Sailors became a starter, the pace of their game was accelerated, he demanded their full attention at all times, and practice sessions were mostly devoted to fundamentals. One of the drills dealt with footwork, but when the ball was thrown to Sadowski and Clifford called for a "back pivot," Big Ed didn't move.

"The guy had no idea what I was talking about," said Clifford. "He'd always gotten by on his size and his strength. When I tried to explain things, he got huffy. He maintained that fundamentals were high school stuff and he didn't need them. I tried everything, but there was no way that Sadowski was going to change."

Since Sadowski scored points by the dozen, he quickly became too popular with the fans to be traded again, but Clifford burned up the telephone wires trying to reshape the rest of his squad. "We had two groups of players," Clifford said, "the old guys and the young guys, and they simply couldn't work and play well together."

Clifford ended up signing one of his old Western Reserve players. "Hank Lefkowitz joined us in midseason after he had graduated," said Clifford. "He was a tough, six-foot-two kid who could run, and he wasn't afraid to knock around in the lane with the big boys."

The Rebels' fortunes were slow to turn. They'd win two, lose two, win three, lose two. Through it all, even the old-timers (except for Sadowski) learned to respect Clifford and attend to his advice, and the new coach quickly gained his players' loyalty (except for Sadowski), because he always stood up for them.

Clifford related, "The fans in Cleveland would razz me whenever a player made a bad play. 'Hey, get that so-and-so out of there!' One night, Ray Wertis had trouble handling the ball, and one of the leather-lunged fans started screaming at me to bench him. But I really liked Wertis. He was well educated, a true gentleman, and he always worked hard. Besides, sometimes even the best players made mistakes. So, this time, the fan's screaming got me really mad. Instead of yanking Wertis, I turned around to face the stands and thumbed my nose at the guy who was making all the noise. I was coaching the team, not him. Not only that, I left Wertis in for the rest of the game. He came over and thanked me for this afterwards."

Pleasing the fans was a season-long struggle that wasn't helped by Sutphin's uncharacteristic stinginess. "There was a sixty cents' tax on all tickets," Clifford said, "and Sutphin insisted that we collect this amount even on complimentary tickets. Early in the season, I was manning the box office when a fan came up and presented his comp ticket. When I told him about the tax that was due, he told me to go to hell, ripped up the tickets, and threw them at me. It didn't take long for the word to get around town that free tickets to Rebels' games cost sixty cents."

Under Clifford, the Rebels were 13–10 and finished the regular season at 30–30. Attendance had been disappointing, but Sutphin hoped to recoup his losses during a lengthy run in the playoffs.

Cleveland Rebels

	G	FGM	FGA	Pct.	FTM	FTA	Pct.	Asst.	PF	Pts.	Avg.
Ed Sadowski	43	256	682	.375	174	262	.664	30	152	686	16.0
Mel Riebe	55	276	898	.307	111	373	.642	67	169	663	12.1
Frankie Baumholtz	45	255	856	.298	121	156	.776	54	93	631	14.0
Kenny Sailors	58	229	741	.309	119	200	.595	134	177	577	9.9
George Nostrand	48	146	520	.281	74	149	.497	21	123	366	7.6
Bob Faught	51	141	498	.295	61	106	.575	33	97	343	6.7
Nick Shaback	53	102	395	.265	38	53	.717	29	75	242	4.6
Leo Mogus	17	73	226	.323	63	88	.716	28	50	209	12.3
Ray Wertis	43	41	195	.210	33	54	.611	21	53	115	2.7
Dick Schultz	16	43	176	.244	20	31	.645	17	29	106	6.6
Ben Scharnus	51	33	165	.200	37	59	.627	19	83	103	2.0
Irv Rothenberg	29	36	167	.216	30	54	.556	15	62	102	3.5
Hank Lefkowitz	24	22	114	.193	7	13	.538	4	31	51	2.1
Kleggie Hermsen	11	18	67	.269	7	15	.467	10	32	43	3.9
Ned Endress	16	3	25	.120	8	15	.533	4	13	14	0.9
Leon Brown	5	0	3	.000	0	0	—	0	2	0	0.0
Pete Lalich	7	0	1	.000	0	0	—	0	1	0	0.0
Ken Corley	3	0	0	—	0	0	—	0	0	0	0.0

Postscript

Sutphin closed up shop after the playoffs. A closer look at Cleveland's demographics would have saved him much time, effort, and money. In 1920, Cleveland had been the country's fifth-largest city. By 1946, it was thirty-third. Also, its population base of 900,000 was rapidly shrinking as tens of thousands fled to the suburbs. To make matters worse, the city-based industries were in the midst of a brief but serious postwar decline.

Sutphin had deluded himself into thinking that because the Cleveland Rams had moved to Los Angeles, his Rebels would be an irresistible wintertime attraction. In so doing, he failed to pay sufficient attention to the Cleveland Browns in the newly formed All-American Football Conference.

Frankie Baumholtz never played pro basketball again but went on to have an outstanding ten-year career in the major leagues with Cincinnati, Chicago, and Philadelphia. Twice he batted more than .300 (his best was .325 in 1952), and he finished with a lifetime mark of .290.

Kenny Sailors played another four years in the BAA/NBA with Chicago, Philadelphia, Providence, Denver, Boston, and Baltimore, establishing himself as a solid scorer (12.6 for his career) and passer (2.8).

The Bottom Line

Average paid attendance	2,259
Net receipts	$64,638
Estimated loss	$200,000

The Professor and the
St. Louis Bombers

Talk about split personalities! Before signing on to coach the Bombers, Ken Loeffler earned a law degree from the University of Pittsburgh, was a talented pop pianist, and wrote poetry. Here's his favorite rhymed composition:

> What makes the game? Not perfect play,
> But golden chances thrown away.
> The errant play, the sad mistake,
> Which men however skillful make.

He'd also been a star basketball and baseball player at Penn State, as well as a defensive ace for the semipro Pittsburgh Morries, in the Central Pro League. "We got twenty-five dollars a game," he said, "and we could beat every team in the country except the Original Celtics." In the summers, Loeffler gave tennis lessons to the Kennedys at their compound in Hyannis Port.

During the war, he was assigned to the Pentagon, where his primary duties were to represent defendants in court-martial trials. "I always took the juiciest cases," he said, "the ones that had to do with murder, rape, or homosexual charges." Later, he was assigned to lead a preflight cadet training program at Butler University, before being summoned back to Washington to join the Special Service staff of General Hap Arnold. After his tour, Loeffler coached the basketball team at Yale.

His characteristic tweed jacket and blue bow tie seemed to reflect his intelligence, charm, and sophistication. He looked more like a college professor than a basketball coach.

Once the game began, though, Loeffler turned into an arrogant, rude vulgarian. Loeffler was well aware of the dramatic changes in his personality and attempted some cursory damage control. "Don't pay any attention to what I say an hour before games," he warned his players. "That also goes for the games themselves, and an hour after games."

He had fixed ideas of how the game should be played and how it should be coached. "Basketball is a game of evasion," he said prior to the Bombers' season, "and it's the fast plays, both on the attack and sometimes defensively, that make it so. We're going to show St. Louis fans a game of movement and finesse and, above all, *speed.*"

Loeffler chose to abandon the old-fashioned game that would hobble teams such as Boston, Pittsburgh, Cleveland (under Dehnert), and Toronto (under Sadowski). At age forty-three, Loeffler shunned the past and looked to the future.

At the same time, he had a retrogressive view of how a coach should coach. "In order to achieve team unity and singleness of purpose," he believed, "all the players should hate the coach."

To that end, Loeffler goaded his players with ruthless sarcasm, while remaining so aloof that they were convinced he either didn't like them or, worse, didn't care about them at all. Loeffler set the tone as his players gathered for their initial practice session: "You guys are great basketball players. Most of you have been all-Americans. You've all had great coaches in your college careers. But I'm not your coach. I'm your boss." No wonder that his players either adored him or detested him.

No wonder, too, that the roster that Loeffler recruited included only one player with any professional experience.

That would be John Barr, a husky, 6'3", 205-pound guard from Penn State, who had played a few games for Wilkes-Barre in the Eastern League.

The rest had played only college and service ball:

The best of these was John Logan, 6'2", 175, out of Indiana, a terrific two-handed set shooter and passer (although he tended to be reckless with his long passes). Logan's hustle set the standard for his teammates, as did his friendly manner. He was also one of the Bombers who took full advantage of the local nightlife in every city on the circuit.

Bob Doll, 6'5", 195, from Colorado, was the shortest center in the BAA. Nevertheless, his aggressive fronting defense was the bane of all the other pivotmen. With a salary of $6,000, Doll was the Bombers' highest-paid player.

George Munroe, 5'11", 170, out of Dartmouth, was highly intelligent (a Phi Beta Kappa) and a valued conversationalist who was especially good company on long train rides. "I'd had some good games against Yale when Loeffler was coaching there," said Munroe, "so I guess that's what interested him. My salary was four thousand plus a couple of hundred extra if we made the playoffs. It was OK money, and totally appropriate, because I never thought of myself as anything more than an OK player. At the time Loeffler contacted me, I was hoping to start my second year in law school but lacked the necessary funds. Playing ball seemed like an enjoyable way to replenish my wallet."

Count Munroe as one of the Bombers who didn't cotton to Loeffler. "I don't recall him having much humility," said Munroe, "and he wasn't exactly my favorite person. Aside from his personality, he was an OK coach."

Don Putman, 6'1", 170, from Denver, made up for his lack of superior talent with relentless energy.

Giff Roux, 6'5", 195, from Kansas, was an earnest rebounder and defender and was the fastest player on the team, if not in the entire league.

Cecil Hankins, 6'1", 175, was a veteran of Oklahoma A&M's initial NCAA championship in 1945 and was more of a driver than a shooter. "Cecil was a devil-may-care bachelor," said Munroe. "We often played seven-card poker on the trains, and Cecil never folded."

Aubrey Davis, 6'2", 175, from Oklahoma Baptist, lived to play defense.

Don Martin, 6'7", 210, from Central Missouri, couldn't jump or run, but he took up a lot of space in the shadow of the basket. Martin's day job was coaching basketball at Jennings High School, and he was unable to accompany the Bombers on long road trips.

Herschel "Herk" Baltimore, 6'4", 190, also hailed from Penn State.

Deb Smith, 6'3", 180, from Utah, was a steady floor man who rarely made mistakes. Smith was a Mormon (and a bachelor) and endured constant teasing from his teammates about the possible dangers and delights of polygamy.

Fred Jacobs was a 6'3" 170-pounder from Denver.

Finally, there was Ralph Siewert, 7'1", 230, from Dakota Wesleyan, a lumberjack who had never played basketball before and who had two nicknames. One was "Moose," because he was so clumsy that, as Munroe observed, "whichever side you were playing for, it was always dangerous to be on the floor with him." The other nom de hoop, "Timber," was applied after Siewert tripped over the foul line during a practice session and hit the floor so hard that everybody present thought the roof had caved in.

The most emphasized part of Loeffler's game plan was ferocious defense—the Bombers ended the season as the BAA's third-best defensive squad, yielding 64.0 points per game, only .2 of a point behind the league-leading Washington Capitols. On offense, the Bombers employed weaves and back screens, as well as pass-and-screen-away and give-and-dive-cut maneuvers that featured all five players in constant motion from a spread formation. Not including Siewert (who lasted only a few weeks), St. Louis was the smallest team in the league. To compensate for this deficiency, all of the Bombers were adept scorers in the pivot—which allowed Loeffler to specifically attack any weak post defenders they faced.

The Bombers' opener, a 56–51 victory over Pittsburgh before 4,507 fans, was a commercial success but an artistic disaster. In pregame advertisements, the Bombers promised "Thrills—Spills—Action—Speed." Thanks to the slick surface of the court, the "spills" generated the most attention. Thus the main headline in the *Globe-Democrat*: "Bombers Glide to 56–51 Victory," with the subhead "Slippery Floor More Slippery to Pittsburgh." The article concluded with, "George Carson, general manager of Arena hockey, said the Bombers proposed to bring St. Louis professional basketball come 'rain or shine.' He wasn't fooling. The rain was there in spirit and in condensation." The accompanying photograph showed John Logan and Press Maravich sprawled on the floor.

A subsequent win in Detroit was succeeded by a home loss to the Knickerbockers. Then came a controversial 70–69 home-court victory over Washington. Because of injuries, the Capitols were able to suit up only nine players, and when five of them fouled out, the visitors were forced to play the last few minutes of the game with only four players on the court. In the confusion, it was later discovered that a discrepancy in the official scorebook credited the Bombers with only 68 points. The Caps threatened to file a protest but never did—primarily because of the cost—so the final score stood.

Washington	FG	FT	Pts.
McKinney, f	2	7	11
Norlander, f	7	8	22
Negratti, f	5	0	10
O'Grady, f	0	3	3
Gillette, f	0	1	1
Mahnken, c	0	1	1
Torgoff, c	1	1	3
Feerick, g	2	4	8
Scolari, g	2	6	10
Totals	**19**	**31**	**69**

St. Louis	FG	FT	Pts.
Putman, f	4	0	8
Smith, f	3	0	6
Logan, f	2	3	7
Baltimore, f	4	0	8
Doll, c	2	6	10
Hankins, c	8	2	18
Munroe, g	1	0	2
Roux, g	0	0	0
Davis, g	0	0	0
Jacobs, g	2	3	7
Barr, g	0	0	0
Martin, g	2	0	4
Totals	**28**	**14**	**70**

The Bombers continued their winning ways. During a 65–53 win against the Celtics, Bob Doll and Art Spector were ejected for "a fistfight." Just two days before, Johnny Logan had been booted from a game for blatantly elbowing an opponent in the chops. The local scribes were actually delighted and hailed the Bombers as a reincarnation of the brawling St. Louis Cardinals teams of the 1930s that earned the sobriquet of "Gashouse Gang." The Bombers' banished center was even identified as "Gashouser Doll."

With a November 23 win in Providence, the Bombers sported a record of 8–2 and were ensconced in first place in the Western Division. According to Loeffler, the reason for the team's success was that his players were giving "the old college try." The real reason, however, had more to do with Loeffler's game plan.

Whereas every other team in the league employed an eight-man rotation, Loeffler routinely played his entire roster. His idea was to enhance his team's intention to keep running and moving, and thus to wear down the opponents' core players.

By the end of November, Loeffler had refined his substitution pattern. The Bombers' starters were usually Doll, Logan, Putman, Jacobs, and Davis. Then, sometime late in the first quarter, he would insert his second team en masse—Hankins, Munroe, Roux, Barr, and either Martin or Baltimore. The starters were more physical, while the second unit was quicker and played better overall defense. It would be years before other pro coaches fully understood the benefits of this tactic. Not only did the sudden influx of fresh legs put additional pressure on opponents, but also, by Loeffler's utilizing two distinct units, other teams were forced to prepare for the Bombers by instituting two separate defensive schemes.

On December 12, St. Louis lost in Chicago by 88–68, but what was noteworthy about the game was the fact that the Stags tossed up 100 shots from the field (making 37), while the Bombers let loose with 133 (making 25). St. Louis's prodigious attempts remained a league record for the next ten years.

By Christmas, the Bombers were 16–7 and in the middle of a six-game winning streak. Even those Bombers who were offended by Loeffler's game-time personality began to appreciate his expertise. They were particularly impressed with his ability to prepare his team for each opponent, as well as his uncanny knack for coming up with some strategic trick that would push them over the top in close contests, whether it was an unexpected switch in defensive assignments, sending Logan into the pivot, playing without a center, or playing with two of them.

Loeffler freely admitted to his "trickery." It was the only way he could overcome a roster that lacked "star-studded players."

The Bombers were still riding high on January 5, with a mark of 20–8, when Fred Jacobs left the team. The word was that he had just received notice that he'd passed a written exam he'd taken for an unspecified government post. Now he was required to take an oral exam in Denver for the same mysterious job. His teammates speculated that Jacobs was an apprentice spy. While he was away from the team, Jacobs said that he would do some scouting.

On February 4, the Bombers were 25–12 and leading the Stags by a mere one and a half games for the top spot in the Western Division. Despite the

Bombers' good showing so far, Loeffler believed that his team lacked a true center and a reliable scorer, and he was always on the lookout to improve his team at any and all positions. Enter Belus Smawley, 6'2", 195, from Appalachian State.

"I was teaching and coaching at a high school in Forest City, North Carolina," said Smawley. "I was also playing with a barnstorming team out of Asheville that paid two-fifty a month plus expenses. We'd play against AAU and company teams all over Georgia, Tennessee, and the Carolinas. The games were mostly at night on weekends, and on Monday mornings, I always managed to get to school just in time."

During the war, Smawley had played ball while stationed at naval bases in Honolulu and then at Norfolk. Among his teammates in Norfolk was Johnny Barr.

"I didn't know much about the BAA," said Smawley, "except that the league existed. About the specific teams, players, and coaches I knew not a thing. I'd just gotten married and was ready to settle down. I had absolutely no ambition to play pro basketball."

Smawley was in uniform for Asheville and was warming up for a charity game in Spartanburg, South Carolina, when he was informed that he was wanted on the telephone. "I took the call in the arena's box office," Smawley recalled, "and it was Loeffler. He said that Barr had recommended me and asked if I was interested in coming to St. Louis. I told him that I surely wasn't. Then he started talking about money. When he got up to five thousand, I suddenly became interested. I mean, I was getting only eighteen hundred from the school plus a couple of thousand from the Asheville team. I talked it over with my wife, and then I went to the principal of my school and asked about getting a leave of absence. When he agreed, off we went."

Smawley's repertoire featured a soft two-handed jumper as well as a two-handed set that he released from a deep crouch. His trademark, however, was a ducklike shuffle that earned him the nickname of "Waddlefoot."

"I'd been on the team for only a few days when we had a game in Philadelphia," Smawley said. "I hadn't played but a minute, and we were getting beaten by a lot, when Loeffler came storming into the dressing room. He'd pace back and forth and smoke up a storm while he chewed us out. Then he turned on me. I said, 'Hold on, Coach. Talk to the guys that are playing. Don't get on my back when I'm sitting on the bench.' From then on, Loeffler never gave me any trouble."

Smawley was quick to get the pulse of the team. "Lots of guys despised Loeffler, but they also respected him," he said. "His way was to use certain guys as whipping posts, and they all came to accept this. Sometimes he'd even apologize after unloading on us. Through it all, Loeffler was an excellent coach, the best I ever played for. He was a great tactician, and nobody could plan for a specific game against a specific opponent like he could. I'll bet we had more out-of-bounds plays than all the rest of the teams combined."

Smawley was also pleased at what good company his new teammates were. "I was saving my money to buy a home for me and my wife," said Smawley, "so I never went out clubbing and drinking and womanizing like some of the others did. But we all got along like brothers."

However, even with Smawley providing some firepower for the second unit, the Bombers began to run out of gas as the season rounded the clubhouse turn in early March. A four-game losing streak dropped them to 32–22 and put first place out of reach. Not even the return of Fred Jacobs could revitalize the team. (He reported finding no suitable prospects.)

"I've run out of tricks," Loeffler said. "All we have left is the old college try."

That trying was succeeding as the Bombers won six of their final seven games, to finish at 38–23.

Next up was a three-game playoff series with the second-place finisher in the Eastern Division, the Philadelphia Warriors.

St. Louis Bombers

	G	FGM	FGA	Pct.	FTM	FTA	Pct.	Asst.	PF	Pts.	Avg.
Johnny Logan	61	290	1,043	.278	190	254	.748	78	136	770	12.6
Bob Doll	60	194	768	.253	134	206	.650	22	167	522	8.7
George Munroe	59	164	623	.263	86	133	.647	17	91	414	7.0
Don Putman	58	156	635	.246	68	105	.648	30	106	380	6.6
Giff Roux	60	142	478	.297	70	160	.438	17	95	354	5.9
Cecil Hankins	58	117	391	.299	90	150	.600	14	49	324	5.9
John Barr	58	124	438	.283	47	79	.596	54	164	295	5.1
Aubrey Davis	59	107	381	.281	73	115	.635	14	136	287	4.9
Belus Smawley	22	113	352	.321	36	47	.766	10	37	262	11.9
Don Martin	54	89	304	.293	13	31	.419	9	75	191	3.5
Herk Baltimore	58	53	263	.202	32	69	.464	16	98	138	2.4
Deb Smith	48	32	119	.269	9	21	.429	6	47	73	1.5
Fred Jacobs	18	19	69	.275	12	25	.480	5	25	50	2.8
Ralph Siewert	7	1	13	.077	2	5	.400	0	8	4	0.6

Postscript

Loeffler coached the Bombers for another season, finishing atop the Western Division with a mark of 29–19. He resigned on May 28, 1947, because of a dispute with management over a $1,000 bonus. (The Bombers lasted until 1949–50 before disbanding.)

Loeffler went on to an illustrious career at La Salle, winning the NIT in 1952 and the NCAA in 1954 (with Tom Gola leading both championships). Later, he coached at Texas A&M, and after retiring from coaching, he taught business law at Monmouth College, in New Jersey.

Johnny Logan was found dead in his apartment on September 16, 1977, apparently the victim of a robbery.

Bob Doll committed suicide on September 18, 1959.

The Bottom Line

Average paid attendance	3,120
Net receipts	$113,808
Estimated loss	$75,000

The Short Flight of the Detroit Falcons

om King enjoyed writing about sports nearly as much as he did playing them. Barely six feet tall and 165 pounds, he'd achieved first-team
all-state status in both basketball and football as a high schooler in Lansing,
Michigan. "I was proud of that," King said, "because I was so small, but the
physical competition didn't quite satisfy me."

That's why King wheedled his way into becoming a stringer for the *Detroit
Free Press* and the *Lansing State Journal*. "We played our football games on
Friday nights," he said, "and the Catholic schools played on Saturdays and
Sundays, so I was able to cover them. I never won a Pulitzer Prize, but by my
senior year, I had my own byline."

King's next stop was the University of Michigan, where he became a star
basketball player. "It was at Michigan that I became more interested in the
business side of sports," he said, "so I chose to major in business administra-
tion. Writing still had its attractions, and in my junior year, I was the sports
editor of the school newspaper."

As with most of his contemporaries, his career prospects were interrupted
by the war. "I joined the Marine Corps," he said, "and they sent me to the
University of Michigan to train troops. I stayed stateside for the duration and
came out a captain."

King also played plenty of basketball during his stint in the military.
"Enough," he said, "to keep my game sharp. Then in the spring of 1945, I
was given leave to play in the College All-Star Game against the Fort Wayne
Zollner Pistons, who were the reigning world champs. We had Bobby
McDermott, Bob Kurland, and Ernie Calverley, but they had more experi-
ence, so they beat us. I had a good game, and we were well scouted."

Immediately after his discharge, King was approached by the Toledo franchise in the NBL as well as the Detroit Falcons, and he became the object of a mild bidding war. "My father had played basketball at Notre Dame," said King, "and somewhere along the line, he'd met up with Walter Kennedy, who was then the public relations director for the BAA. Kennedy got into the act and convinced me that my future was with the new league. I signed with the Falcons for eight thousand dollars plus a five-hundred-dollar signing bonus."

As training camp commenced, King was focused on simply making the team. Yet he was surprised by the poor physical condition of coach Glenn Curtis.

Curtis was renowned in the Midwest as the "old fox" of prep basketball. His teams had won four Indiana High School Championships (Lebanon in 1918; Martinsville in 1924, 1927, and 1933) and had made two other trips to the finals (Martinsville in 1926 and 1928). He'd moved on to Indiana State University in 1938, and in the spring of 1946, he had led ISU into the finals of the small-college championships.

"Curtis was a delightful man," said King, "but he was severely handicapped by ill health. He looked absolutely wasted, like he had some kind of cancer. It came out later on that that's exactly what his problem was. During our preseason practices, he'd just throw out the ball and tell us to scrimmage."

Smoking a cigar, Curtis would sit in the stands and watch his players freelance. His theory was to play the players who could play together. Anybody who was inordinately selfish or who caused even the least bit of dissension was cut.

In addition to King, here are the key players Curtis chose:

John Janisch, 6'3", 200, from Valparaiso.
Ariel "Ace" Maughan, 6'4", 190, from Utah State.
Bob Dille, 6'3", 190, also from Valparaiso, one of the Falcons' senior citizens at twenty-nine years old. "Bob was very outgoing," said King, "and his insistence on always working hard made him the leader of the team."
Grady Lewis, 6'7", 215, from Oklahoma, King's best friend.
Harold Brown, 6'0", 155, out of Evansville.
Chet Aubuchon, 5'10", 137, from Michigan State. At thirty years old, Aubuchon was over the hill. In any event, he was more interested in becoming a teacher than in playing basketball full-time, and he didn't finish the season.

Milt Schoon, 6'7", 230, another Valparaiso guy. Schoon couldn't shoot himself in the foot, but he was big and bighearted. Also, Schoon was still a matriculated student at Valparaiso and wasn't scheduled to graduate (with a degree in physical education) until later in December. Until then, he played with the Falcons only on weekends.

George and Henry Pearcy, both 6'1", 170. Both had played for Curtis at Indiana State.

The best player on the squad, Stan Miasek, 6'5", 210, hadn't attended college.

"I was born and raised in the Bronx," said Miasek, "and I didn't make my high school team because the coach didn't like my style, so I started playing with various semipro teams in and around New York. I got ten bucks a game and played pretty good, even against superior teams like the Rens. It was in the service where I got most of my experience. This was with the Ottumwa, Iowa, Naval Air Station, and we competed against Notre Dame, the University of Indiana, and a really good team out of Great Lakes."

Miasek was also a power-hitting baseball player with tremendous potential. "When I mustered out in 1945," he said, "I signed with the Giants to play first base and the outfield with a farm team of theirs in Rome, New York. While I was there, I was contacted by several teams from the BAA, the most persistent being Detroit and New York."

Why did Miasek opt for the Falcons instead of the hometown Knicks? "Detroit offered me eight grand, and New York offered five. New York and several of the other teams said that I'd have a hard time surviving the final cuts, because I was so inexperienced. They said that going up against old pros and top-notch college players would be too much for me. The Falcons' offer, like everybody else's, was conditional on my making the team, but Detroit laid it on the line: they said they desperately needed a big man, and they were running out of time to find one, so the job was mine to lose. I couldn't believe there could be such a big difference in the offers, so going with Detroit was a layup that I couldn't miss. Also, I was in such great condition from playing baseball that I could run rings around all the other big guys. Agility and quickness: those would be my edges all season long."

Long before the season began, Tom King sized up the Falcons' organization and came to a distressing conclusion. "We had a coach, a trainer, players, a gym, and uniforms," said King, "but that was about all. The Olympia

Stadium was staffed with people who were very interested in ice shows and hockey teams, but not really in basketball."

Arthur Wirtz and Jim Norris were absentee owners. Nick Landes was the overall supervisor of the Olympia but spent most of his time promoting boxing and wrestling matches. Charlie Escoe ostensibly handled player personnel for the Falcons, but he was also the team's ticket manager and was likewise responsible for overseeing the day-to-day management of the arena. Fred Huber was publicity director of the Red Wings and was supposed to do the same for the Falcons, but he had no interest in, or understanding of, basketball.

The Falcons were the neglected stepchild of Wirtz's sports franchises. They didn't even have any traveling plans for the upcoming season. "I wrote a memorandum to Wirtz to inform him of his organization's shortcomings," said King, "and also of my qualifications. After a brief face-to-face meeting, he hired me as the Falcons' publicity director and traveling secretary. Wirtz then signed me to a separate contract for an additional eight thousand dollars."

The Falcons opened at home with an embarrassing 50–33 loss to Washington. Not only would their point total prove to be the lowest for any team in any game for the entire season, but also the Olympia's court had the same water-condensation problems as elsewhere.

"We were strictly a finesse team," said King. "If we couldn't run our way into a shot, we had no patterns to rely on, so we needed quick stops and cuts to be effective. With the court so slippery, we were helpless. I mean, I stopped short one time to take a shot and wound up sliding like I was trying to steal third base. The Capitols were bigger, more powerful, so their movements were slower and under much more control than ours. Meanwhile, the Detroit fans were amazed; we were supposed to be the world's greatest basketball players, and we couldn't keep from falling all over the place."

The Falcons' disorganized offense proved easy marks for most of the team's early foes. After losing to St. Louis and Toronto, they secured their first win on November 11 in beating the hapless Celtics. Later in November, they strung together three consecutive wins—over Chicago, Cleveland, and Providence—before embarking on a road trip that lasted from November 27 to December 26 and included thirteen games.

The reason for this record-setting journey? So that the Olympia might accommodate Sonja Henie and her ice review.

On the road, King was responsible for distributing meal money—$4.50 per diem—to the players. He also wrote postgame stories for the wire services. "The Associated Press and International News Service paid me by the word," said King. "It came out to about twenty dollars per game, but I would have done it for nothing."

Still in uniform, King would find a chair in the corner of the dressing room, lift the cover off his ancient Remington portable—"a present from my mother when I was in high school"—and type out his stories.

Here's what else he did on the road: "Hustle to get train tickets to all the players; then hustle to get taxis from the train station to the hotel. During our first trip to Toronto, I ran around like a crazy man rounding up taxis, only to discover that the hotel was directly across the street from the train station."

Once the team was settled in the hotel, King would call radio stations trying to arrange interviews and on-the-air plugs. "I'd also go to the offices of all the newspapers," he said. "I always carried pictures of all the Falcons and came equipped with several ideas for possible feature stories. I got the best results in Cleveland and Toronto, because the media people there weren't very sophisticated. Getting any airtime or press coverage was the toughest in New York. After all my running around, I'd get to the arena, get taped, play the game, then write stories for the wire services."

Somewhere, King also had to find the time to write advance stories for the afternoon dailies in Detroit: the team would be returning home at such and such a time on such and such a day; Miasek's sprained finger was better; Maughan's knee was achy.

For home games, King's duties also required him to make certain that the pressroom, the press table, and the press credential were in order. "I had my own office in the Olympia," he said, "with my own secretary."

In this respect, King considered himself lucky that he wasn't an outstanding player. "My teammates knew that I was acting in a professional manner regarding what I chose to write about," he said. "They knew that I had everybody's best interests at heart, that I wasn't on an ego trip, and that I had an ambition to get into journalism. On the court, I hustled, hit the open man, and tried to avoid taking bad shots. If I had a good game, the box score would speak for itself. My relationship with the other guys would have been more difficult if I'd been a better player."

The Falcons were 3–10 on their lengthy road trip and returned home with a record of 8–16. One of the lowlights of the trip was a 75–64 loss in

Washington during which King got into an altercation with Red Auerbach, the Caps' infamously obnoxious coach.

"Red was a master of matchups," King recalled. "I'd normally do a good job defending Fred Scolari, because we were about the same size, but Red always managed his moves so that I spent much of the game guarding Feerick, who was six-three and one of the best scorers in the league. It wasn't surprising that Feerick gave me fits, especially during that particular game. I was frustrated by chasing Feerick at the same time that Red was frustrated by some of the refs' calls. On one play, I ran into Washington's bench in pursuit of a loose ball, and Red took objection to this. As I was getting to my feet, he pushed me in the back and sent me sprawling again. I responded by pushing him, and for a moment, we squared off. Fortunately, for him rather than me, his players interceded and separated us."

The Falcons' return home was marred by a loss to Toronto, 52–48, that extended the latest losing streak to seven games. The contest featured still another on-court brawl that characterized so many of the BAA contests. With Mike McCarron setting the tone, the Huskies were infamous for their eagerness to stop playing and start punching. (Just two days later in Chicago, Toronto's Bob Fitzgerald would KO Chick Halbert, and McCarron would pummel Max Zaslofsky.) This time, McCarron was a spectator as the fisticuffs between Milt Schoon and Bob Fitzgerald led to their banishment. Curtis, however, was encouraged by the feistiness of his players in the face of their wearying and spectacularly unsuccessful road trip.

As the New Year approached, the Falcons' season was already an irrevocable disaster. "Coach Curtis simply wasn't up to the task," said King. "The traveling was too much for him, and he really didn't understand the fine points of the pro game. He gave us the same speech before every single game. When we had the ball, he told us to have poise and confidence. On defense, we were supposed to be like cats and dogs. Before one game, he announced six starting players."

Even so, the players enjoyed each other's company. "There was absolutely no monkeying around," said King. "We'd sit on the trains and talk about everything under the sun, from sports to politics. Since none of us were dedicated barhoppers, there were no problems with curfew. Milt Schoon was the team comedian, but when you lose forty games, how funny can things be?"

On New Year's Day, the Falcons were a half game out of the Western Division basement as they prepared to face the mighty Capitols, who not only had the best record in the league but also were riding a seventeen-game unbeaten streak. The Falcons' players, however, were heartened by the fact that, although they hadn't overcome the Caps in any of their three previous meetings, they expected that Washington was looking ahead to its battle in St. Louis the very next evening against the always tough Bombers. Nobody knew it at the time, but (although King was out with a minor injury) the Falcons' subsequent 62–57 victory would constitute the highlight of the team's season.

Washington	FG	FT	PF	Pts.
Feerick, f	2	2	5	6
Mahnken, f	3	4	4	10
McKinney, c	3	1	5	7
Norlander, g	1	2	2	4
Scolari, g	7	5	4	19
Torgoff, g	4	3	4	11
Gillette, g	0	0	3	0
O'Grady, g	0	0	0	0
Totals	**20**	**17**	**27**	**57**

Detroit	FG	F	PF	Pts.
Janisch, f	6	3	5	15
Dille, f	6	4	5	16
Miasek, c	4	9	5	17
G. Pearcy, g	2	9	4	13
Lewis, g	0	0	3	0
Maughan, g	0	0	0	0
Johnson, g	0	0	0	0
Brown, f	0	0	0	0
Aubuchon, g	0	0	1	0
Schoon, c	0	1	1	1
Totals	**18**	**26**	**24**	**62**

Halftime score: Detroit 35, Washington 17.

Missed free throws: Detroit (9)—Brown, Miasek 4, G. Pearcy 2, Janisch 2. Washington (6)—Feerick, Mahnken, McKinney 2, Scolari, Torgoff.

It should be noted that in the Falcons' practices prior to the game, Curtis had emphasized free-throw shooting; also, because Janisch, Dille, and Miasek had fouled out early in the fourth quarter, the Falcons were forced to play their scrubs. Subsequently, Detroit was outscored by 21–8 in the final period and barely finished with its lead intact.

Despite the resounding upset of the Caps, home attendance showed no increase, and King responded with various promotions. For one game, any party of twelve that included an individual named Miasek would be admitted free. When no Miasek appeared, King repeated the process for fans whose last name was Dille. This time, three groups of a dozen fans each gained free admittance.

Another of King's brainstorms was to have a tryout for the team's costumed mascot. "People thought it was a setup," said King, "when Eddie Escoe, the general manager's son, won, but the decision came about honestly, because he was clearly the best of the lot."

Two-for-one admissions, autograph nights wherein players were available to sign whatever was thrust in front of them, camera nights that enabled fans to have their photos snapped with the players, halftime shooting contests for fans, pregame contests for local high schools and YMCA teams—all of these failed to sufficiently arouse the public's interest. "The only promotion that worked," said King, "was the morning skills clinics for high school and junior high school kids. All of the players participated, and they were able to teach basic fundamentals that most high school coaches couldn't teach."

Because of the disappointing attendance, King made sure that costs were minimized. "We kept the salaries of ushers and ticket takers as low as possible," King said. "The Red Wings, for example, had eight ticket-selling stations that required sixteen workers at each game. We only had two stations and employed four ticket sellers. We were always bottom-line conscious, and we definitely had the correct financial approach."

When the Falcons' schedule permitted, King would also represent the team at league meetings in New York. "I had no vote," he said, "and was only there so that the franchise could be represented by someone who knew something about basketball. Basically, the meetings boiled down to differences between the haves and the have-nots."

On every issue, the have-nots sought to survive, while the haves sought to improve their position. Even President Podoloff was alarmed at the lack of cooperation among the owners.

Meanwhile, the Falcons' miseries continued unabated. Finally, with their record standing at a dismal 12–22, Curtis was forced to resign and was replaced by Phil "Cincy" Sachs.

The Falcons' new coach had been born in Cincinnati and had moved to Detroit in 1933, making his reputation by leading several semipro and YMCA teams to championships in various leagues. "He did a great job from the outset," said King. "Sachs was an Xs-and-Os guy, but it was difficult for him to try to install a system so late in the season, especially since we were basically a group of individuals, rather than a team."

Miasek wasn't affected by the change. "Under Curtis," he said, "we'd mostly throw the ball from guard to guard and then follow the ball. The receiver could step back and shoot, or pass to another guy coming up from the baseline. We didn't do too much picking away from the ball. Sometimes I'd get the ball in the pivot, and guys would crisscross looking for a handoff. Sachs tried to get us moving in a more coordinated way, but we were too far gone. In fact, my game didn't change much at all. I was strictly a transition player, and I could outrun the majority of the centers I faced. I used to get a lot of lead passes on the run. I'd rebound, outlet, and then take off. My speed and my stamina were my biggest advantages."

Miasek was easily the most inexperienced of the Falcons, and despite his earnest work ethic, he was also stubborn. "I could run all night long, and that's all that I wanted to do," said Miasek. "Besides, if a team set up and started to grind out a patterned offense, they were at a great disadvantage. That's because once defenders got position, the refs would let them do whatever they wanted to do to keep their position. The bigger centers would just bang the hell out of me whenever I tried to settle into the pivot. Hell, you had to blow somebody out of the arenas to get called for a charge. So, I had good reason not to want to slow down."

The Falcons greeted Sachs with three consecutive losses, and the team's fortunes didn't improve much thereafter. A brief win streak against three of the league's weaker franchises—Pittsburgh, Cleveland, and Providence—gave the Falcons a glimmer of hope, but then came three consecutive losses, followed by two more wins and then a painful nine-game losing streak.

The Falcons went 8–18 under Sachs and finished at 20–40. Only Pittsburgh had a worse record.

"I had a great time," said King. "I loved playing pro ball and felt it was a privilege. I would have done it for nothing. Aside from our record and our attendance, my main regret is that I wasn't a better player."

Miasek likewise enjoyed the season. "Everything about the season was terrifically exciting," he said. "I just loved playing, especially at such a high level. Once the season started, money retreated into the background. Our record, however, was a huge disappointment. We all thought we'd do much better than we did. I guess for whatever reasons, we just didn't have the right combination of talent and coaching."

Detroit Falcons

	G	FGM	FGA	Pct.	FTM	FTA	Pct.	Asst.	PF	Pts.	Avg.
Stan Miasek	60	331	1,154	.287	233	385	.605	93	208	895	14.9
John Janisch	60	283	983	.288	131	198	.662	49	132	697	11.6
Ariel Maughan	59	224	929	.241	84	114	.737	57	180	532	9.0
Robert Dille	57	111	563	.197	74	111	.667	40	92	296	5.2
Tom King	58	97	410	.237	101	160	.631	32	102	295	5.1
Grady Lewis	60	106	520	.204	75	138	.543	54	166	287	4.8
Harold Brown	54	95	383	.248	74	117	.632	39	122	264	4.9
Milt Schoon	41	43	199	.216	34	80	.425	12	75	120	2.9
Art Stolkey	23	36	164	.220	30	44	.682	38	72	102	4.4
George Pearcy	37	31	130	.238	32	44	.727	13	68	94	2.5
Henry Pearcy	29	24	108	.222	25	34	.735	7	20	73	2.5
Chet Aubuchon	30	23	91	.253	19	35	.543	20	46	65	2.2
Moe Becker	20	19	107	.178	3	10	.300	15	33	41	2.1
Howie McCarty	19	10	82	.122	1	10	.100	2	22	21	1.1
Harold Johnson	27	4	20	.200	7	14	.500	11	13	15	0.6

Postscript

Arthur Wirtz folded the franchise in the summer.

Stan Miasek was chosen by the Chicago Stags in the dispersal draft. "During the summer of 1947," he said, "I kept hitting the ball and moving up in the Giants' farm system. My plan was to play both baseball and basketball, but the Stags' management told me I had to choose between the two. I was only making two hundred and fifty dollars playing baseball, and my wife just had a baby, so I chickened out and stayed with basketball."

Miasek played an additional five years with Chicago, Baltimore, and Milwaukee, without losing a step and without losing his effectiveness.

Tom King had a career choice to make after the season. "The Stags heavily recruited me," said King. "I'd played well against them and also against Ohio State when Ole Olsen coached there. In retrospect, I realized that all the distractions in Detroit had affected my game, so I was eager for another go at playing. Then Nick Landes called and offered me a front-office job in the Chicago Stadium. I'd be involved in everything that took place there, from the ice show to the Stags, from the Blackhawks to college games. Olsen responded by guaranteeing me a spot on the team. OK, I thought, but what about the year after that? For the sake of my and my family's future, I opted to devote myself to an administrative career. And it was a decision I never regretted."

The Bottom Line

Average paid attendance	1,239 (the lowest in the league)
Net receipts	$48,238
Estimated loss	$120,000

The Ethnic Knicks

There was little doubt that New York was the sports capital of the country, if not the world. The city boasted three major-league baseball teams—the Yankees, Giants, and Dodgers—together with a major-league (the Rangers) and a minor-league (the Rovers) hockey team, two pro football teams (the Giants and the Americans), and three of the country's most successful college basketball programs (LIU, St. John's, and NYU). In addition, Madison Square Garden hosted the Millrose Games and the prestigious NIT as well as championship boxing matches. Rounding out the action were several racing tracks for both trotters and Thoroughbreds.

Indeed, given the stock exchange, the publishing houses, the ten daily newspapers, the United Nations headquarters (which was under construction), and the tens of thousands of veterans returning with their pockets stuffed with money, New York was the foremost city in the entire world.

Surely the metropolitan sports fans would eagerly support a professional basketball team. Ned Irish would do everything within his considerable powers to make this a certainty.

Irish had become acting president of the Garden in the spring of 1946 when General John Reed Kilpatrick was recalled to active duty. Unbeknownst to the public, Irish subsidized the BAA's office expenses and salary expenditures from his own pocket. Yet, despite his private largesse, he was an aloof man, one more used to giving than obeying orders. It followed that he insisted on micromanaging his new ball club.

As soon as the BAA's charter had been completed and approved by all eleven franchises, Irish convened his staff to determine his team's nickname. "We all met in Ned's office," said Fred Podesta, Irish's right-hand man. "That would be Ned, me, Lester Scott, who would be the team's public relations director, and a few other staff members. At Ned's suggestion, we each wrote down the name we thought would be the best fit; then we dropped the paper chits into a hat. Most of them said 'Knickerbockers,' after Father Knickerbocker, a fictional character with a long history in New York."

The name harked back to the seventeenth century and referred to the pants worn by the city's Dutch settlers. Rolled up just below the knee, they were commonly called knickerbockers or knickers. The Knickerbocker name was first used in the world of sports in 1845, when Alexander Cartwright's Manhattan-based baseball team—the first organized team in baseball history—was named the New York Knickerbockers, also called the Knickerbocker Nine.

Over the years, Father Knickerbocker, with his cotton wig, three-cornered hat, buckled shoes, and knickers-style pants, became the unofficial symbol of New York. Irish ordered that the team's logo show Father Knickerbocker dribbling a basketball. He further decreed that the city's colors—orange, blue, and white—be installed as the team's colors.

Choosing a coach wasn't quite as easy. Irish desperately wanted to hire Joe Lapchick, a former Original Celtic and without question the most respected basketball strategist in the metropolitan area. But Lapchick was still contractually obliged to continue coaching at St. John's for another year.

Since his first choice was not yet available, Irish turned to Neil Cohalan, one of Manhattan College's all-time-best athletes and coaches, with the understanding that Cohalan would only be keeping the seat warm for Lapchick.

As an undergraduate, Cohalan had earned varsity letters in basketball, baseball, football, and track-and-field. He became the Jaspers' basketball coach in 1929 and produced several outstanding teams (the best being 18–3 in 1942–43, while his total record was 165–80). The war siphoned off many of the school's varsity athletes, and when the basketball program was shut down, Cohalan enlisted in the navy in March 1944. After one year of sea duty, he was transferred to the Armed Guard Center, in Brooklyn, as an athletic officer. While there, he coached the Armed Guard five to a record of 29–2, including the Third Naval District title.

Cohalan was smooth and polished and was still hailed in the press as Manhattan College's "number one glamour boy." In some ways, he had a little too much glamour, which manifested in an excessive fondness for alcohol.

Even so, Lapchick not only heartily endorsed Cohalan but also worked closely with the Knicks' coach, even to the point of taking an active part in the team's training camp in the Catskills. Once the season was under way, Lapchick traveled with the Knicks whenever his schedule permitted and also scouted rival ball clubs.

As noted earlier, the accepted wisdom among the franchise directors was that radio coverage of the ball games whetted the public's appetite and eventually increased attendance. The lure of radio was so great that most of the teams gladly paid for the privilege of being broadcast and then tried to recoup their cash outlay by selling game-time advertising.

So, when Irish and Podesta lunched at Toots Shor's with Bert Lee, the program director of WHN radio, and Marty Glickman, the prospective play-by-play announcer, Irish's first question was, "How much will these broadcasts cost me?"

To Irish's utter delight, Lee's response was, "Not only will they not cost you anything, but we'll pay you two hundred and fifty dollars per game."

"It's a deal," Irish said, before Lee could change his mind.

While the radio broadcasts most likely did enhance the Knicks' attendance, they also produced considerable distress among the members of the fourth estate. The sheer immediacy of radio forced the local sportswriters to investigate the "whys" of a particular ball game rather than merely reporting the whos, whats, whens, and wheres.

The site of the team's preseason camp was the Nevele Country Club, a luxurious Catskills resort in upstate Ellenville. The meals were so fantastic that the players didn't mind having to play on a concrete-surfaced outdoor court that turned routine floor burns into bleeding wounds. "We had two-a-days, did a lot of roadwork, and we were in great condition," said Sidney "Sonny" Hertzberg, a slick two-handed set shooter from CCNY. "We were there by ourselves for the first two weeks, and then they let our wives join us. But Cohalan wasn't satisfied with the way we were progressing."

Nor were the scribes who witnessed the early practice sessions. To a man, they believed that New York's elite college squads could have their way with the Knickerbockers. It wasn't until the pros drubbed the collegians in a series of unofficial scrimmages that the Knicks gained some respect from the sportswriters.

While Irish was reputed to have unbridled respect for Lapchick, he believed that he himself knew much more about basketball than did his temporary coach, Neil Cohalan. Accordingly, Irish didn't hesitate to overrule Cohalan when it came to the final composition of the roster. By Irish's lights, "good" players were those who would bring more fans through the turnstiles. He had no other criteria. To Irish, this meant local players.

Of these, Hertzberg—5'10", 175—was the best. Hertzberg had graduated from CCNY in 1942 and, concurrent with his military service, had then played four seasons in the ABL with the New York Jewels (later the Gothams).

"Red Auerbach was the first to contact me," said Hertzberg, "and he offered five thousand plus a twenty-five-hundred-dollar signing bonus to join his team in Washington, but I was involved in an optical business in New York, and my wife was pregnant, so I really didn't want to leave the city. I negotiated a forty-five-hundred-dollar salary with Irish, because we both anticipated that I'd be able to supplement this with my earnings in the business. It didn't turn out that way, because the Knicks' schedule was so heavy, so Irish gave me a fifteen-hundred-dollar bonus at the end of the season. I still could have made more in Washington, but under the circumstances, I was much better off staying put in New York."

What kind of player was Hertzberg? "I was a good shooter and a good playmaker," he said. "I think the best thing about my game was that I was so steady."

He was joined by other locals of note:

Leo "Ace" Gottlieb, 5'11", 180, was another CCNY alumnus.
Tommy Byrnes, 6'3", 175, out of Seton Hall, was a racehorse type of player.
Ossie Schectman, 6'0", 185, LIU, was an all-American and a member of LIU's NIT championship teams in 1939 and 1941.
Ralph Kaplowitz, 6'2", 170, another New York native, had starred at NYU before enlisting in the Army Air Corps. As a fighter pilot, Kaplowitz earned three air medals and also flew the fighter escort for the *Enola Gay* on its journey to drop the atomic bomb on Hiroshima.
Nat Militzok, 6'3", 195, was born in New York and transferred from Hofstra to Cornell. In line with nearly every other player in the BAA, he gained valuable on-court experience while playing in the military.

"I remember when I went to the Garden to negotiate a contract," Militzok said, "Ned Irish offered me four thousand. He was sitting there with Neil Cohalan, and Cohalan said, 'Let's give him five thousand, because he'll be the best defensive ballplayer in the league.' So, through Cohalan, who'd been my coach in the navy, I was able to get an extra thousand. I was very, very pleased. I'd just gotten out of the service, and I'd never seen that kind of money. I thought it was the epitome of all salaries and that I'd never earn more than that for the rest of my life."

The more marginal local players included Hank Rosenstein, 6'4", 185, who attended CCNY but didn't play there; and Bob Mullens, 6'1", 175, from Fordham

The Knickerbockers also fielded several major imports:

Stan Stutz, 5'10", 172, was a record-setting scorer at Rhode Island State under Frank Keaney (he'd once tallied 36 points in sixteen minutes) and was therefore a runner and a gunner. After graduating from RIS, he had his name legally changed to Stutz from Modselewski.

Bob Cluggish, 6'10", 240, was twice an all-conference center at Kentucky and had played three seasons in the ABL.

Jake Weber, 6'6", 225, from Purdue, was a veteran of five games with Indianapolis in the NBL.

Notice not only the many New Yorkers on the roster but also the number of Jewish players. This was also part of Ned Irish's design.

Virtually all of the Jews who'd made their mark in sports (which provided a quick and enjoyable way to become Americanized) were the offspring of immigrant parents. The most celebrated Jewish athlete of the day was Hank Greenberg, a home-run slugger for the Detroit Tigers and then the Pittsburgh Pirates. College football featured the likes of Benny Friedman at Michigan, Marshall Goldberg at Pitt, and Sid Luckman at Columbia. Noteworthy Jews in boxing included Benny Leonard, Max Baer, Barney Ross, and Sammy Mandell.

Unlike many of their compatriots in other athletic fields of endeavor, most of the Jewish basketball players grew up in New York's Lower East Side ghetto, where baseball and football fields, along with expensive equipment, were unavailable. For sport, trash cans served as basketball goals, and in lieu of balls, they had stockings stuffed with rags. "We could only advance the so-called ball," said Nat Militzok, "with passes or with air dribbles." No wonder sleight of hand was the name of the game. The only available basketball courts were at the neighborhood settlement houses and were typically long, narrow, low-ceilinged courts that likewise put a premium on passing, dribbling, and cutting.

As a consequence, outlanders came to believe that all Jewish cagers were intellectual and cunning. They were said to avoid physical contact in favor of playing with finesse and guile. Years later, Hall of Fame coach Hubie Brown would describe the style of play that evolved in the settlement houses as "Jew ball."

Despite, or perhaps because of, Irish's talent evaluations, the ball club was old and slow, the big men were unathletic to the point of being clumsy, and Cohalan was in over his head. "Neil knew the college guys his Manhattan teams had played against," said Hertzberg, "but he wasn't at all familiar with either pro players or the pro game. He was used to teaching fundamentals to boys, and in college, the procedure was to go with your five best players until somebody got hurt or fouled out. The pro game was more about balance and matchups and required much more in-game management: now you might need defense or rebounding; now you'd need scoring."

The schedule was similarly difficult for Cohalan to accommodate. "In college," said Hertzberg, "you might have one big game every week. In the BAA, we had three or four every week. Neil had trouble preparing us on a game-to-game basis, and being always on the go, moving from city to city, also wore him down in a hurry. Add it all up, and Neil was not a very good coach for us."

Cohalan's rather stagnant offense called for weaves and give-and-goes that eventuated in either layups or set shots, mostly the latter. On defense, the Knicks were encouraged to grab and hold as much as possible, under the theory that the refs couldn't, and wouldn't, whistle every such infraction.

Still, the players were a tight group. After home games, they'd go over to somebody's house for beer and pizza or chicken while they rehashed the game. "We were so cohesive that it didn't make much difference who roomed with who on the road," said Hertzberg. "We never had any fights or even arguments, which was a very rare situation in those days."

After their history-making victory in Toronto on November 1 to launch league play, the Knickerbockers entrained to Chicago, where they were gored by the Stags, 63–47, the very next evening. A rousing win in St. Louis had the Knicks at 2–1 in advance of their home opener against Chicago on Monday, November 11 (Armistice Day).

The Knickerbockers' first appearance at Madison Square Garden was not the biggest sporting news of the long weekend. That distinction went to the Army–Notre Dame football game played on Saturday afternoon at Yankee Stadium, which ended in a scoreless tie.

On Sunday, the football Giants defeated the Philadelphia Eagles, 45–17, at the Polo Grounds. There was horse racing at Jamaica, in Queens, and Roosevelt Raceway, in Yonkers, that was distinguished by the recent installation of automatic starting gates. Even baseball was in the news when the Brooklyn Dodgers' manager, Leo Durocher, announced that he had turned down a lucrative offer to manage the New York Yankees.

Elsewhere in the city, November 11 marked the changeover from trolleys to diesel-powered buses along Tenth Avenue (from Fifty-ninth Street to 125th Street and West Twelfth Avenue). The fare remained at five cents.

Lambert Brothers offered fourteen-karat-gold wedding rings for $50. Roger Kent offered stylish raincoats for $20. Gimbel's had a sale on silk ties, all of them going for $2 each. The big movie at the Strand Theatre on Broadway was *Nobody Lives Forever*, with John Garfield and Faye Emerson. Radio City Music Hall presented *The Jolson Story*, starring Larry Parks and Evelyn Keyes. Helen Hayes had just opened in *Happy Birthday* at the Broadhurst Theatre. Laurence Olivier was acting in *Henry V* at the Golden Theatre.

Nationally, President Truman led an Armistice Day salute for the dead of two world wars. Also, it was announced that General Dwight David Eisenhower, chief of staff, was to resign from active service (due to a budgetary shortage) and become ambassador to Great Britain.

Despite all of the other distractions, the public's interest was piqued by the Knicks' home opener, and the Garden (the "old" version, on Eighth Avenue) was crowded with 17,205 curious fans. Irish had arranged a gala affair befitting an opening night.

At halftime, the fans were entertained by a parade of models wearing the latest in fur fashions. Then came a brief basketball game matching the New York Football Giants and several of the Original Celtics (including Nat Holman, Johnny Beckman, Joe Lapchick, Chris Leonard, and Pete Barry). The game was officiated by Pat Kennedy and comedian Al Schact, whose clowning imitations of Kennedy's overwrought calls brought down the house. The game ended in a 1–1 tie, with the points being scored by Lapchick and the Giants' Howie Livingston, a two-way halfback and defensive back.

(The upbeat festivities, however, did not extend to the Knicks and the Stags, who had to use locker rooms designated for hockey teams. As such, the spaces were cramped with uniforms and equipment hung up for drying, and hanging over all was the odor of stale perspiration.)

Later, Lapchick was asked by the press to comment on what he'd seen during the first half of the Knicks-Stags contest. "The game is much cleaner than ours used to be," said Lapchick, who was understandably loath to knock any aspect of his next career, "and the officiating is much tighter. Both the Knicks and the Stags are much better than the best college teams, and the caliber of play in this new league will only get better as the season progresses."

As for the main feature of the evening, the Knicks controlled most of the game and actually led by 14 points midway through the third quarter, before Chicago made its move. It took a long one-handed shot at the buzzer by Ossie Schectman to send the game into overtime, but Schectman's desperation basket only delayed the inevitable as the Stags emerged victorious by 78–68.

The metropolitan newspapers were not unduly impressed by the game, the various sideshows, nor the near-capacity crowd. The next day's coverage of the Knicks' debut took second place to stories about the mad demand for tickets to upcoming college games. The *New York Times* buried the results of the game under stories about the Columbia University football team and the major-league baseball draft of minor-league players.

Irish was dismayed but not totally surprised. In fact, because many of the Garden's prime dates had previously been booked for surefire draws such as the ice show, the circus, and the rodeo, and because he was still doubtful about the viability of the new league, the Knicks were scheduled for a total of only six appearances at MSG.

Five days later, the Knicks beat the Ironmen, 64–62, at the Sixty-ninth Regiment Armory, which seated only 5,200 spectators. (The top ticket went for $3.50, as compared with $5 in the Garden.) This antiquated military installation had been brought up to date with refurbished seats, locker rooms, backboards, time clocks, and overhead lighting, as well as a new playing surface. Even so, the building had a well-used look that was decidedly bush league.

After downing Pittsburgh, the Knicks went on a nine-game winning streak (that extended to a twelve-out-of-thirteen burst), creating sufficient momentum to essentially carry them through most of the season.

The second-class status of the BAA, though, was reinforced on December 18, when the Knicks hosted the Cleveland Rebels at the Armory and Sonny Hertzberg was kicked in the nose during a third-quarter melee in pursuit of a loose ball. As there were no physicians on hand, Hertzberg (and his pregnant wife) had to take a cab over to the Garden, where a doctor was covering a fight card. Speed was deemed to be essential, so Hertzberg climbed into his civilian clothes without taking a shower.

The doctor snapped the nose back into place and said, "It's nothing." As a precaution, though, he sent Hertzberg over to St. Claire's Hospital for x-rays. When no concussion was revealed, Hertzberg—with two black eyes, a grossly swollen nose, and his skin and clothing all grimy, holding his Knicks travel bag on his lap, with his wife beside him—endured a long subway ride out to his apartment in Manhattan Beach (near Coney Island, in Brooklyn).

The same game, however, also marked the first appearance of a player who represented legitimate class. This was Bud Palmer, late of Princeton University and also a powerful team out of Chapel Hill, North Carolina, that had represented the Navy Air Corps.

After finishing his flight training in Chapel Hill, Palmer flew B-26s in the Caribbean until his discharge in December of 1945. He then went into business in Spartanburg, South Carolina, but soon sold the enterprise and returned to his home in Princeton. One day shortly after the Knicks had opened their season, Palmer showed up at a workout and asked for a job. Cohalan told him to get out on the floor and toss a ball around. Though Palmer might have been out of shape, he showed sufficient promise to warrant further trial. For the next three weeks, he scrimmaged with various local colleges until he was in tip-top playing condition.

"Bud was an authentic Ivy Leaguer," said Hertzberg, "and Ned Irish was in a tizzy over him. But Bud was also a good player. He had a two-handed jump shot, was an excellent rebounder, always competed, and dove for loose balls whether we were winning by twenty or losing by twenty."

Cohalan, however, wasn't initially impressed. Soon after Palmer was inserted into the game, he took a jump shot and missed. When he missed two more, Cohalan summoned him to the bench.

"What kind of a shot is that?" Cohalan wanted to know.

Palmer shrugged. "It's a shot I use most of the time."

"Well, don't use it anymore on my ball club. Sit down."

For the rest of the game (which the Knicks lost to Cleveland, 56–53), Palmer attempted only layups and hook shots. "After a couple of practice sessions," Palmer said, "I was able to convince Cohalan that it was a pretty good shot after all."

It didn't take Palmer long to adjust to the on- and off-court idiosyncrasies of the pro game. "There was a good neighborhood bar we went to after games," he said. "Sometimes there were more people in the bar than there had been at the game."

Despite the Knicks' gaudy, 14–3 record, the New York press remained a tough customer. "We would scrimmage all the local colleges at their gyms just to prove that we could beat them," Palmer said. "The press would be invited and were eventually won over. No matter how well we did during our league games, it was those scrimmages that established our credibility."

The Knicks' win streak was succeeded by a five-game losing binge, most of which occurred during an extended road trip. Looking back after so many years, the players had contradictory stories to tell about their traveling routines.

"Just about everything was done in a first-class manner," said Nat Militzok. "When we traveled by train, we would have our own railroad car. Each player would have both an upper and a lower bunk, and you would throw your luggage in the upper bunk and sleep in the lower. I think we were the only team that was able to travel that way."

Bud Palmer told a vastly different tale: "We'd have berths in the sleeping cars, just like all the other passengers, and we'd have constant arguments about who got the upper bunks and who got the more desirable lower bunks. Should this be based on size or seniority?"

Others remembered bringing multiple cases of beer along for lengthy train rides. The players would adjourn to the bathroom area at the end of the sleeper cars, which was furnished with washstands, toilets, and benches. What with playing cards and drinking beer, everybody would be drunk by two or three in the morning.

One overnight trip from Toronto (December 20) to Providence (December 21) was particularly memorable. "Right after losing to the Huskies," said Hertzberg, "three taxis picked us up at the Maple Leaf Gardens and drove us to a railroad station just outside of Toronto where we were supposed to catch a train to Providence for a game the next night. The last car in the procession had the starting five, because we were the last to shower and dress after the Toronto game. Well, that was the car that broke down and got stuck in a mountainous area. I happened to be in that last car, and we had to get out and push it up the mountains; then we'd coast down, get out, and push it up the next mountain. Anyway, the first two cars were waiting for us at the station, because the train had already left by the time they got there. So, we hired three more taxis to drive us to Buffalo, which was an eight-hour trip."

The ordeal wasn't over yet. Militzok picked up the story: "The train to Providence was also long gone, so we found a restaurant near the station that was open all night. By that time, it was really late, about four A.M. When the owner saw a bunch of big guys walking into his place, with each us of carrying a small bag, he thought we were about to hold him up, so he called the mounted police. A few minutes later, here come the Mounties, charging into the restaurant with their guns drawn. We finally explained our situation, and they even helped us hire four more taxis that would take us to Providence. Don't you know that two of the taxis got lost en route? The first two cars got to the Providence Arena while the Steamrollers were concluding their pregame warm-ups. The fans were there, and we had half our team, so we went ahead and started the game. After leading most of the way, and with the game seemingly won, the older players finally arrived, put on their uniforms, and got into the game. We wound up losing by 63–61."

The Knicks concluded this memorable road trip in St. Louis. "For some reason," Palmer recalled, "there were lots of Princeton grads in St. Louis. On this night, about seventy of my buddies came out to see me play, but I sprained my ankle within three minutes of the opening tip-off. This was the only time I ever sprained an ankle playing basketball. My buddies started booing and yelling, 'Throw the bum out!' Then they got up and left. Since they constituted half the crowd, the rest of the game was played in relative privacy."

On January 15, New York lost a 65–63 squeaker in Washington, and Cohalan was wowed. He had recently castigated his own squad for taking too many long shots and also singled out Cluggish for being out of shape, but his negativity was overwhelmed by the Capitols. Ignoring his own team's outstanding effort, Cohalan could only say that the Caps were "the greatest team I've ever seen—anywhere at any time."

By now, the many Jewish players on the ball club had become an issue. In Pittsburgh, the fans greeted the Knicks' appearance on the court by singing their own version of a popular song: "East Side, West Side, here come the Jews from New York."

In other cities, when the Knicks had the ball, the fans took to shouting, "Abe! Pass the ball to Abe!"

These reactions prompted Cohalan to complain to Irish about the predominance of Jews on the team. Cohalan thought they were cliquish and invited too much fan abuse on the road. Before long, Militzok was traded to Toronto (for Bob Fitzgerald); Kaplowitz was dealt to Philadelphia (for Moe Murphy); and Rosenstein and Weber were sold to Providence.

The season crawled along, with the Knicks exhibiting a frustrating inconsistency. They'd win one; then lose three; win two; then lose four or five. After the Knicks were embarrassed at the Armory by the Bombers (71–46), New York's once awesome record had plummeted to 19–19. But help was on the way.

On Sunday, February 2, Lee Knorek—6'7", 215—was a matriculated student at the University of Detroit and a member of the school's basketball team. It chanced that the Knicks were in town for a game against the Falcons, and Knorek contacted Cohalan to voice his intention to quit school and join the Knickerbockers. When Knorek did report to the Knicks several days later, Lloyd Brazil, the school's athletic director, sent a vigorous protest to

Podoloff. Employing Knorek before his graduation, Brazil said, was "irregular and unethical."

In response, Podoloff traced Knorek's lengthy college career: He had played for DeSales College from 1939 through 1942, after which he transferred to the University of Detroit and played there for the 1942–43 season. During the 1943–44 season, Knorek played as a Navy V-12 student at Dennison College. Podoloff also noted that, having already completed five years of college competition, Knorek had previously signed a professional contract to play for the Knicks on August 13, 1946. Podoloff reminded Brazil that he had advised him of Knorek's signing at the time. Despite Knorek's having declared himself a professional, the University of Detroit had permitted him to continue playing with its varsity team.

In supporting the Knicks' right to employ Knorek, Podoloff concluded:

> After a player has had four years of amateur competition as a regular member of a college student body and has, in addition, one year's competition as a member of a student body seeking special training, it can hardly be said that eligibility remains, so far as college athletics are concerned under any definition of the term. . . . Even by the wildest stretch of the imagination, and the most forced construction of terms, Knorek cannot be considered an amateur.

While Knorek turned out to be a useful player for the Knicks, his off-court antics were even more noteworthy. Knorek had been born in Poland, as had the parents of Stan Stutz, and both men could therefore speak Polish. "We were on a road trip," said Palmer, "and Lee bought two derby hats, one for him and one for Stutz. Anyway, we get to Cleveland, and Lee and Stan decide to switch derbies just as we arrive at the hotel. Lee's derby comes down over Stan's eyes, while Stan's derby makes Lee look like a pinhead. One thing leads to another, and the six-seven Lee and the five-eleven Stan now exchange coats. You can imagine how ridiculous they each looked. So, the team is checking in to the hotel, when up step Lee and Stan. Stan starts yelling at the poor gal behind the desk in Polish, and, of course, she has no idea what he was saying. That's when Lee offers himself as a translator. In a mixture of Polish and broken English, he tells her that Stan is a commissar from the Soviet Union, a very important man, and he was demanding a suite and a limo—immediately. Through it all, Lee and Stan are talking to each other in Polish, which the clerk couldn't distinguish from Russian. So, they both wound up with a suite and a limo. While we rode the bus to the arena and later on to the airport, Stan and Lee rode in the limo."

Since Palmer and Knorek were roommates on the road, the Ivy Leaguer also observed more personal aspects of Knorek's character: "Lee loved Snickers candy bars, to the point where he could eat a dozen at a time, and without getting sick! Lee also liked to fly, and he was the only player who couldn't wait to bend into the DC-3s that were the only planes we ever took. He prevailed on the stewardesses to let him make all of the announcements over the PA system. He'd also help them serve beverages and meals and then help them clean up. Meanwhile, most of the other guys were trying to keep from throwing up as the planes bounced all over the sky."

Another new addition to the roster at around this time was Frido Frey, 6'2", 195, from LIU, who was purchased from the Brooklyn Gothams, of the ABL. Unfortunately, Frey had been strictly a pivotman in college and couldn't make the transition to a wing position.

Then, about two weeks later, Bill "Butch" van Breda Kolff also became a Knick. VBK and Palmer had played together at Princeton for one season before Butch flunked out and joined the marines. After forty-two months in the service, van Breda Kolff returned to Princeton, flunked out again, and finally graduated from NYU in 1946. At 6'5", 185, VBK was an accomplished rebounder and defender. "I had slob skills," is how he defined himself.

By the time he joined the team, the Knicks were in disarray—mired in mediocrity and arguing among themselves. "The first day that Butch got there," said Palmer, "we had a players' meeting where everybody was accusing everybody else of something. 'You're a son of a bitch, a ball hog.' 'You never pass.' 'You never get back on defense.' 'Goddamn it, I get all the rebounds and never get the ball back.' So it went for nearly an hour. I was the only guy on the team that Butch knew, so he started crying to me, 'Christ, what the hell am I doing here? Why the hell did I ever join this stupid team?' But he turned out to be a really good player for us."

Both Knorek and VBK were good enough to help the Knicks regain their winning ways. After embarking on a five-game winning streak, the team had compiled a record of 30–24, when disaster struck. In the closing minutes of a March 19 game in Chicago (won by New York, 65–57), the visitors were freezing the ball, when one of the Stags made a desperate lurch and fell on top of Ossie Schectman.

"We knew it was bad right away," said Palmer, "because of the screams of pain that came from Ossie, who was always a quiet, stoic kind of guy. It turned out to be a ruptured spleen, and they had to operate immediately. And that was the end of Ossie's basketball career."

Without their leading assist man and playmaker, the Knicks soldiered on. Their most memorable victory of the season came two games later, on March 22 in Washington, when they simultaneously terminated a pair of the Caps' incredible streaks: fifteen consecutive wins, and twenty-seven consecutive wins at home.

New York	FG	FT	PF	Pts.
Palmer, f	8	1	4	17
Frey, f	2	2	3	6
Fitzgerald, f	1	0	2	2
Knorek, c	0	4	2	4
Cluggish, c	1	2	0	4
Stutz, g	3	2	4	8
Hertzberg, g	9	5	5	23
Gottlieb, g	2	0	0	4
Byrnes, g	0	0	0	0
Totals	26	16	20	68

Washington	FG	FT	PF	Pts.
Norlander, f	2	4	4	8
McKinney, f	3	1	1	7
Torgoff, f	2	0	1	4
Passaglia, f	0	0	1	0
Mahnken, c	3	4	5	10
Gantt, c	0	0	0	0
Feerick, g	6	1	5	13
Scolari, g	9	3	4	21
O'Grady, g	0	0	0	0
Totals	25	13	21	63

SCORE BY QUARTERS	1	2	3	4	Total
Washington	20	4	20	19	63
New York	12	12	22	22	68

Missed free throws: New York (5)—Frey, Knorek 2, Cluggish, Stutz. Washington (4)—Feerick, Torgoff, Mahnken, Passaglia. Officials: Schoenfeld and Nucatola.

When the horn sounded ending the game, the Knicks tossed their warm-up jackets into the air, embraced each other, and then nearly crushed Cohalan in their efforts to congratulate him. A goodly portion of the fans at the Uline Arena likewise poured onto the court to offer their felicitations.

The unexpected conquest of the Caps put the Knicks only a half game behind the second-place Warriors. But a 3–3 finish, coupled with Philadelphia's concluding rush of five straight wins, left the Knicks with a 33–27 record and the prospect of facing Cleveland in the third-place playoffs.

New York Knicks

	G	FGM	FGA	Pct.	FTM	FTA	Pct.	Asst.	PF	Pts.	Avg.
Sonny Hertzberg	59	201	695	.289	113	149	.758	37	109	515	8.7
Stan Stutz	60	172	641	.268	133	170	.782	49	127	477	8.0
Tommy Byrnes	60	175	583	.300	103	160	.644	35	90	453	7.6
Ossie Schectman	54	162	588	.276	111	179	.620	109	115	435	8.1
Bud Palmer	42	160	521	.307	81	121	.669	34	110	401	9.5
Leo Gottlieb	57	149	495	.302	36	55	.665	24	71	334	5.9
Bob Cluggish	54	93	356	.261	52	92	.571	22	113	238	4.4
Ralph Kaplowitz	24	71	274	.259	52	71	.732	25	57	194	7.2
Lee Knorek	22	62	219	.283	47	72	.653	21	64	171	7.8
Nat Militzok	36	52	214	.238	40	73	.548	28	91	144	4.0
Hank Rosenstein	31	38	145	.262	57	95	.600	19	71	133	4.3
Frido Frey	23	28	97	.289	32	56	.571	14	37	88	3.8
Bob Fitzgerald	29	23	121	.190	36	60	.600	9	67	82	2.8
Bob Mullens	26	27	104	.260	22	34	.647	18	23	78	2.9
Dick Murphy	24	14	58	.241	4	5	.800	5	9	32	1.3
Butch van Breda Kolff	16	7	34	.206	11	17	.647	6	10	25	1.6
Moe Murphy	9	8	25	.320	8	12	.667	0	3	24	2.7
Jake Weber	11	7	24	.292	6	8	.750	1	20	20	1.8
Frank Mangiapane	6	2	13	.154	1	3	.333	0	6	5	0.8

Postscript

Butch van Breda Kolff continued with the Knicks for three more years before joining the coaching fraternity. Over the next sixty years, VBK coached on the college level at Lafayette, Princeton, Hofstra, and the University of New

Orleans; he also coached the Los Angeles Lakers, Detroit Pistons, New Orleans Jazz, and, in the American Basketball Association, the Memphis Tams. In addition, van Breda Kolff coached the New Orleans Pride, in the former Women's Professional Basketball League, and at Picayune Memorial High School, in rural Mississippi. He died on August 24, 2007.

It was VBK, a self-confessed basketball junkie (not the self-promoting Pete Carril), who invented and refined the "Princeton offense."

Sonny Hertzberg played one more season in New York, followed by two with the Celtics and two more with the Baltimore Bullets. Upon his retirement, Hertzberg resumed his career as an optician. In his spare time, he did some scouting for the Knicks, and he even coached the team for four games in 1954–55 when Joe Lapchick was ill.

Ossie Schectman went into the garment business and then retired to Florida. Several of the surviving old-timers (including Nat Militzok, Hank Rosenstein, and Sonny Herztberg) took to meeting for breakfast once every month.

Ned Irish became one of the Brahmins of the NBA—and one of the richest men in sports. In the late 1960s and early 1970s, the Knicks featured future Hall of Famers Walt Frazier, Willis Reed, Earl Monroe, and Bill Bradley, winning two championships and becoming the first NBA team to generate national interest and iconic status.

The Bottom Line

Average paid attendance	3,406
Net receipts	$204,043
Estimated profit	$20,000

Gotty, Jumping Joe, and the Philadelphia Warriors

If Philadelphia was justifiably celebrated as being a hotbed of professional basketball, then Eddie Gottlieb had set the fire. The popularity of Gottlieb's Sphas convinced Pete Tyrell (who ran the Philadelphia Arena and the AHL's Philadelphia Rockets) that the new BAA team would be boffo at the box office. Since it wouldn't do for the "Sphas" nickname to be resurrected, because of its connection with the South Philadelphia Hebrew Association, there was no question that the new franchise would be named the Warriors, after Philadelphia's entry in the ABL (1926–28). In the same vein, Tyrell had no qualms about putting the entire operation into Gottlieb's capable hands.

Gottlieb was proud and even thankful that he was a bachelor, since this status allowed him to work twelve hours a day. "He was married to basketball," said Harvey Pollack, who started as the Warriors' stat man before becoming their longtime public relations man. "Gotty did the Warriors' recruiting, negotiated the contracts, took care of all the traveling arrangements, booked the hotels, schmoozed the sportswriters and the local politicians, and, in his spare time, coached the team."

Most of the players signed by Gottlieb had three background experiences in common: several were local to the Philadelphia area and were graduates of either Temple or St. Joseph's, virtually all had played service ball, and the majority were veterans of the ABL. Here's a rundown:

Angelo Musi, 5'9", 145, from Temple University, was celebrated for his uncanny set shot, his dribbling skills, and his playmaking ability. Musi was a seasoned veteran of the ABL and had also paced the Forty-first Division Juglers to the Pacific Service basketball championship.

"Red Auerbach contacted me first," said Musi, "but I signed with Gotty because Philly was my hometown. I got fifty-five hundred for the season, which probably made me the highest-paid player on the team. I didn't know for sure, because we never compared salaries."

Art Hillhouse, 6'7", 220, out of LIU, had led the ABL in scoring while playing with the Sphas during the 1945–46 season. "Art was a relentless rebounder," said Musi. "He got a lot of points in the ABL from put-backs and stuff like that, but he really wasn't a strong offensive player."

Matt Goukas, 6'3", 195, from St. Joseph's, was the Warriors' most experienced player. A veteran of four seasons in the ABL, Goukas had also been an outstanding performer in the tough U.S. Army circuit.

"Matt was the best passer and the best dribbler on the club," said Musi. "He was so unselfish that we had to encourage him to shoot."

Goukas had played center in the ABL and was delighted with Gottlieb's promise that he'd be able to play facing the basket with the Warriors. "I was the first player that Gotty signed," said Goukas. "He put a contract down in front of me that said my salary would be twenty-five hundred dollars and said, 'Sign it.' So, I did."

Petey Rosenberg, 5'10", 165, from St. Joseph's, was a sharpshooting guard who'd played with the Sphas in the ABL and was also the mainstay of one of the best service teams while at Camp Luna, New Mexico. "Petey didn't play much for us," said Musi. "He was a two-hand set shooter and an excellent dribbler, but the best part of his game was an exceptional right-handed hook shot off the drive."

Jerry Fleishman, 6'2", 190, from NYU, had played with the Sphas and with a celebrated team at Fort Jackson that had won thirty-eight straight games in military competition. Speed and a high basketball IQ were his trademarks. "Jerry was a lefty," said Musi, "which was a huge advantage back then, because lefties were so rare. He was only a fair outside shooter, but he could pass well and was a rugged defender."

George Senesky, 6'2", 179, from St. Joseph's, led the country in scoring during the 1942–43 season before graduating into the army. In addition to being a dynamic scorer, Senesky was renowned as a defensive ace—hence his nickname, "the Octopus."

"In college, George was the only player on his team who could shoot the ball," said Musi, "and that's why he was such a big-time scorer. When he got to play with the rest of us, he understood that several of us were better scorers than he was, so he voluntarily made the transformation into being a defensive player. And he was a great one, definitely one of the best in the league. George was totally unselfish and a pleasure to play with for all concerned."

Jerry Rullo, 5'10", 165, was an all-around player who was fresh out of Temple University.

Fred Sheffield, 6'2", 165, had been the NCAA's high-jump champion in 1944 and 1945 while enrolled at Utah.

By far the most noteworthy player signed by Gottlieb was Joe Fulks, 6'5", 190, who eventually became the BAA's first superstar.

Born October 26, 1921, in a farmhouse on the banks of the small Tennessee River community of Birmingham, Kentucky, Fulks first encountered basketball one autumn afternoon in 1929 when he aimlessly wandered into town. Stopping to watch the local high school team practicing, he immediately became enamored with the sport. As much as he wanted to learn the game, his family was too poor to buy him a basketball. However, the determined youngster came up with his own solution.

Although he'd previously been an avid fisherman, his instant passion for basketball sent him to the school's outdoor court, where he practiced throwing tin cans, rocks, and bricks at the hoop until the sun set. When the coach of the high school team noticed that the outdoor backboard had been scratched and gouged and the nets shredded, he became alarmed. One afternoon, he and several other concerned school officials hid in an adjacent classroom to try to discover the culprit. They were amazed when they saw young Fulks so accurately tossing rubble through the hoop, and they immediately found an old battered, lopsided basketball for him to use. The next day, the eyewitnesses raised $2.19 and ordered a new basketball from Sears, Roebuck and Company in Memphis, which they then presented to the youngster.

Fulks went on to become the star of the Birmingham Elementary School team. But the town was flooded in the summer of 1932 to make way for the construction of the Kentucky Dam, so the Fulks family moved to nearby Kuttawa. By Fulks's junior year at Kuttawa High School, he had grown to nearly 6'5", and a year later, he led the school to a state championship. In so doing, he broke every Kentucky schoolboy scoring record and was hailed as the "Kuttawa Klipper."

Following his graduation in 1940, he turned down a chance to play for the legendary Adolph Rupp at the University of Kentucky, choosing instead to enroll at Millsaps College, in Jackson, Mississippi. Before attending classes, though, Fulks switched to Murray State Teachers College, where he averaged 13.2 points per game in forty-seven contests during his two-year varsity career. His achievements were rewarded by his being named as a Kentucky Inter-Collegiate Athletic Conference All-Star, and also being named to the National Association of Inter-Collegiate Athletics All-American team in 1943. Despite these accolades, his talents were largely unknown outside of his native state.

In the summer of 1943, Fulks joined the marines and saw combat action in Iwo Jima and Guam. After his active service, he played a marginal role with the Marines All-Star basketball team that made a short tour of the United States.

"Nobody'd ever really heard of Fulks when he played in college," said Petey Rosenberg, "but I'd played against him in a service tournament in Hawaii. Fulks was a sub on his team, but when he played, he'd pop the ball into the basket like it had eyes. He could dribble, run fairly well, hit hooks with either hand, and he had a one-handed jump shot that couldn't be defensed. If Fulks couldn't play a lick of defense, well, back in those days, the only guys who did came from the Eastern Seaboard. Anyway, as soon as I could, I wrote a letter to Gotty telling him about Fulks. 'If you sign this kid,' I wrote, 'you could win a championship in any league you could imagine.' Fortunately, Gotty took my advice to heart."

It took Gottlieb a week to find Fulks once he was discharged from the service, and he offered him a $5,000 contract. Fulks resisted before signing for $8,000 and a new car. A few days after Fulks inked his contract, the Knicks tracked him down and put a larger deal on the table. As soon as Ned Irish discovered that the Warriors had beaten him to Fulks, he telephoned Gottlieb to say that Philly had just signed "the best basketball player in the country."

The Warriors were a clean-living group, with the notable exception of Fulks, who was a big-time drinker, though an affable one. "Even when he was in his cups," said Rosenberg, "Fulks was still a likable guy."

Musi described Fulks as unassuming. "That's what made him so easy to be with. None of the publicity he got ever went to his head. We used to kid him about being a hillbilly, and he'd laugh along with the rest of us."

When Fulks first arrived in Philadelphia, he became enamored of riding elevators up and down the city's skyscraping office buildings. "Goddamn!" he'd yelp, much to the amusement of his new teammates.

His thick Southern drawl, however, wasn't quite as entertaining. "It took me three weeks before I could understand him," said teammate Howie Dallmar.

Fortunately, the Warriors' training camp lasted exactly three weeks, during which the players were quartered in the Broadwood Hotel. Their only permanent court, however, was the Broadwood's ballroom. This led to the team's shuttling around the Philadelphia area in search of more suitable gyms. Several venues were willing to accommodate them, with the proviso that the Warriors scrimmage the host team.

"We scrimmaged against high schools like the Germantown Academy, whose home court was in a boathouse," said George Senesky. "We also scrimmaged against other high schools, like Penn Charter and Lower Merion, as well as some of the local colleges, like Temple and Villanova. But the scrimmages were useless for us, because the kids were all hopped up, and for us it was like going to work. We lost more games to high school and college teams than we did during the entire BAA season. Our so-called training camp was a mishmash."

Still, the three-week session enabled Gottlieb and his players to bond. "He had an astute basketball mind," said Dallmar, "and he was incredibly intense. Gotty was so lovable that it was almost impossible not to like him."

Moreover, the ability of Fulks to put the ball in the hole was a revelation. "He had an awkward money shot that nobody could defend," said Senesky. "The ball we used was so big and got so heavy with sweat in such a short time that we really had to pound it into the floor to dribble it with some control. To help him keep the ball steady, Joe would start his shot with his left hand underneath it and his right hand in back. He'd wind up shooting his jumper with his right hand but with lots of support from his left hand. And he could get his shot off on the move, while he was twisting in the air and going both left and right. His nickname, 'Jumping Joe,' came about because of his shot, not because he was a great leaper."

Back then, any player who converted one-third of his field-goal attempts was deemed to be a superior shooter. Tom Fox, of the Detroit Falcons, explained why: "Shooting techniques were poor. The ball was heavy and lopsided. Defense was extremely tenacious, and the refs tended to call only the most blatant fouls. Everybody boxed out, so there were very few cripples or easy put-backs. As a result, we all wound up taking a lot of what would be considered to be bad shots in the modern game."

According to Rosenberg, the Warriors never considered themselves to be among the BAA's most talented squads. "We were tough, though, and everybody pulled for each other," he said. "Even though Gotty didn't like to substitute and would have been happy to play five guys every minute of every game, nobody was jealous about their lack of playing time, or about Joe's shooting all the time. We all respected Gotty and never answered back to him. And the guys were so tight that we all hung together at home and on the road."

It was Fulks's sensational point making that forced Gottlieb to change his habitual game plan. Whereas his Sphas outfits had been known for playing team-oriented ball with an emphasis on passing and cutting and a minimum of dribbling, the Warriors' offense centered almost exclusively on getting the ball to Fulks.

"We didn't have any Negroes on the team," said Goukas, "so we didn't throw the ball away like those guys usually did. It was understood that Gotty let us pass and cut to our heart's content, as long as the ball eventually wound up in Joe's possession."

Gottlieb felt that pay-for-play players already knew the game and didn't require much additional instruction. "He never put an X or an O on the blackboard," said Goukas. What Gottlieb did bring to the bench was intensity. He savored each victory above all other considerations, while he suffered after each defeat as though another world war had just been declared.

Gottlieb was happy as he could be when the Warriors opened their season by besting Pittsburgh 81–75 at home. Fulks stunned the home crowd by scoring 25 points on 9-for-19 shooting and 7-for-10 from the foul line.

The game was also marked by a deviation from the rules that was instigated by Gottlieb. The Ironmen had showed up with only nine players in uniform, and because of the whistle-happy refs, five of them fouled out. The last banishment left the visitors with only four available players for the final three minutes of the game. Gottlieb asked Johnny Muscatel to allow one of Pittsburgh's disqualified players to return to action for the duration, but the veteran referee refused. So, Gottlieb obligingly withdrew one of his own players, and the game concluded with the teams playing four-on-four.

Afterward, Gottlieb petitioned Podoloff to raise the foul limit from five to six. (By changing the existing rule, Gottlieb would then be able to reduce the number of player substitutions he was routinely required to make.) He also suggested that a team be allowed to play with five men even if that meant reinstating a player who'd previously fouled out. His suggestions were declined in a telephone vote of the owners.

Regardless, Gottlieb was still licking his chops, since the Warriors would play five more times in Philly before embarking on their first road game. He had every reason to anticipate that his team would take full advantage of this favorable schedule and get a jump on the rest of the conference. Those expectations were reinforced when the Warriors bested the Capitols on November 14 to extend their record to 2–0.

Then the roof fell in. Losses to St. Louis, Chicago, Detroit, and the Knickerbockers (at New York) were sandwiched around a victory over the hapless Celtics. The Warriors evened their record at 4–4 with a home win over Providence, only because Fulks tallied the astounding total of 37 points.

Through Philadelphia's initial eight games, Fulks averaged 20.1 points. Despite the disappointment over the team's so-so record, Gottlieb knew that he had control of a promoter's dream—the best gate attraction in the league. If the Warriors were indeed a humdrum outfit, it didn't mattter; Gottlieb would maximize Fulks's scoring heroics and get the turnstiles spinning all around the BAA.

After Fulks, Howie Dallmar was the Warriors' most significant player. At 6'4" and 200 pounds, Dallmar was an exceptional ball handler, rebounder, and playmaker deluxe who'd led Stanford to the NCAA championship in 1942. After joining the navy, Dallmar was first posted to St. Mary's College preflight school in Ottumwa, Iowa. That's where he came under the tutelage of Hank Luisetti, an instructor in the physical conditioning program. Playing for Stanford in the late 1930s, Luisetti had been the first collegian to score 50 points in a game and was universally celebrated as being one of college basketball's icons. It was Luisetti who refined Dallmar's pass work and court vision. Dallmar eventually wound up in a Navy V-7 program at the University of Pennsylvania, where he was allowed to compete on the varsity basketball team, leading the Quakers to the Ivy League championship in 1945.

"Nothing that Howie did was spectacular, but he was good in everything," said Musi. "He was a big guard who could rebound, pass, set good screens, and throw a fast, accurate outlet pass that let us fast-break. He also happened to be one of the greatest guys anyone could ever hope to meet."

As soon as Dallmar was discharged from the service, the Chicago Stags offered him $9,000 to play for them. "Then they let all the other teams know about it to discourage them from even talking to me," said Dallmar, "but it was kept secret from the other players in the league. When Gotty came up with ten grand, I jumped at it. That made me one of the highest-paid guys in the league."

According to Dallmar, Fulks's scoring totals were critical to the success of the franchise: "The house count was very important to Gotty. He was interested in anything or anyone who could help that cause. He didn't go so far as actually saying that we should give the ball to Joe—I mean, it wasn't spelled out in a telegram—but there was no mistaking his intent. For instance, Joe would stay in the game no matter what the score was. If we were up by twenty, down by twenty, or if Joe was stinking up the court, he'd still be in there. It was clear as day that Gotty wanted Joe Fulks to lead the league in scoring."

Even though Fulks only had eyes for the basket, his teammates were not resentful. "Joe had a license to do whatever he wanted and to go wherever he wanted," said Dallmar. "If he went into the pivot, then the center would move out to the wing and anticipate going after an offensive rebound. He seldom passed, but we thought that was OK, because we were an unselfish bunch. Also, after our slow start, we started winning, so things seemed to be working out. If we had continued to lose, I'm sure Joe's selfishness would have been a problem."

Naturally, the league office also took notice of Fulks's scoring prowess. Podoloff totally agreed with Gottlieb that Fulks could turn out to be the young league's savior. Accordingly, the last thing that Podoloff wanted was to have Fulks's playing time curtailed because of personal fouls. So, the word was passed to the league's officials to avoid calling fouls on Fulks. This was an easy-enough undertaking, since Fulks disdained playing defense and was rarely within hacking distance of his man. The refs were more than willing to cooperate and thereby help promote the stability of the league and their own job security.

Joe Lapchick came down from New York to scout the Warriors-Steamrollers game in Philadelphia on December 3. He was duly impressed by seeing Fulks score 37 points. "His eye is uncanny," Lapchick said at the time, "and he has a wonderful knack of twisting himself into positions affording a clear shot. I wish I had him at St. John's."

The old-time cager also voiced some misgivings. "In bygone days, professional basketball looked for good defensive players," said Lapchick. "Today they don't care about defensive basketball. If a boy can hit that basket with great regularity from almost anyplace on the floor, they'll grab him, and he fills the bill. Take this boy Joe Fulks here. That fellow has a lot to learn about defensive basketball. Why, he wouldn't even get a seat on the bench back in the old days."

Lapchick then backtracked, most likely remembering how much his own future was tied to the success of the BAA: "But Fulks makes up for his defensive deficiencies ten times as much with his offensive play."

A week later, the Warriors made their first trip to Toronto. Right off, Gottlieb's decision to showcase Fulks seemed to be hugely successful even north of the border. "We took taxis from the airport straight to the Maple Leaf Gardens," said Dallmar, "and we saw fans lined up four abreast outside the box office. Gotty was beaming, and the players couldn't help being impressed: basketball was really taking hold there, and Joe was a sensational draw. Then we learned that the fans were lined up to buy hockey tickets for a game that would be played in two days."

Once those road trips began, the Warriors did more flying than any other team in the league. "If the weather was really stormy, we'd take a train," said Matt Goukas, "but if it was iffy, we'd fly. The Mogul must have had some kind of a deal with the airlines. Some of the flights could be scary. There was one time that a door flew open while we were airborne. Newspapers and stuff were flying out of the plane, and guys were screaming bloody murder. I was sitting closest to the open door, so I grabbed on tight to a seat support, reached outside the plane, grabbed the door handle, and closed the damned thing. The Mogul said he was glad that a short-armed guard hadn't been sitting where I was."

As the season wore on, the Warriors struggled to win more games than they lost. Even so, Fulks's high-octane scoring made him the most publicized player in the BAA. Time magazine called him "the Babe Ruth of basketball," and wherever the team played, at home or away, they always drew sizable crowds.

Most of the fans were curious, but some were cynical. There must be something funny about the BAA game; how else could one player be averaging more than 23 points per game while the league's second-best scorer (Bob Feerick) wasn't even notching 17 per? Were the defenses lying down? Were the refs crooked? Among basketball purists, mostly devotees of the college game, these suspicions lingered all season long.

Meanwhile, Fulks was living the high life, chasing (and catching) women and drinking too much bourbon. To subdue his frequent hangovers and get himself ready to play, he had to imbibe huge quantities of Alka-Seltzer before virtually every game. Gottlieb was aware of Fulks's over-the-top lifestyle, but as long as Fulks was filling the basket and filling arenas, the Mogul was almost happy.

Almost.

"Gottlieb hated to lose," said Petey Rosenberg. "Afterwards, he'd curse and rant and rave. And he'd keep on talking about the game, griping about all the things that we'd done wrong from the start to the finish. I mean, he'd replay the game countless times on the train or on the plane. He'd just go over and over the goddamn game, dissecting every play again and again. After a loss, we tried to stay out of his way."

They could try, but Gottlieb would always find a way to corral his team and berate them just one more time. For instance, Angelo Musi described what occurred on the evening of January 11. "We were in the middle of a long, difficult stretch," said Musi, "six games in eight days. It was a Saturday night, and we'd just lost an overtime game in Detroit. What happened was that I'd missed a technical foul shot late in regulation time that would've won the game, and I'd also missed a last-second set shot when I'd gotten belted by one of the Falcons and a foul hadn't been called. So, Gotty was really steamed."

After the aggravating loss, the team had to rush to the airport to catch a flight to Chicago, where Philly would be playing the very next night. "We had about thirty minutes before the flight took off," Musi continued, "but Gotty just had to have a team meeting. The only private space at hand was a men's room, so he herded us in there and locked the door. He even stood leaning against the door to make sure we couldn't escape."

The loss left them with a 14–12 record, and after cursing out all of his players, Gottlieb softened and asked them what they thought was wrong with the team. "But he was clearly in a frame of mind where he really didn't want to be given any advice from any of us," said Musi. "It was the best time to keep our mouths shut, but Matt Goukas couldn't resist saying a few things: this was wrong, and that was wrong. From then to the end of the season, Matt was on Gotty's shit list."

After Goukas said his piece, Gottlieb resumed his tirade—when suddenly there was a desperate knocking on the door. Gottlieb cracked the door open, peeked outside, and saw a man with a strained look on his face.

"What the hell do you want?" Gottlieb barked.

"I got to take a leak."

Without saying a word, Gottlieb slammed and relocked the door; then he continued his diatribe.

The meeting failed to rouse the team, which lost another nail-biter in Chicago, 75–72. However, a 41-point explosion by Fulks (a record for the new league) enabled Philadelphia to overcome the Huskies in Toronto by 104–74 on January 14. Despite the lopsided score, Fulks once again played the entire game.

The game in Toronto also illustrated Gottlieb's unquenchable quest for perfection. The Warriors were leading by 26 points with less than a minute left to play, when one of them threw an errant pass. Gottlieb jumped to his feet and roared for his team to call a time-out.

He was apoplectic as the players approached the bench. "What the hell was that?" he wanted to know.

"Cool down, Mogul," Goukas said. "We're a mile ahead, aren't we?"

"Does that mean you're allowed to get careless?" Gottlieb snapped. "Do something like that again and you'll all walk home."

On January 16, the Warriors lost to Chicago, 84–78. This result fit the pattern, as Philadelphia would end up losing five of its six regular-season games against the Stags. The Warriors had now lost their last two home games and four of their last five overall.

On the bright side, a team recruited from the Philadelphia Fire Department had played a squad representing the Philadelphia Eagles in a preliminary game. The outcome compelled Maurice Podoloff to issue Bulletin 69, which concluded, "The net house was $9,730.00." Accordingly, Podoloff encouraged the other franchises to match attractive teams as preambles to their regularly scheduled ball games.

Even without any bonus games, the Warriors continued to lead the league in home attendance, and Gottlieb knew why this was so. It was all about supply and demand: "As long as the fans want to see spectacular shots and a steady stream of points, we're going to try to please them. Present-day spectators appreciate defensive gems, but they wouldn't come out to as many games if the contests were mainly defense." He added, "That was the reason why the BAA outlawed the zone defense when the fans booed its use."

The league's referees had their own opinion of the Warriors' hometown fans. "The fans in Philadelphia were vicious," said Sid Borgia. "There were no cops or security guards to escort the refs on and off the court, and the fans would line up and wait for us to pass. If the Warriors lost, or if Fulks didn't get to the foul line enough to satisfy the fans, they'd think nothing of kicking us and spitting at us. We just took the punishment and got the hell out of there as quickly as possible. Why didn't we have any protection? Because the league didn't give a damn about the refs. It took another five years and a series of assaults on the refs for the league to finally do something to keep the fans away from us. Cops cost money, and besides, refs were easily replaced."

On or about January 20, Gottlieb engineered a trade for Ralph Kaplowitz (for Moe Murphy), which helped turn the Warriors' season around. A loss in Washington on January 22 put the Warriors' record at 16–15, but Kaplowitz's outside shooting and timely pass work seemed to energize the ball club.

The results were dramatic: the team was off on a 7–1 spurt, which included five consecutive wins. Kaplowitz was able to feed Fulks enough to satisfy Gottlieb but was also able to lay clever passes on Dallmar and Musi. While Fulks continued to fill the basket, suddenly the Warriors' attack became somewhat more diverse.

Then, on February 13, the Warriors hosted the Cleveland Rebels. A pre-liminary rematch of the Firemen versus the Eagles was a considerable draw, but most of the 5,698 fans came to see Joe Fulks score his 1,000th point of the season. After missing his initial eight shots, Fulks finally found the range, but it wasn't until his thirty-third shot of the game that he managed to nail a twisting jumper that registered his 1,000th and 1,001st markers.

The fans gave him a standing ovation, time-out was called, players and coaches from both teams clustered around the hero, and the historic ball was removed from the game. (Instead of presenting the ball to Fulks, Gottlieb had it placed inside a glass case and positioned in the lobby of the arena.)

The only other professional basketball player who had surpassed the same one-season's total had been Willie Kummer, who'd played for Connellsville, Pennsylvania, in the Central Pro League in 1911–12. Over the course of sixty-two games, Kummer had tallied 1,404 points, the caveat being that, under the prevailing rules, Kummel had shot all of his team's free throws—a total of 938 from the stripe.

For the game, Fulks wound up with 19 points. Reporters who interviewed him and his wife after the game were hard pressed to glean any meaningful quotes. How did it feel to score that historic field goal?

"It was just like any other field goal," Fulks said.

The missus was even more closemouthed, saying only, "It was nice."

The next day's newspapers quoted "one veteran observer" who objected to Fulks's high-scoring heroics: "The way I see it, the Warriors are always feeding Fulks, even at the expense of taking layups of their own."

Ever the promoter, Gottlieb was quick to capitalize on Fulks's achieve-ment. The Warriors announced that fans could submit guesses as to how many points Fulks would have at the conclusion of the regular season. The guesses were to be jotted down "on a penny postcard" and mailed to the team's publicity department "today." The winner would receive twenty tickets to a postseason playoff game.

Unaffected by all the fuss, Fulks blithely resumed his assault on the score-boards. Sometimes he was practically unstoppable—as in a home game against the pitiful Ironmen on February 20:

Pittsburgh	FG	FT	Pts.
Abramovic, f	7	4	18
Maravich, f	3	0	6
Mills, f	0	1	1
Gunther, f	2	6	10
Bytzura, f	2	1	5
N. Jorgensen, c	0	0	0
Milkovich, c	4	0	8
Noszka, g	5	1	11
R. Jorgensen, g	0	1	1
Kappen, g	1	4	6
Totals	24	18	66

Philadelphia	FG	FT	Pts.
Musi, f	3	0	6
Rullo, f	1	0	2
Fulks, f	13	8	34
Hillhouse, f	4	4	12
Dallmar, c	1	2	4
Goukas, c	1	0	2
Fleishman, g	0	2	2
Kaplowitz, g	3	1	7
Senesky, g	4	0	8
Rosenberg, g	0	1	1
Totals	30	18	78

Halftime score: Philadelphia 38, Pittsburgh 26.

Missed free throws: Pittsburgh (10)—Abramovic, Maravich, Mills 3, Gunther 2, Milkovich 2, Noszka. Philadelphia (11)—Fulks 4, Hillhouse 2, Dallmar 3, Fleishman 2.

The Warriors concluded the regular season at 35–25, with Fulks's having established several league records:

Total points, season—1,389. (Bob Feerick was next with 926.)
Field goals, season—475. (Feerick was runner-up with 364.)
Foul goals, season—439. (Behind Fulks was Leo Mogus with 235.)

Total points, single game—41. (Fulks also had the next-best performances, with 37 three times and 36, 35, and 34 twice each.)

Average points per game—23.2. (Far behind Fulks in second place was Feerick's 16.8 ppg.)

But as the Warriors prepared to play St. Louis in the first round of the playoffs, several players were unhappy.

"There were plenty of guys who didn't want to play in the playoffs," said George Senesky. "It was especially tough for the married guys who had to live away from home and pay for rent and for all of their meals. Once the regular season was over, we were off the payroll and had to depend on whatever bonuses we could win. Even before the playoffs started, we had to fork over two months' rent in advance just to stay put. Most of us paid about two hundred bucks a month for our lodging. We would've made something like three hundred fifty dollars if we'd gotten knocked out in the first round, which would've put us down fifty bucks, not including meals. Plus, we wouldn't be getting any of the playoff money until the playoffs were over, so there was plenty of out-of-pocket expenses. Even Joe Fulks wound up broke after the season, and he had a wife and three kids. No, sir—the playoffs had no appeal for me and most everybody else on the team."

Philadelphia Warriors

	G	FGM	FGA	Pct.	FTM	FTA	Pct.	Asst.	PF	Pts.	Avg.
Joe Fulks	60	475	1,557	.305	439	601	.730	25	199	1,389	23.2
Angelo Musi	60	230	818	.281	102	123	.829	26	120	562	9.4
Howie Dallmar	60	199	710	.280	130	203	.640	104	141	528	8.8
George Senesky	58	142	531	.267	82	124	.661	34	83	366	6.3
Art Hillhouse	60	120	412	.291	120	166	.723	41	139	360	6.0
Jerry Fleishman	59	97	372	.261	69	127	.543	40	101	263	4.5
Ralph Kaplowitz	30	75	258	.291	59	80	.738	13	65	209	7.0
Petey Rosenberg	51	60	287	.209	30	49	.612	27	64	150	2.9
Jerry Rullo	50	52	174	.299	23	47	.489	20	61	127	2.5
Matt Goukas	47	28	104	.269	26	47	.553	9	70	82	1.7
Fred Sheffield	22	29	146	.199	16	26	.615	4	34	74	3.4
Moe Murphy	11	3	15	.200	2	3	.667	0	5	8	0.7

Postscript

Fulks had several more prime years. He led the BAA in scoring in 1946–47 with 22.1 ppg and then peaked out at 26.0 the subsequent season but dropped from the top spot with the arrival of George Mikan. Fulks lasted until the 1953–54 season, when his alcoholism caused his game to collapse in a hurry.

Fulks then returned to Marshall County, Kentucky, where he lived in relative seclusion until March 21, 1976, when he was shot to death in an argument over a handgun.

Eddie Gottlieb became the owner of the franchise in 1953. In 1959, he selected Wilt Chamberlain, a native of Philadelphia, as a territorial pick in the college draft. Chamberlain immediately proved to be a modern-day Joe Fulks—averaging 50.4 points per game in 1961–62, scoring 100 points against the Knicks on March 2, 1962, and attracting curious customers wherever the team played.

In 1963, Gottlieb sold the team to a group of investors in San Francisco, and the Warriors relocated to the West Coast. Gottlieb continued his connection to the league as a consultant and was unilaterally responsible for plotting out the schedules from season to season. The Mogul went on to his greater reward on December 7, 1979.

"There simply wasn't enough money to justify wasting a year of our lives," said George Senesky. "If I had it to do all over again, I wouldn't do it at all. After our careers were over, we knew we'd never have a big enough of a grubstake to last us while we figured out some other way to earn a living. There just wasn't much call for dribbling a basketball."

Senesky played with the Warriors through the 1953–54 season.

The Bottom Line

Average paid attendance	4,300 (best in the league)
Net receipts	$191,117
Estimated loss	$30,000

16

The Washington Capitols and the Apprenticeship of Red Auerbach

Arnold Jacob Auerbach was Brooklyn born (September 20, 1917) and Brooklyn bred. As such, he dabbled in all of the usual neighborhood sporting activities—stickball, punchball, baseball, Johnny on the pony, kick the can, box ball, off the bench (or stoop or curb)—but his first love was always basketball.

"I learned my basketball at a gym built outdoors," he said in a 1983 interview, "on the roof of Public School 122. Unless it snowed or rained, we played. In high school, I made the all-Brooklyn second team." Later, whenever he was kidded about that second-class status, Auerbach's response was, "What people don't know is that we had more good basketball players in Brooklyn in those days than there were in all the rest of the United States."

The next stop for Auerbach was George Washington University, in the nation's capital. "I had a tough time making the basketball team there," Auerbach said. "There were six backcourt men trying out for the varsity and only one spot open. I had four fistfights in the first two weeks of practice, but I got the job. The point is, I guess, I was always a bit brash."

After graduating, Auerbach was good enough to play in the ABL for the Washington Huerich Brewers. Over the next few years, he also coached various local high school teams—starting with St. Alban's Prep School and finishing at Roosevelt High. Once the war erupted, he landed in the navy and became assistant coach of the crackerjack Norfolk Naval Training Station quintet of 1943–44. "We had Fred Scolari and Bob Feerick and were one of the best teams in the country," he said. "On weekends, we'd do some local barnstorming for fifty bucks a game, and sometimes I'd play with them." In 1944–45, Auerbach coached an all-star service team that walloped the

Washington Bears, who had won an open tournament in Chicago and were considered to be the world's professional champions. "The Bears were an all-black squad made up of guys from the Globetrotters and the Rens, and they were truly great players, but they'd never seen guys like Feerick who could shoot from the hip."

When Auerbach mustered out of the service early in 1946, he went back to coaching the kids at Roosevelt High School while completing his master's degree at GW. "At the same time," he said, "I also coached a team made up of some football players from the Washington Redskins, guys who were looking to make a few extra bucks in their off-season. It was a barnstorming thing, and we'd mostly play a team from the Philadelphia Eagles. A couple of times, we'd played in Uline's arena and had to deal with some of Uline's staff. That's how I first met him."

Auerbach's penchant for self-promotion served him well when he set his sights on advancing his coaching career: "I was twenty-nine and right out of the navy when I just walked in on Mike Uline and told him I was the guy to coach his Washington team that was being organized for the new league. I was a little nothing high school coach." Auerbach's primary credential was the time he'd spent coaching in the navy, which led to his promising Uline that he'd be able to assemble an outstanding ball club by recruiting the best players he had either coached or coached against. When Auerbach proceeded to name the players, Uline—who didn't know a pick-and-roll from a kaiser roll—was impressed.

"Uline was a tall, soft-spoken Dutchman in his middle seventies," Auerbach recalled. "He offered me a one-year contract for five grand, saying that he'd had bad experiences signing some of his hockey coaches to longer-term deals. My school job paid twenty-nine hundred, and I also had to teach hygiene and physical education, so I jumped at his offer."

Auerbach did most of his recruiting by telephone, and he had his own idea of which players he wanted. "I disagreed with what some of the other franchises were doing—taking mostly local players to try to boost their attendance," he said. "My belief was that certain geographical areas tended to produce players who excelled in certain areas of the game. Players from big cities, for example, were usually good ball handlers; so, that's where my guards came from. With few exceptions, forwards and guards who could run and drive came from the Midwest. You got your rebounders from wherever you could, but not from New York, which was mainly noteworthy for its guards. The majority of the one-handed shooters, of course, came from the West Coast."

The roster that Auerbach subsequently assembled included the following players:

Bob Feerick, 6′3″, 185 pounds, who'd been an all-American at Santa Clara University in 1941 and went on to become the high scorer of the Norfolk Naval Station outfit. Both teammates and opponents agreed that Feerick was the best all-around player in the BAA.

Horace "Bones" McKinney, 6′6″, 180, who'd played at North Carolina State and then at the University of North Carolina. (His nickname came from his having played a character called Beau Brummel Bones in a high school play.) His lean physique belied his muscular board game, and he was also noted for his trick shots and trick passes. McKinney's ability to palm the large, heavy ball enabled him to fool opponents and please the fans with a variety of ball fakes.

While at N.C. State, McKinney was prone to giving himself audible pep talks as he ran up and down the court. He also gravely thanked the referee every time a foul was called on his opponent, and he elaborately checked the scorer's table whenever he sank a basket, to make sure he got credit for it. This all added up to making him a crowd favorite wherever he played.

"I actually didn't sign with the Caps until after training camp was under way," said McKinney, "and this is how it happened: I was working in the personnel department of Hanes Hosiery in Winston-Salem and playing for the company basketball team when I got a call from Earl Shannon, a guy I'd played with in the army. Shannon had signed with Providence, and he talked me into coming up to his home in Greensboro and signing a contract to join him with the Steamrollers. So, that's what I did, but when I got back to Winston-Salem, I decided that I'd made a mistake. I was married and had a kid, and I realized that Providence was too far away. So, I went back up to Greensboro, got the contract from Earl, and tore it up."

Shortly thereafter, Arthur Wirtz called McKinney and offered him $7,000 to play with the Stags. McKinney agreed and made plans to travel to Chicago, but the night before he left, Auerbach called.

"Why not stop over in D.C. on your way to Chicago?" Auerbach said. "I've got a bunch of guys on the team that you played with and against in the service. I've got a spot reserved for you as a backup to John Mahnken."

Once again, McKinney was agreeable. "I met Red at the Blackstone Hotel on Seventeenth Street," said McKinney. "Then I went with him over to

Georgetown University to watch the team practice. Right away, I knew that I was better than Mahnken."

After practice, McKinney dallied with Auerbach back at the hotel and listened to Auerbach's pitch. Washington was a lot closer to home than was Chicago, and Bones could easily bring his family with him. The presence of Feerick and John Norlander assured McKinney that the Caps would be a competitive team. Besides, what awaited him in Chicago? Who would be his teammates there, and how good would the Stags be?

"After a while, I had to go to the bathroom," McKinney remembered, "and Red followed me there. And that's when he put the finishing touches on his arguments, saying that he'd match the seven thousand that Wirtz had promised. That was good enough for me. The date was October 15, 1946."

Despite his playful attitude, McKinney was a serious student of basketball, and as soon as training camp commenced, he realized that he knew much more about the pro game than did Auerbach.

Irv Torgoff, 6'1", 195, a fine shooter, a savvy playmaker, and a stout defender out of LIU and the Philadelphia Sphas.

Fred Scolari, 5'11", 180. Scolari had played for the University of San Francisco and was a dynamic scorer and underrated defender. With his fleshy hips, bulging stomach, spindly legs, and soft thigh muscles, he didn't look much like a professional athlete. Still, he was both quick and strong, and his peers touted him as the best all-around guard in the BAA.

John Norlander, 6'3", 180, a sharpshooter from Hamline College and a record-setting scorer with the Bainbridge Naval Station team. After his discharge, Norlander played with the Baltimore Clippers, champions of the ABL. Starting with training camp and continuing throughout the season, Norlander earned a few extra bucks by taping his teammates' ankles.

John "Stretch" Mahnken, 6'8", 225, a capable scorer but mostly celebrated for his defense.

Francis "Buddy" O'Grady, 5'11", 160, a native of Staten Island. A former teammate of Mahnken's at Georgetown, O'Grady played his service ball in the army.

"O'Grady used to call guys who didn't get off the bench rinky-dinks," said McKinney. "As we were warming up before a game, he'd turn to somebody like Bob Gantt and say, 'Sit down, boy, you ain't gonna play a damn lick. It's not even worth the trouble to work up a sweat.'"

The rest of the squad was composed of benchwarmers, including the following:

> Marty Passaglia, 6'1", 170, also from Santa Clara. In fact, one of Feerick's demands was that Auerbach sign up his ex–college teammate. "Marty was a one-handed shooter," said McKinney, "which was typical of West Coast players, but since Red didn't play a lot of people, he mostly sat and watched."
> Albert Negratti, 6'3", 200, from Seton Hall.
> Gene Gillette, 6'2", 205, from St. Mary's (California).
> Bob Gantt, 6'4", 205, from Duke.

In addition to recruiting the players, Auerbach negotiated their salaries. Feerick ($9,000), McKinney ($7,000), and Mahnken ($6,500) all earned more than their coach. Scolari was a bargain at $4,500, as was Norlander at $3,500. O'Grady made $4,000. The rest averaged about $3,000.

"The biggest problem," said Auerbach, "was that some of the players were about my age. I used to play with some of them, and all of us who had been in the service were certainly peers, but to maintain my authority, I had to keep my distance. So, sometimes I'd go to a movie with them when we were on the road, but that was the extent of my socializing. I made sure to stay away from their parties and their apartments. I knew I couldn't be picking some guy's kid up on my knee and then cut the guy two days later."

Auerbach also sought to emphasize that he was indeed the boss: "Some guys would start an argument every time I took them out of a game. So, I'd take these guys aside and say, 'Your job is to play, and my job is to coach. If I'm going to fail, it'll be because I can't coach and not because of your attitude. I'm not going to blow this job because I'm scared of you or anyone else. That's the way it is. Take it or leave it.'"

Training camp lasted the requisite three weeks, with the players residing at the Blackstone Hotel and given $5 per diem for their meals. Auerbach knew that Uline wasn't totally committed to his rookie coach and that the team had to be successful in a hurry for him to keep his job. So, he ran his players dizzy with nonstop drills and sprints.

"I wanted them to be a fast-breaking team," he said, "so we had to be in great shape anyway. Most coaches believed that guys should play themselves into shape. My idea was for them to be in great shape to begin with, and if we were in midseason condition when the season started, then we'd have a huge advantage over everybody else. This was especially important since our first six games were on the road."

Another critical ingredient in Auerbach's up-tempo game plan was a series of nearly full-time, full-court traps and presses. "The prevailing principle," he said, "was that these kinds of pressure defenses were to be used only in desperate situations—when a team was down by ten with two minutes to go—but my aim was to wear down the opponents and throw their rhythm off right out of the box. So, I ran my players, and ran them, and ran them some more."

Auerbach also prided himself on being a hands-on coach. "Instead of just telling them that I wanted them to block out," he said, "I'd go out there and show them exactly how I wanted them to do it."

After racing to season-opening wins at Detroit (50–33) and at Pittsburgh (71–56), the Caps began to stumble—losing a squeaker in St. Louis (70–69), getting blasted in Cleveland (92–68), and then suffering another tough loss in Philadelphia (68–65).

Being on the road for two weeks was also hazardous to the physical and emotional well-being of Auerbach and his players. "On the longer trips, we flew in the old DC-3s," Scolari recalled. "They were excellent planes, and the pilots were damned good, but the technology was so primitive that they mostly had to fly by the seat of their pants. Because of our tight schedule, we frequently had to fly in bad weather, so there were lots of close calls—like running out of gas while aloft, or an engine catching fire, or having to land in a snowstorm where we couldn't see the runway. All of these things happened more than once."

McKinney was extremely sensitive to the risks of flying and categorically refused to board an airplane. "If God had meant us to fly," he insisted, "he'd have given us wings." Whenever the team flew, McKinney traveled by train.

"Being a good friend," said Scolari, "I would accompany Bones on his train rides. We'd leave early and meet the rest of the team in the next city. But after a while, I couldn't take it anymore, so I deserted him. Bones just shrugged and kept on riding the rails by himself."

Even the teamwide train trips could be annoying. "We tried to sleep a lot, but the berths were cramped for the bigger fellows like me," said McKinney, "and that made us kind of testy. I mean, we'd sleep, chatter, play cards, drink beer, eat, drag ourselves over to the next hotel in the next city, sleep, eat, play a game, go to a movie on a free night, sleep, chatter . . . We didn't do much else because there wasn't much else to do, and since most of us were right out of the service, we didn't have much clothing—maybe two shirts and one pair of pants. Besides, the uniforms had a rough texture, so we all had jock itch. We had no trainer on the road, so we were responsible for washing our uniforms. Fat chance of that with all the goings and comings. Our jerseys were so full of salt that they could stand up by themselves. And losing didn't help either."

The early-season three-game losing streak also caused some dissension. "At the start," said Scolari, "some of the more experienced players knew more about the game than Red did. He relied on them for scouting reports, how to play this guy or that guy."

One of the Caps who felt he would have been a better coach than Auerbach was Bob Feerick. It was Feerick who often called time-outs when the opponents went off on a ministreak. Mumbling as he headed to the bench, Feerick would criticize Auerbach for making the wrong substitutions or for calling the wrong plays. Since Feerick was the team's best player, Auerbach pretended that he didn't hear Feerick's grousing.

After a 73–65 victory in Chicago, the Capitols finally returned home with a respectable record of 3–3. "Red wouldn't let us recuperate," said McKinney. "We got off the train at about eight or nine in the morning, and we had to be at American University by eleven for a practice. He ran us through fast-break drills, long-pass drills—and, oh Lord, did we scrimmage. After that, we played half-court—two-on-two for twenty-one baskets. Gosh knows we ran and ran until I thought he'd kill somebody."

For their home opener on November 20, neither the Caps nor the visiting St. Louis Bombers did much running. That's because, as with virtually every other venue in the league, the floorboards at the Uline Arena were laid directly over an ice hockey surface.

To make matters worse, Uline had stubbornly insisted that the baskets and backboards be assembled according to his own specifications. The result was that the metal wedge securing the heel of the rim to the glass backboard was nine inches long, three inches longer than regulation. Also, the wires holding the backboards steady were anchored to sections of the mezzanine within reach of the frenzied Caps fans.

Here's what a local newspaper had to say about the spectacle:

Players couldn't get traction and both teams had to resort to long-distance shooting at swaying targets suspended from guide wires. After the game, which Washington's Capitols won, 54–51, a St. Louis official stormed into the office of Caps' publicity manager, Paul B. Rothgeb, deplored the condition of the court and demanded that it be remedied.

"I will not bring my team to Washington again unless you give me a written guarantee that it has been remedied," he added.

By the Caps' next home game, a 74–50 routing of the Huskies three days later, waterproof Celotex paper was placed beneath the floorboards and successfully absorbed the moisture. To further discourage condensation, the heat in the arena was lowered, but this led to the players' having to put newspapers or towels under their feet, or sometimes even don overcoats, while they sat on the bench.

During the second quarter of the win over Toronto, Scolari tossed up an errant flip shot that got stuck in the enlarged space between the basket and the backboard. According to the rules, the result should have been a jump ball, but McKinney quickly jumped and tapped the ball through the hoop. Despite the Huskies' stormy objections, the refs let the score stand. Said McKinney, "It was the easiest basket I ever made."

The Uline Arena was plagued with still another problem. "The building was close by the railroad tracks," Auerbach said, "and because of the food scraps dumped from passing trains, and the popcorn seeping down through the floorboards during hockey games, the place was full of rats. I mean, rats as big as cats. Every morning when the building was opened, workmen would turn on the lights and hunt the rats with .22s. Thankfully, the rats never came into the locker rooms."

The building was also inhabited by an alley cat the players named Little Bones. McKinney noted, "This was a big, mean cat that none of us wanted anything to do with. It was big and mean enough to whip any rat. One day, Little Bones had kittens, and we stopped the game while she led her brood right across the middle of the court. The fans applauded like mad. Bob McClain, a writer for the *Evening Star*, did a story about me and the cat. There was a picture of Little Bones in fighting position next to one of me in a defensive stance. In a lot of ways, the cat was more popular with the fans than I was."

After the Caps beat the Bombers in their home opener, McKinney was given a good luck charm by a friend. "The guy knew how superstitious I was," said McKinney. "It was a Chinese doll made of wood, and it stood about three inches tall—sort of like a Buddha, with a big belly and a smile. It even came with a name: Yehudi. Well, after we next beat the Steamrollers in Providence and Toronto back home, I decided that Yehudi was a keeper. So, I started carrying him around wherever I went, always in my left pants pocket. Then we beat the Huskies up there and Chicago at home, and most of the guys on the team agreed that Yehudi had a lot to do with those wins. By then, we'd incorporated Yehudi into our pregame ritual: the guys would line up and kiss Yehudi's belly."

Suddenly the Caps seemed invincible. By downing the Huskies in Toronto and then the Stags at home, they extended their winning streak to six games.

What with the team's success, and with Yehudi in tow, McKinney began having some fun. If the Caps had a game totally under control, he'd often shoot his free throws with his back to the basket. Whenever a player slid along the floor trying to rescue a loose ball, McKinney would rush toward him yelling, "Out!" or "Safe!" If a vendor chanced to be at hand when McKinney was called to the bench, he'd grab a few bags of popcorn or peanuts and hawk them as he walked through the crowd. He once sat on a woman's lap in Boston and posed there, patting her head. Another time, he toweled the sweating brow of a courtside fan, saying, "You need this more than I do." In Detroit, while attempting to capture a defensive rebound, he crashed into a row of temporary seats and then helped the maintenance men reset the chairs, all the while ignoring the game action as it continued at the other end of the court. Once the chairs were reassembled, McKinney ambled onto the court just in time to catch a long pass from Scolari and score an uncontested layup.

As McKinney entertained fans all over the league, the Caps kept on winning. Home wins versus Pittsburgh, Providence, and Detroit extended the streak to nine games. Their tenth win was enabled by John Mahnken's stifling defense on Stan Miasek as the Caps re-routed the Falcons in Washington. Next came victories over Philadelphia and Cleveland. St. Louis was the thirteenth victim, but the Caps had a scare when Feerick sprained an ankle late in a 68–47 win over the Bombers.

According to Morris Siegel, of the *Washington Post*, the injury was more than an accident. He reported, "The former Santa Clara set-shot specialist was roughed up in the closing moments of the rough and tumble affair, which saw the Missourians abandon basketball tactics and resort to everything but actual fisticuffs in a hopeless effort to cut down the Caps."

The early prognosis was that Feerick would miss a week's worth of games. His absence might have presented a huge problem, since Auerbach was wont to use only six or seven players. (He barely even spoke to the benchwarmers.)

To the Caps' relief, Feerick returned to action in time to tally 15 points as the Warriors became the fourteenth consecutive vanquished foe.

After the Philadelphia game, Uline turned down Walter Brown's offer of $50,000 for Norlander, Feerick, McKinney, and Mahnken. The quartet kidded Scolari about being left out of the proposed deal.

Next to go down were the Steamrollers, for fifteen straight wins. Then, as the Caps prepared to host the Knicks, Uline sought to capitalize on the streak by issuing the following announcement: "Due to the importance of the game, and the widespread demand for seats, the Ladies' Night policy of admitting ladies for fifty cents has been suspended but will be resumed later."

In fact, the front office's suspending of this bargain rate was often done with minimal warning and was always done when the best teams came to town or when the Caps' latest winning streak became big news. Dozens of irate women (and their male escorts) turned away from the box office when unexpectedly apprised that they'd have to pay the undiscounted ticket price, and many of them would never again attend a Caps game at Uline.

The mishandling of the Ladies' Night feature went along with another grievous error that kept too many fans at home. "Television was new to Washington," said Joe Holman, the team's public relations director, "and the only television station in town—ATTG-TV, Channel 5—was contracted to carry all thirty of the ball club's home games. Our gate was really hurt by basketball rooters choosing to stay home and watch the games for free."

Moreover, the scorecards on sale at the arena were more misleading than informative. Uniform numbers were wrong, and players' names were misspelled. The scorecards were printed before the season began, and no corrections were ever made.

Although the front office might have operated in bush-league fashion, the team on the floor was proving to be the class of the league.

The streak reached sixteen as the Knicks were blasted by 70–49 before a sellout home crowd of 5,570. The blowout was extraordinarily satisfying for Auerbach because of a longtime grudge he harbored against Ned Irish. It seems that in 1940, Auerbach's senior year at George Washington, Irish had guaranteed the team a bid to the NIT, but because the Colonials developed into a powerhouse ball club, one that was much better than the New York teams in the tournament, Irish changed his mind at the last minute.

Besides the ritual kissing of Yehudi, several of the Caps developed other personal idiosyncrasies to try to keep the streak alive. Auerbach took to carrying a silver charm on his watch chain that was engraved with "For Red for

Luck" and given to him by his wife. McKinney made sure that the players left the dressing room in a certain order: Feerick first, and then Mahnken, Norlander, Gillette, Ken Keller, and Torgoff, followed by Scolari, O'Grady, and, last but not least, himself. Scolari wore the same orange socks and the same loud necktie to every game. Other players always ate the same pregame meal.

Auerbach, naturally enough, believed that the streak owed more to his innovative game plan than to the various superstitions. "I was the first one to line up the players four across in vertical or horizontal lines for inbounds plays," he said. "Other coaches designed their half-court plays to produce layups, but I was the first to use set plays to generate set shots or else high-percentage shots from fifteen feet."

Auerbach also preached his own variation of fast-break basketball. "Not like Keaney at Rhode Island," he pointed out. "That was firehouse basketball, where the rebounders just threw the ball downcourt, and whoever was free took the shot. Mine was derived from Bill Reinhart, my college coach, and was an organized fast break. We had lanes for the rebounder, the trailer, and the wings. We had a designated triggerman. And we ran drills to make everybody aware of everybody's responsibilities."

When the break was not available, the Caps would usually freelance. "We didn't have many set plays," Auerbach recalled. "A high-post alignment that wound up with a double pick for Bones and a subsequent handoff to him. That was called the McKinney Play. Our bread-and-butter play was the One Play that involved more high-post stuff and double picks for the guards, but with the constant possibility of backdoor cuts."

Auerbach also claimed to be the innovator of having players other than centers play the pivot. "Feerick would go inside against certain opponents," he said, "and Scolari would sometimes take Kenny Sailors into the pivot. What's the difference if a six-three guys slips into the pivot if he's guarded by a six-footer?"

When opponents extended their defensive pressure on the Caps' guards, Auerbach had no compunction about having one of his forwards carry the ball across the time line. "I was always unconventional," he said.

Auerbach's radical thinking extended into his motivational techniques. "Sometimes Red was charming," said Scolari, "and sometimes he pissed us off. He would ask us to beat different teams for different reasons. Maybe he didn't like the other coach. Or the other coach had told the press that we were vastly overrated. He had all kinds of ways to psych us up for games. This was new to me and to most of the other guys. We always played to win because that was what the game was all about. We didn't need any artificial reasons. Some of the older guys, like Feerick and Bones, just ignored him."

Even so, Auerbach felt that Scolari needed to be periodically goosed to play his best. "He was always making me mad," said Scolari. "I thought I was having a good year, but he was always deflating me. 'Hey, you little bastard,' he'd sneer. 'You think you're pretty good, do you? But I can take you any time, any day.' So, one day after a practice session at the arena, we played a game of one-on-one. I was so mad that I wouldn't let Red score, and I beat him twenty-four to nothing. That kept him quiet for a while. Oh, he'd still needle me, but he never challenged me to play him again."

While Auerbach aroused mixed emotions in his players, virtually all of the other coaches blatantly detested him. (Honey Russell was the notable exception that proved the rule.) "They were all veteran coaches," Auerbach said, "and much older than me, and they resented being constantly beaten by a little nobody like me. Take Ole Olsen: When the Stags took a train, he had his own drawing room. Me, I was lucky to have a seat all my own. So long as I was beating them, I really didn't care how they regarded me, but the guys with big reputations like Loeffler and Olsen also let it be known that they had input as to which refs would work which games. So, I had to fight like hell with the refs just to get a fair shot."

Auerbach subsequently felt justified in stomping, shouting, and spitting at and cursing the refs whenever a call went against the Caps. His antics were designed to intimidate the refs by rousing up the home fans, but he also created bad feelings among opposing players. "Red was always a clown," said Sailors, the mainstay of the Cleveland Rebels. "He'd do anything to get attention. All the other coaches hated him, because he thought he was such a genius, but it was Bones McKinney who actually ran the team. Bones kept the other guys in line, told Red when and who to substitute, and told Red what ought to be done against the other teams. We all thought that Red was little more than a figurehead—and an obnoxious one at that."

On December 30, the Caps squared off against the Celtics in Boston, looking to extend their run to seventeen games. Inspired by 2,628 shrieking fans, the home team rebounded and defended with a passion the players had rarely exhibited thus far in compiling a 5–20 record. Connie Simmons was on the mark with his hooks and looping one-handers, and Dutch Garfinkel was a passing wizard. A last-minute tally by Simmons evened the score at 55 and sent the game into overtime.

"We might have taken the Celtics too lightly," Auerbach said after the game. But some serious heroics by McKinney and Norlander in the extra period clinched the game.

Washington	FG	FT	PF	Pts.
McKinney, f	10	2	3	22
Norlander, f	7	4	0	18
Mahnken, c	2	1	5	5
Torgoff, c	4	0	2	8
Feerick, g	4	5	2	13
O'Grady, g	0	0	2	0
Scolari, g	2	0	0	4
Totals	29	12	14	70

Boston	FG	FT	PF	Pts.
Brightman, f	6	0	3	12
Spector, f	3	0	5	6
Wallace, f	2	1	3	5
Connors, c	0	1	0	1
C. Simmons, c	7	5	2	19
Kottman, c	0	0	0	0
Gray, g	5	0	2	10
Garfinkel, g	1	0	0	2
Kelly, g	0	1	5	1
Fenley, g	2	0	2	4
Totals	26	8	22	60

SCORE BY QUARTERS	1	2	3	4	OT	Total
Washington	15	10	22	10	13	70
Boston	15	16	7	19	3	60

Halftime score: Boston 31, Washington 25.

Missed free throws: Washington (11)—Norlander 5, Mahnken, Feerick 3, Torgoff 2. Boston (6)—Connors 2, Gray, Brightman, Fenley, Wallace.

With their record now standing at 19–3, the Caps had firmly established themselves as the BAA's best ball club. Still, the Washington press was restrained.

"Washington had the Redskins and the Senators," said Auerbach, "and the media looked at us like unwanted newcomers. They knew next to nothing about basketball and were either very tough on us or, like Shirley Povich, simply ignored us totally. Their attitude was that if a guy was tall, a string bean, he could automatically play basketball; being a good athlete had nothing to do with it. The writers eventually came around when they'd interview baseball and football players and the guys would mention that they'd played baseball or football with so-and-so in high school and he's now in the BAA. Gradually they came around, but it was a tough sell."

The Caps' streak was finally snipped in Detroit on New Year's Day. The following night, the Caps also lost in St. Louis. They quickly regrouped and reeled off another ministreak of five games.

The capper of this spurt came in New York on January 15. With the Caps leading by 10 points and only minutes left, McKinney provided an encore of his back-to-the-basket shots from the free-throw line. The crowd howled with delight as both shots went in, and McKinney ran back on defense grinning and waving to the fans like a politician. Auerbach, of course, approved of McKinney's humiliating the Knicks, but the mood on the Caps' bench changed when New York rallied to close the final margin to 65–63.

On January 16, the Caps were thrashed by the Celtics, 47–38, and Auerbach was furious. How could a team of his score only 38 points? And against one of the worst defensive outfits in the league? In his rage to the press, his preposterous declaration was that his players were out of shape.

The players were upset. An anonymous player leaked the team's complaints to the newspapers: The consensus was that because Auerbach so desperately wanted to win every game, the burden fell on the team's best players. Meanwhile, the subs cooled their heels on the bench while their self-confidence eroded. The source warned that the Caps' mainline players would eventually wilt from the strain, and the reserves would not be prepared to pick up the slack. It was also noted that all of the starters had suffered considerable weight loss—some as much as forty pounds (most likely Scolari)—and the season was only half over.

Auerbach paid no attention to these gripes. It was business as usual on the court, as the Caps won five, lost one, won three, lost three, and then generated another fifteen-game unbeaten streak. The only disappointment took place in Washington on March 22, when the Knicks ended up on the long end of a 68–63 ball game.

Whereas all the league's teams concluded the regular season by winning 57 percent of their home games, the loss to New York was the only home-court blemish on the Caps' record. They finished at 29–1 at the Uline Arena and 49–11 overall.

The BAA's second-best mark was 39–22 posted by the Chicago Stags. Since Washington had taken five of the six games played with the Stags, the first round of the playoffs was expected to be a breeze for the Caps.

Washington Capitols

	G	FGM	FGA	Pct.	FTM	FTA	Pct.	Asst.	PF	Pts.	Avg.
Bob Feerick	55	364	908	.401	198	260	.762	69	142	926	16.8
Freddie Scolari	58	291	989	.294	146	180	.811	58	159	728	12.6
Horace McKinney	58	275	987	.279	145	210	.690	69	162	695	12.0
John Norlander	60	223	698	.319	180	276	.652	50	122	626	10.4
John Mahnken	60	223	876	.255	111	163	.681	60	181	557	9.3
Irv Torgoff	58	187	684	.273	116	159	.730	30	173	490	8.4
Buddy O'Grady	55	55	231	.238	38	53	.717	20	60	148	2.7
Marty Passaglia	43	51	221	.231	18	32	.563	9	44	120	2.8
Bob Gantt	23	29	89	.326	13	28	.464	5	45	71	3.1
Albert Negratti	11	13	69	.188	5	8	.625	5	20	31	2.8
Ken Keller	25	10	30	.333	2	4	.500	1	14	22	0.9
Gene Gillette	14	1	11	.091	6	9	.667	2	13	8	0.6
Al Lujack	5	1	8	.125	2	5	.400	0	6	4	0.8
Ben Goldfaden	2	0	2	.000	2	4	.500	0	3	2	1.0

Postscript

Auerbach coached the Caps to records of 28–20 in 1947–48, and 38–22 in 1948–49. When Uline continued to refuse his coach's requests for a multiyear contract, Auerbach quit—and was replaced by Feerick. The Caps folded on January 9, 1951, in the middle of the season.

After a brief stint as assistant coach at Duke University, Auerbach returned to the BAA (now called the NBA) to coach the Tri-Cities Blackhawks (28–

29 in 1949–50). The following year, he began his Hall of Fame career in Boston—eventually coaching the Celtics to nine NBA championships.

Bones McKinney played pro ball for five more seasons, rejoining Auerbach (in Boston) through the 1950–51 season. McKinney then went on to become a highly successful collegiate coach at Wake Forest.

Fred Scolari enjoyed a productive nine-year career with Washington, Syracuse, Baltimore, Fort Wayne, and Boston. In 1952, while Scolari was the player-coach of the Baltimore Bullets, he scored 10 points in the second all-star game ever played. Following in the footsteps of McKinney, he spent his last season (1954–55) with Auerbach in Boston.

After retiring from basketball, Scolari sold insurance and then became the executive director of a boys' club in San Ramon, California.

The Bottom Line

Average paid attendance	2,189
Net receipts	$98,901
Estimated loss	$125,000

The Playoffs

1946–47 BAA Final Regular-Season Standings

Eastern Division	W	L	Pct.	GB
Washington Capitols	49	11	.817	
Philadelphia Warriors	35	25	.583	14
New York Knicks	33	27	.550	16
Providence Steamrollers	28	32	.467	21
Boston Celtics	22	38	.367	27
Toronto Huskies	22	38	.367	27

Western Division	W	L	Pct.	GB
Chicago Stags	39	22	.639	
St. Louis Bombers	38	23	.623	1
Cleveland Rebels	30	30	.500	8.5
Detroit Falcons	20	40	.333	18.5
Pittsburgh Ironmen	15	45	.250	23.5

In conformance with the postseason model of both major hockey leagues, the BAA divided its inaugural playoffs into five series:

SERIES A: Between the two first-place teams in each division—Chicago and Washington—in a best-of-seven matchup. The winner would advance directly into the championship round, while also splitting a $14,000 prize. The consolation package totaled $12,000. Even before this series began, the Stags and the Capitols each received $200 per man for finishing atop their respective divisions.

SERIES B: Between the second-place finishers—Philadelphia and St. Louis—in a best-of-three confrontation. The winning team would split $5,000, and the losing team would get $4,000. In addition, each player received a bonus of $150 to reward the second-place finish.

SERIES C: Between the third-place finishers—New York and Cleveland—in a best-of-three series, the winners to divvy up $3,500, the losers to split $3,000. For finishing in show position, each player would get a bonus of $100.

SERIES D: Between the winners of Series B and Series C in a three-game matchup, the winners to get $5,000 and the losers $4,000.

SERIES E: The best-of-seven championship series pitting the winners of Series A and Series D for a $14,000 prize. The losers' share would be $12,000.

However, prior to the opening of the postseason tournament, the league's owners were already contemplating serious alterations. They had come to believe that the starting date of April 2 for the playoffs was too late in the sports calendar to attract the landslide of publicity necessary to ensure the league's continued survival—if only because the baseball season was also getting under way.

In addition, the early-April date coincided with the beginning of the hockey playoffs in both the AHL and the NHL. This made the scheduling a nightmare—even for Eddie Gottlieb. After the BAA playoffs were under way, the league was still scrambling to find available and agreeable dates in the various arenas.

The idea that was floated was to start next season's playoffs while the major-league teams were still involved in spring training. This would mean reducing the 1947–48 BAA schedule to fifty games.

Still, since the teams were not obliged to pay the players extra for postseason games, and since the prize money had already been set aside, and the owners were liable only for traveling and operating expenses, the playoffs were highly profitable. Contributing to that end, the players would receive only $5 per diem, and the limit for overnight hotel accommodations was set at $3.50.

Series C: Cleveland (30–30) vs. New York (33–27)

During the regular season, the Rebels had captured four of the six games they'd played against New York, but because of the Knickerbockers' superior overall record, New York would enjoy the home-court advantage in Games 2 and 3.

Cleveland's chances to advance were further damaged by the fact that Frankie Baumholtz, the team's second-best scorer (14.0 points per game), was down in Florida attending spring training with the Cincinnati Reds. "Physically and mentally, I was unable to play professional sports year-round," said Baumholtz. "To make things even worse, the basketball season and the baseball season overlapped. Since I had to choose one or the other, I decided that baseball offered a more secure future for me and my family. And that's exactly the way it worked out. I played in the major leagues for ten years, collected a pension, and put my kids through school. Both of my daughters are schoolteachers, and my son is a dentist in Hawaii. There's no way I would have been able to manage this if I'd stayed with basketball."

With Baumholtz in Florida, the Knicks were considered to be a shoo-in.

But on April 2, the Rebels bloodied and battered the Knicks on their way to a lopsided, 77–51 win. The difference in the game was the inability of New York's centers—Bob Cluggish and Lee Knorek—to contain Ed Sadowski's bullish attacks on the basket. Nor were the Knicks able to deflect Kenny Sailors's hot-stepping drives into the lane.

In addition, the Knicks sorely missed ace playmaker Ossie Schectman, whose career had been tragically terminated by the severe spleen injury he suffered near the tail end of the season. The Knicks' chances for success took another hit when the team's high scorer, Sonny Hertzberg, was shut out by the determined defense of Nick Shaback.

> **Game 1:** Cleveland (1–0) over New York (0–1), 77–51.
> **High scorers:** Cleveland—Sadowski 24, Sailors 13, Wertis and Riebe 10 each. New York—Knorek 10, Gottlieb 9, Byrnes 8.

Afterward, Hertzberg had this to say: "Cleveland's floor wasn't the best to play on. There were nails and splinters and whatnot. I ripped my arm, and somebody else suffered a cut leg. Every call went to Cleveland. I don't know whether the crowd influenced the referees, or if it was just bad judgment. At any rate, we sulked into the locker room convinced that we had been hosed. There was no question about it: we should have won the game."

While the players were stewing, Coach Neil Cohalan shared these words of wisdom: "Fellows, I hope there's plenty of beer on the train."

For sure, Cohalan's remark lifted the gloom, but Hertzberg wasn't impressed by his coach's season-long interest in alcohol. "Getting his mitts on some beer was very important to Neil," he said. "So, that gives you an idea."

Three days later, the Knicks and Rebels faced off at the Sixty-ninth Regiment Armory. Once again, Sadowski dominated the middle with his powerhouse hook shots, but Bud Palmer and Stan Stutz also had their mojos working, and Hertzberg finally broke loose from Shaback's adhesive defense.

The first half was fiercely contested. The score was knotted at 41, when Shaback unleashed a desperate fifty-foot heave just before the buzzer sounded to end the second quarter. The sensational shot dropped through the net, and the Rebels celebrated as though they'd already won the game and the series.

But Stutz was on fire as the third period began, scoring three field goals within the first minute of play, and then accounting for 11 of the Knicks' first 13 points. His set shots and clever drives were literally unstoppable.

Keyed by the trio of Stutz, Palmer with his accurate two-handed jump shooting (which Cohalan heartily approved), and Schectman, the Knicks ran away with the game, winning by 86–74.

> **Game 2:** New York (1–1) over Cleveland (1–1), 86–74.
> **High scorers:** New York—Stutz 30, Palmer 22, Hertzberg 14.
> Cleveland—Sadowski 26, Nostrand 12, Shaback 10.

Five days intervened between Game 2 and the rubber match. During that interval, the Rebels lost whatever slim chance they had to win the series. "Kenny Sailors's wife got very sick," said Roy Clifford, the Rebels' coach," so he left the team to go back to Cleveland. Without Baumholtz and Sailors, we didn't have a chance."

Game 3 drew a considerable crowd of 5,124 at the Armory, and the Knicks were in control from the opening tip to the final buzzer. With Palmer once more off to a sizzling start, the home team jumped to a 27–9 lead after the first quarter. Sadowski and Bob Faught rallied the Rebels during the second quarter, reducing the Knicks' lead to 45–35 at the intermission. But when play resumed, Palmer and Stutz still had hot hands, and the Knicks put the game away for good, winning by 93–71.

Game 3: New York (2–1) over Cleveland (1–2), 93–71.
High scorers: New York—Palmer 26, Stutz 25, Knorek 11, Hertzberg 10. Cleveland—Sadowski 21, Faught 14, Nostrand 12.

Series B: Philadelphia (35–25) vs. St. Louis (38–23)

Since the Warriors and the Bombers had split their six regular-season meetings, it was expected that St. Louis's aggressive defense (which allowed only 64.1 points per game, third-best in the league) as well as its home-court advantage would easily be the deciding factors.

Two days prior to the series (and the day after the conclusion of the regular season), Eddie Gottlieb took his entire team for a gala day of beach, sun, and beer at Atlantic City. "We were all impressed that Gotty wanted to win so badly that he covered all of our expenses," said Angelo Musi. "It was a great move on his part, one that really brought us all together." As a further incentive, Gottlieb vowed to chug down five martinis if Philadelphia prevailed over St. Louis.

Before the opening game, general manager Pete Tyrell presented Joe Fulks with the keys to a brand-new Chevrolet in appreciation of his stellar performance during the season. "Thank you very much," the taciturn Fulks responded. "This is a swell team to play with, and I like it here in Philly."

The investment in Gottlieb's treat and promise and Fulks's latest new car paid immediate dividends when the Warriors edged the Bombers, 73–68, before a sellout crowd of 8,273. The game was close from end to end. The Warriors, however, rallied behind Musi's long-range set shooting and Howie Dallmar's pinpoint passing to take command of the game midway through the second quarter. Time and again, Philadelphia succeeded in beating back determined rallies by the visitors.

Even though Musi outscored and outperformed Fulks (who was kept in check by the defensive diligence of Bob Doll), it was Fulks who provided the game's most memorable moment: At 10:30 of the third quarter, Fulks sank a free throw that tied the all-time single-season scoring record of 1,404, which had been set in 1912 by Willie Kummer with Connellsville (Pennsylvania), of the Central Pro League. (Back then, as has been noted, the rules were such that Kummer shot all of the free throws that were awarded to his team.) Fulks broke the record thirty-eight seconds later with a twisting jump shot that dropped through the net without touching the rim. Play was halted while the fifty-eight-year-old, bespectacled Kummer hustled out onto the floor and pumped Fulks's hand as the photographers crowded around them.

> **Game 1:** Philadelphia (1–0) over St. Louis (0–1), 73–68.
> **High scorers:** Philadelphia—Musi 19, Fulks 17, Hillhouse and Dallmar 10 each. St. Louis—Logan and Munroe 16 each, Smawley 14.

After the game, the Bombers complained about the distractions caused by the smoke-filled arena and the raucous fans. In fact, they believed that the constant roaring of the partisan fans unduly biased the referees.

The Bombers' coach, Ken Loeffler, stated, "Our players have always let the Philly fans get the best of them. They listen to the fans who are after them all the time, but there will be a different story when we return to St. Louis."

Loeffler also predicted that the Bombers would win the series. "The Warriors are not so hot as a road team," he said, "and I figure they will fold up in the next two games."

Loeffler's predictions were on the money in Game 2. After a tight beginning, the Bombers rolled to an easy 73–51 win that was witnessed by 7,182, the second-largest crowd in the league's young history.

Critical to the home team's showing was the masterful job that Doll did on Fulks. The BAA's most proficient scorer didn't notch his first field goal until the latter half of the fourth quarter. Overall, Fulks shot only 2 for 5 from the field.

Fulks's low yield was likewise due to his picking up four fouls during the initial sixteen minutes of play. Only one infraction short of disqualification, Fulks fumed on the bench until the start of the last quarter. Local scribes, however, were quick to note that the referees, John Muscatel and Hagen Anderson, had whistled twenty-one fouls on each squad.

Game 2: St. Louis (1–1) over Philadelphia (1–1), 73–51.
High scorers: St. Louis—Smawley 17, Roux 14, Doll 11, Munroe 10. Philadelphia—Musi 12, Fulks 9, Senesky and Kaplowitz 7 each.

Because the Warriors had played so poorly in Game 2 just the day before, they had the blues as they prepared for the deciding contest. For the first and only time during the season, Pete Tyrell entered the pregame locker room and gave his team a pep talk. "This game is not a matter of life and death," said the Warriors' general manager. "The season is already a success, and it doesn't matter whether we win or lose." Tyrell's brief comments instantly relaxed the players.

The opening half of the game was extremely close, concluding with the visitors grimly clutching a 33–30 lead. But the Warriors resumed the game with an 11–0 spurt, and the Bombers never closed the margin to less than 10 points.

Fulks finally broke away from Doll's tenacious defense, and Musi had another good outing. Even so, the hero of the game was George Senesky, who held Johnny Logan scoreless for forty minutes. The Warriors prevailed, 75–59.

Game 3: Philadelphia (2–1) over St. Louis (1–2), 75–59.
High scorers: Philadelphia—Fulks 24, Senesky 16, Musi 14. St. Louis—Smawley 21, Logan 10, Munroe 8.

On the flight back to Philadelphia, the teetotaling Gottlieb kept his promise and chugged five consecutive martinis, but the players were sorely disappointed when the drinks had no discernible effect.

Series A: Chicago (39–22) vs. Washington (49–11)

The winner of the series would advance into the championship round, while the loser would go home. Despite the high stakes, the Caps were bursting with confidence as they prepared to host the Stags for the back-to-back games that would inaugurate the series. After all, they had taken five of six from Chicago during the regular season, the last victory being a 105–77 blowout in Washington just seven days prior.

This time around though, the Stags' coach, Ole Olsen, had a brand-new trick up his sleeve. During their previous matchups, Olsen had been well aware that the 6′ 6″ Bones McKinney had overwhelmed his opposite number—Mickey Rottner, a quick-handed guard who stood only 5′10″. Olsen's brainstorm was to replace Rottner in the starting lineup with a seldom-used substitute—Chuck Gilmur, a 6′4″, 225-pound defensive specialist who usually played center. Rottner enthusiastically supported the idea. "Anything for the good of the team," he said.

Olsen's strategy was successful, but while Gilmur stymied McKinney, Fred Scolari, Johnny Norlander, and Bob Feerick were mostly on target, and after a dozen lead changes, the Caps managed to limit their halftime deficit to 33–31. Then Tony Jaros found the range in the third quarter while Gilmur and Chick Halbert controlled the backboards, and the Stags ran away with the game. The final tally was 81–65 and marked the Caps' second, and worse, defeat at the Uline Arena.

Both coaches had explanations for the upset. According to Auerbach, his boys merely suffered an off game, but he also admitted that his team "had too much confidence; that didn't help a bit."

Olsen concurred, but he turned the spotlight on his team's rebounding edge and also on Gilmur's holding McKinney to only one field goal and 7 total points.

Neither coach mentioned the real reason why the Caps had played so sluggishly: after playing fast-break basketball for five months with only six or seven players being trusted to play meaningful minutes, the Caps' starters were leg weary.

Game 1: Chicago (1–0) over Washington (0–1), 81–65.
High scorers: Chicago—Jaros 29, Gilmur 15, Halbert 11.
Washington—Feerick and Scolari 13 each, Norlander 12,
Mahnken 10.

Game 2 offered more of the same. The Stags owned the boards and ran the Caps ragged. Gilmur smothered McKinney, holding him scoreless from the field (for the first time in Bones's sixteen years of playing the game) and limiting him to a solitary point. And the visitors' defense hounded the Capitols into abysmal shooting—1 for 22 in the opening period, 2 for 24 in the last, and 16 for 91 overall.

Even worse, Feerick slightly reinjured a previously sprained ankle, and Scolari hurt his shooting hand so badly that he remained on the bench for the entire second half.

The Caps were thoroughly embarrassed, losing 69–53.

The losing team sat in stupefied silence in the postgame locker room. Finally, Feerick just about conceded the series when he said to his teammates, "They got our number."

Even the normally verbose Auerbach had nothing to say. While the local sportswriters peppered him with questions, he silently popped a slice of orange into his mouth, shrugged his shoulders, and shook his head.

> **Game 2:** Chicago (2–0) over Washington (0–2), 69–53.
> **High scorers:** Chicago—Zaslofsky 15, Jaros and Carlson 14 each, Halbert 10. Washington—Feerick 19, Mahnken 11, Torgoff 9.

Auerbach and his minions had lots to think about during the four-day recess before playing Game 3 in St. Louis.

"This series isn't over by a long-shot," said John Norlander. "They got the jump on us, but we'll be ready for them on Tuesday."

By Monday, as they were preparing to board their plane, Feerick modified his previous statement of surrender. "We've always had difficulty with a team that crowds us," he said, "but on Tuesday, we're going to be moving fast. At least, we hope so."

After swearing that his players weren't tired, Auerbach noted that both Feerick and Scolari had fully recuperated from their injuries. He also praised the play of Torgoff and indicated that in Game 3, the rugged forward would be starting in place of Norlander. "They won't wear us down," Auerbach promised as he also announced his intention to go deeper into his bench. "We'll run as much as they will."

John Mahnken got off to a strong start, and the Caps jumped to an early 8–4 lead in Game 3. Then Chicago rallied behind the sharp shooting of Max Zaslofsky to forge to a 19–12 margin at the end of the first quarter. With

Gilmur's defense still blanketing McKinney (holding him to a pair of field goals and only 7 total points), Feerick registered 16 second-quarter points as Washington closed the gap to 33–32 at the half.

But the third quarter was a disaster for the visitors. That's when Don Carlson developed a hot hand, dropping 14 points to ice the game for the home-standing Stags.

The final count was 67–55, which boosted Chicago to a commanding 3–0 lead in the series.

If the Caps grudgingly admitted to being "tired" after Game 1, and "surprised" after Game 2, they were speechless with despair after their latest loss. Only Johnny Norlander kept the faith: "We know that we can beat them four straight."

Game 3: Chicago (3–0) over Washington (0–3), 67–55.
High scorers: Chicago—Carlson 22, Zaslofsky 20, Halbert 9.
Washington—Feerick 16, Torgoff 10, Scolari and Mahnken 9 each.

The Caps were inspired both by their return to Washington and by Auerbach's tweaking of his game plan, and they began Game 4 in their up-tempo mode and then switched to a grind-it-out pace in the second and third quarters before resuming their run-and-gun style. These variations greatly discomforted the Stags and short-circuited their defensive focus. Auerbach also utilized his bench players more than he had before, and they all responded with good efforts—-particularly Buddy O'Grady and Marty Passaglia. And with McKinney finally escaping from Gilmur's defensive clutches, the Capitols copped Game 4 by 76–69.

Feerick credited the support of the hometown fans for the Caps' turnabout. "Here we came from Chicago, after losing three straight, expecting to get booed off the floor, but they cheered us instead. That really was a big help."

Game 4: Washington (1–3) over Chicago (3–1), 76–69.
High scorers: Washington—Mahnken 18, Feerick 16, McKinney 15, Scolari 11. Chicago—Carlson and Zaslofsky 21 each, Halbert 17.

With the Caps still facing elimination, the series moved back to Chicago, and Game 5 was a dogfight until the last two minutes.

Carlson was held in check, but Jaros and Zaslofsky matched McKinney and Feerick point for point, while McKinney and Mahnken ate up the available rebounds. After Zaslofsky bagged a set shot to bring the Stags to within a single digit of the lead (55–54), McKinney, Norlander, and Feerick simply took over the game. The threesome scarcely missed a shot as the Capitols blasted off on a 12–1 run that secured the win, 67–55.

> **Game 5:** Washington (2–3) over Chicago (3–2), 67–55.
> **High scorers:** Washington—Feerick and McKinney 18 each, Scolari 9. Chicago—Zaslofksy 20, Jaros 13, Halbert 9.

Now that the Caps needed only one more victory to send the series back to Washington for the deciding game, their confidence was completely restored. As they expected, Game 6 was another hard and furious battle.

This was Scolari's finest performance. With his banged-up hand healed, he filled the basket with one-handed hip shots and also put the defensive clamps on Jaros. For the home team, Halbert's board work and interior scoring set the pace. Then, when Scolari fouled out near the end of the fourth quarter, the Caps' offense stuttered, and Chicago pulled the game out, 66–61, thereby advancing to the championship series.

As Bones McKinney trudged off the court, he angrily hurled Yehudi into the cheering crowd.

The Caps were understandably disappointed, but a few months later, their disappointment turned to rage. Here's Johnny Norlander's testimony:

"There were several reasons why we lost. First off, we were fatigued. And secondly, because Red had never developed his bench players. But there was a third reason that was more important than the others. We were up by six points in that last game with only a couple of minutes to go, and we could taste the win. But from there until the end, the Stags made a parade to the foul line. In fact, they failed to notch a single field goal during that stretch. Just about all of the calls that sent them to the line were clearly ridiculous ones, and they were all made by the same ref: Nat Messenger. The other ref was Pat Kennedy, a guy I knew from the games he worked when I was in college. Pat was always straight as an arrow, and the two of them had reffed every single game in the series, all six of them. As we walked off the court after the final buzzer, Kennedy nodded at Messenger and said to me, 'Wasn't that terrible?' All I could do was to sadly agree."

The real anger overflowed the following August. "That's when we found out," said Norlander, "that Messenger had a substantial amount of money bet on Chicago to win the series. If he'd been straight, we'd have won Game Six and then closed the Bombers out back in D.C. No question about it. We felt like the series, and the championship, were stolen from us by a crooked ref."

> **Game 6:** Chicago (4–2) over Washington (2–4), 66–61.
> **High scorers:** Chicago—Halbert 25, Zaslofsky 18, Jaros 7.
> Washington—Scolari 25, McKinney 12, Feerick 8.

Series D: Philadelphia (35–25) vs. New York (33–27)

With the Warriors having taken four of six from the Knicks during the regular season, and with Ossie Schectman out, Philadelphia was expected to have no trouble advancing into the championship series. And that's just what transpired.

The first game was played in Philly before a raucous gathering of 8,317 partisans. After a relatively competitive three quarters, the Warriors broke away and drew first blood with a convincing 82–70 victory.

The bugaboo for New York was the team's atrocious shooting. Bud Palmer was 6 for 25 from the field. Stan Stutz was 5 for 21, and Sonny Hertzberg was 2 for 17. It was Stutz's bull's-eye shooting that kept the Knicks close in the first half, until George Senesky's chest-to-chest defense totally shut the little guard down. Overall, the Knicks shot 26 for 113, for a collective 23 percent.

The Warriors weren't much better. Their team total of 29 for 97 (29.1 percent) included Fulks's shooting 8 for 32, Dallmar at 4 for 17, and Senesky with 2 for 10. The main difference was Philadelphia's knocking down 24 of its 26 free throws.

Game 1: Philadelphia (1–0) over New York (0–1), 82–70.
High scorers: Philadelphia—Fulks 24, Musi 16, Hillhouse 15,
Dallmar 12. New York—Knorek 20, Stutz and Palmer 16 each,
Gottlieb 10.

On April 14, the Warriors easily walloped the Knicks, 72–53, before 4,607 locals at the Sixty-ninth Regiment Armory. Once again, Senesky's earnest defense locked up Stutz, and the Knicks shot mostly blanks (18.6 percent from the field, and 45 percent from the foul line).

Game 2: Philadelphia (2–0) over New York (0–2), 72–53.
High scorers: Philadelphia—Fulks 16, Senesky 14, Musi 11,
Hillhouse 10. New York—Byrnes 11, Palmer 9, Stutz and
Hertzberg 7 each.

So, it would be the Philadelphia Warriors squaring off against the Chicago Stags for the BAA's first-ever championship.

The First Champions

C hicago Stadium was hosting a circus, so even though the Stags had a better regular-season record than the Warriors, the series opened in Philadelphia. Stags fans weren't particularly concerned about forfeiting the home-court advantage, since their team had a lopsided edge in the season's competition, five games to one.

Warriors supporters were just as quick to point out that all of the games had been close, with the margins varying by 3 to 8 points. Also, two of their three defeats in Chicago were played on Sunday afternoons when the Warriors were still bruised and weary after having battled the rough-and-ready Falcons in Detroit the previous nights.

During their prior head-to-head confrontations, Philadelphia had been particularly bedeviled by Chuck Halbert and Max Zaslofsky. Of course, Joe Fulks had been the most potent Warrior. In fact, discounting an early-season game (November 21) in which a bad cold had limited Fulks to a mere 10 points, he had averaged 28.0 versus Chicago. Ole Olsen's plan was to sic Chuck Gilmur on Fulks.

As the series progressed, however, Gilmur would have only periodic success against Fulks. Much more decisive a factor would be George Senesky's ornery defense on Zaslofsky.

On April 16, the fourth consecutive sellout crowd in the Philadelphia Arena (7,918) saw the most prolific scorer in basketball history ring up 37 points as the Warriors broke open a tight contest in the last period of Game 1. Fulks started the winning rally by hitting his first eight shots. A stringer for the Associated Press called Fulks's clutch performance "the greatest shooting exhibition ever seen."

Until then, Halbert and Chet Carlisle had kept the Stags in contention with their ferocious inside play. Yet, while the visitors managed to knot the score on several occasions, they never forged into a lead. It wasn't that they didn't uncork enough shots; for the game, the Stags fired up a record number of field-goal attempts—hitting only 26 of 128.

Gilmur fouled out in the third quarter. And the game was officiated by Pat Kennedy and Nat Messenger.

Sure, there had been rumors of players fixing college games for several years. A betting scandal in 1945, for example, involved several players from Brooklyn College, and shortly thereafter, Nat Holman had bounced a player from his CCNY squad for being in league with gamblers. Nevertheless, even the professional wise guys figured that pro refs were on the up-and-up. If Messenger was often seen hanging out with shady characters, well, for some guys, that was part of the lure of the sporting life. Kennedy, for his part, was known to be purer than Caesar's wife.

> **Game 1:** Philadelphia (1–0) over Chicago (0–1), 84–71.
> **High scorers:** Philadelphia—Fulks 37, Musi 19, Fleishman 8.
> Chicago—Halbert 19, Carlisle 11, Carlson 10.

Fulks cooled off considerably the next night, and Game 2 was another cliff-hanger until the last four minutes. Chicago was unable to take full advantage of Gilmur's inspired defense against Fulks because Senesky did an even better job of stifling Zaslofsky, holding him to 4 points.

The Warriors' late splurge was led by Howie Dallmar's crisp passing and also by the play of Art Hillhouse, who scored 7 of Philadelphia's last 10 points. And it was mainly the combination of Dallmar and Petey Rosenberg that preserved the Warriors' 85–74 victory by successfully freezing the ball in the closing minutes.

During the game, Chicago broke its one-day-old BAA record by launching the incredible total of 150 shots from the field. Also, the Stags shot twenty-four free throws, to the Warriors' thirty-six, and the former were whistled for twenty-eight personal fouls, versus the latter's eighteen. Once again, the referees were Kennedy and Messenger.

> **Game 2:** Philadelphia (2–0) over Chicago (0–2), 85–74.
> **High scorers:** Philadelphia—Dallmar 18, Fleishman 16,
> Kaplowitz and Hillhouse 14 each, Fulks 13. Chicago—Carlisle
> 19, Halbert 18, Gilmur 10.

The following morning, the Warriors boarded a four-engine Trans World airplane that was planning to make a historic trip from Philadelphia to Chicago. The idea was to cover the eight-hundred-mile trip in less than four hours, which would constitute a new world record.

"We were up in the air for about ten minutes, when I smelled something burning," said George Senesky. "I asked Dallmar if he had put a cigarette out on the floor. No, he hadn't. Then all this black smoke filled the plane."

After they returned to the airport and switched planes, the record-setting plan was abandoned. Although the remainder of the trip proved uneventful, Petey Rosenberg had seen enough airborne drama. He quit the BAA for good as soon as the series concluded.

With Fulks nailing 11 quick points, the Warriors jumped into an early lead when the series finally shifted to the Chicago Arena for Game 3. The Warriors' defense was the key, keeping the Stags scoreless for the opening seven minutes. However, led by Halbert, Don Carlson, and Zaslofsky, the Stags rallied to reduce their deficit to 18–17. A pair of buckets by Zaslofsky and Carlson then boosted Chicago to its only lead of the game, until Jerry Fleishman's determined drives to the hoop roused the visitors to a 5-point advantage. The half ended with the game even at 31, and both teams struggled to score as play resumed.

Philadelphia was hampered by Gilmur's swarming defense on Fulks, which limited the Kuttawa Klipper to 3 points in the second quarter and 2 points in the third quarter. Senesky more than took up the slack with his determined drives and hustling offensive rebounds, while Ralph Kaplowitz's high-arcing set shots began to find the range. Then Fulks regained his touch in the concluding period, mainly because of Gilmur's continuing foul troubles.

The Warriors' lead burgeoned to 13 with only four minutes left on the game clock, but the Stags refused to yield. With seconds remaining, the margin was narrowed to 71–68, when Fulks provided the clincher by putting back a free throw missed by Dallmar. The Warriors then went into their stalling mode until the buzzer finalized their 75–72 victory to give them a 3–zip stranglehold on the series.

This time, the referees were Kennedy and Jim Biersdorfer.

Game 3: Philadelphia (3–0) over Chicago (0–3), 75–72.
High scorers: Philadelphia—Fulks 26, Senesky 13, Kaplowitz and Fleishman 11 each. Chicago—Zaslofsky and Carlson 15 each, Seminoff and Halbert 14 each.

The Warriors almost closed the series (and the season) the very next evening after Zaslofsky and Carlson had prompted Chicago to a 13-point lead near the end of the third quarter. Fulks had spent most of this critical time on the bench with four fouls, leaving Senesky to do virtually all of the scoring. Fleishman likewise kept Philadelphia's hopes alive by coming up with six steals of the opponents' errant passes that culminated in layups for Senesky and Kaplowitz. Fulks returned early in the fourth quarter to front a fierce comeback that brought Philadelphia within 3 points of the Stags before being tagged with his fifth foul with 1:25 to go in the game.

Despite Fulks's banishment, the Warriors had a last desperate try at winning the game. Two seconds before the final buzzer, Senesky intercepted a pass deep in the backcourt and raced toward the far basket, but he failed to get off a shot. With Kennedy and Biersdorfer again manning the whistles, the Stags were victorious by 74–73.

Later, Gottlieb claimed that had the game lasted ten more seconds, his team would have won the title. "But I'm satisfied to win one of the two games played in Chicago," he added, "and I'm confident that we'll take Chicago back in Philadelphia and end the season then."

> **Game 4:** Chicago (1–3) over Philadelphia (3–1), 74–73.
> **High scorers:** Chicago—Zaslosfky 20, Carlson 18, Seminoff and Halbert 13 each. Philadelphia—Senesky 24, Fulks 21, Kaplowitz and Musi 6 each.

Because of the continuing scheduling difficulties, all subsequent games would be played in Philadelphia. Mindful of the Caps' comeback from a three-game deficit against Chicago, the Warriors were determined to put the Stags to sleep as soon as possible.

Fulks came out smoking, hitting jumpers from all angles and even climbing the offensive boards. After twelve minutes of play, the home team led by 27–13, and the game seemed to be well in hand. It was at this juncture that Tony Jaros finally found his game. He almost single-handedly paced a furious comeback that eventually peaked with Chicago in front by 68–63 at the start of the fourth quarter. Yet the outcome wasn't determined until the final minute.

Throughout the series, Howie Dallmar had been plagued by split calluses under his left foot that were so painful that they had to be cut and trimmed earlier in the day. As a result, Dallmar limped through the game and had made only one of his previous six shots. Indeed, he'd just missed a driving layup that would have broken an 80–80 tie. No matter, as Dallmar's last shot turned out to be the most important of the entire game—a one-hander from fifteen feet with the score still knotted at 80–80. "The ball bounced on the rim at least four times," he said, "before it finally went in."

Petey Rosenberg was sent into the fray to help freeze the ball with his clever dribbling, but when Rosenberg was fouled, Gottlieb sent Kaplowitz, a much better free-throw shooter, to the line instead. Kaplowitz's try missed, and neither of the attending officials (Kennedy and Eddie Boyle), nor any of the Stags, ever realized that Gottlieb had pulled a switch. A successful (and legal) free throw by Kaplowitz subsequently closed the scoring and the season.

> **Game 5:** Philadelphia (4–1) over Chicago (1–4), 83–80.
> **High scorers:** Philadelphia—Fulks 34, Musi 13, Senesky 11.
> Chicago—Jaros 21, Seminoff 12, Carlson 11.

Many of the 8,221 delirious fans on hand swarmed the court after the final gun, joining in the joyful hugging and backslapping. The scene in the Warriors' locker room was even more frenzied, with Maurice Podoloff being the first to extend his felicitations to Gottlieb and to the players.

Gottlieb then praised his team as the media representatives gathered around him: "In all my years, I have never coached a finer group of boys. They were easy to handle, and I never had to fine a single one. They are a credit to the game of basketball."

In the losers' locker room, Ole Olsen likewise praised the victors. "They're a great team," he said, "and there is not a team in the league that I would rather have lost to."

Everybody agreed that Fulks was the hero, not only of the moment but also of the entire season. "I sure am glad to be associated with such a wonderful group of guys," he said.

When asked about when he'd be heading home, Fulks said, "As soon as I can. I'm already two weeks late in planting my potato crop."

Two days later, the arena management hosted a farewell dinner at Raymond's restaurant. During the festivities, Gottlieb was humble when Major Stanley W. Root, the president of the Philadelphia Arena, pronounced the Warriors to be the greatest team in the history of basketball. "I won't go that far," said Gotty. "I will say that this was the greatest team in the United States this season."

Gottlieb modestly accepted praise for his strategy of starting the season slowly and then inevitably building to a peak. The obvious comparison was with the Washington Capitols, who started in high gear and then burned out in the playoffs. In truth, Gottlieb wanted to win every single game, and the Warriors' coming together had more to do with the midseason addition of Ralph Kaplowitz than any conscious plan of his.

In the end, Gottlieb was universally hailed as the BAA's first bona fide genius, and the long, strange first season was in the books.

Barely Alive

On April 24, two days after the playoffs concluded, the BAA announced its all-star team: Joe Fulks, Bob Feerick, Stan Miasek, Bones McKinney, and Max Zaslofsky. The second team consisted of Ernie Calverley, Frank Baumholtz, Johnny Logan, Chuck Halbert, and Fred Scolari. It was further announced that each member of the first team would receive $200, while the second-teamers would get $100.

Whether they received their bonuses remains unclear, especially after it was reported that the only material awards were tie clasps and autographed photos of Maurice Podoloff.

The commissioner and his cohorts had more important shortcomings to deal with. At a postseason press luncheon, the BAA's media mouthpiece, Walter Kennedy, claimed that attendance had been disappointing only at the beginning of the season, when college football had garnered most of the headlines and the fans' support; later in the season, and especially during the playoffs, attendance showed a dramatic increase.

Only the first part of Kennedy's statement had any validity.

The league's official stance was that, including the benefits accruing from the postseason tournament, five franchises had made money—presumably New York, Philadelphia, Washington, Chicago, and St. Louis. This accounting was probably accurate, since all of these teams were the beneficiaries of substantial playoff receipts.

In addition, three were reputed to have broken even, and only the remaining three had finished in the red—a blatant absurdity.

"All told," Kennedy said, "it's been a good season."

Playing his part, Podoloff smiled in public and repeated Kennedy's rosy suppositions. It wasn't until years later that the commissioner confessed his true feelings.

"The first season was a complete failure," Podoloff said. "Detroit, Pittsburgh, and Toronto couldn't have paid their players in the waning months of the season without being bailed out by the other owners. The fans came by the millions and left by the millions—our attendance rapidly decreased as the season progressed—and I couldn't blame them. With all the stalling and endless possessions, the games were lousy. That was my lasting memory of that season—the lousy games. Still, I had no idea why the league had been such a flop. Even Gottlieb couldn't figure it out. When that first season was finally over and done with, I thought that the league would go down the drain, that there wouldn't even be a second season."

It came as no surprise when the Toronto, Pittsburgh, Cleveland, and Detroit franchises quickly folded. That left the BAA with only seven surviving teams—not enough to even formulate a viable schedule for the proposed and hoped-for 1947–48 season.

Moreover, several other critical problems had to be solved:

- On November 1, 1946, there had been a total of 131 players divided among the eleven teams. By season's end, only 70 (or 53 percent) were still with their original teams. These constant alterations negatively impacted the ability of the fans to develop the loyalties and rooting interests necessary for the league's survival. Something had to be done, then, to establish some kind of roster stability.
- It was evident that the franchises that had focused on signing players with professional experience had failed to establish a sufficient fan base. Somehow a fresh batch of college players would have to be recruited to inspire a higher degree of interest and loyalty among the fans in each surviving city.
- The leaguewide net receipts had totaled $1,089,949. One way to expand this sum would be to greatly reduce expenses.
- The season would have to be abbreviated, with the playoffs beginning well before the baseball season was under way.
- Only Philadelphia and New York had attracted more than 100,000 paid admissions, so something drastic had to be done to lure more paying customers.
- Too many star-quality players were fouling out and were therefore unavailable in the closing minutes when tight games were decided.

This last item was the most easily remedied problem: the limit was increased from five allowable personal fouls to six.

A modicum of glamour was claimed by the league when the Knickerbockers announced at a luncheon at Toots Shor's that Joe Lapchick was replacing Neil Cohalan as coach. Lapchick's three-year contract was guaranteed, and it made him the highest-paid coach in the history of professional basketball.

Shortly thereafter, the press proposed and promoted the idea of the BAA's attracting more customers by playing doubleheaders. The most universally advocated suggestion was that the BAA join forces with the ABL, with the BAA's hosting the twin bills on the basis of their larger population centers. This was considered a viable arrangement because both leagues had franchises in Philadelphia and New York; the ABL had a franchise in Baltimore that was in close proximity to Washington; the Jersey City Atoms were situated just across the Hudson River from the Knicks; and the Trenton Tigers were close to the Warriors. Neither league seriously considered the proposal.

What did happen was that after the ABL's Baltimore Bullets had won their way into the league's championship round (versus Trenton), the team had simply pulled out of the competition, choosing instead to participate in the more lucrative World Basketball Tournament, in Chicago. Since the Bullets were halfway out of the ABL anyway—and since the league featured franchises in such small markets as Elizabeth and Paterson, New Jersey, as well as Troy, New York—the team simply jumped leagues and became the BAA's eighth franchise.

Now Gottlieb had a much easier time compiling an equitable forty-eight-game schedule, in which divisional rivals would play each other eight times, and interdivisional rivals would face off six times. Squeezing the eight teams into two equal divisions, however, took some awkward geographical manipulations, and Washington and Baltimore wound up in the Western Division.

The problem of infusing the BAA with new, locally popular players was addressed with the introduction of a college draft. The teams would draft in reverse order of the 1946–47 standings, a procedure that would theoretically strengthen the weakest teams. The draft would also prevent teams from bidding against each other for the services of graduating college stars. The draft was further augmented by a gimmick called the "territorial draft choice," which allowed a team, regardless of its assigned slot, to claim a player who was born within seventy-five miles of the interested franchise or who had played for a local college. Despite these proposed regulations, the BAA teams realized that they would still be competing against both the NBL and the ABL for the brightest of the available college stars.

The particulars of this territorial draft soon became mired in land grabs. Several of the surviving BAA franchises claimed that their territory was nearly as extensive as the Louisiana Purchase. For example, the Washington Capitols considered each of these colleges to be within their domain: Georgia Tech, Vanderbilt, Miami, Washington Jefferson, Catholic University, American University, the University of California, Oregon and Oregon State, Stanford, UCLA, USC, Washington and Washington State, Pepperdine, and the University of San Francisco.

The St. Louis Bombers claimed "the entire state of Missouri" plus the University of Illinois, the University of Kansas, Oklahoma and Oklahoma A&M, Iowa, Kentucky and Western Kentucky, University of Arkansas, and Murray State Teachers College (Joe Fulks's alma mater).

After much bickering and compromising, the territorial draft was eventually instituted in 1949—when St. Louis selected Ed Macauley from St. Louis University, and Minneapolis picked Vern Mikkelsen from Hamline.

Before that, though, the list of players chosen in the BAA's first draft in 1947 contained several players who would become notable performers: Carl Braun (New York), Andy Phillip (Chicago), Red Rocha (St. Louis), and Paul Hoffman (Baltimore). Meanwhile, dozens of other players became available when all those who had played with the defunct BAA teams were declared to be free agents. While the original intent was to encourage these players to sign with the league's most inferior ball clubs, an unrestrained bidding war ensued. Eventually, Ed Sadowski and Mel Riebe landed in Boston, Stan Miasek in Chicago, and Kenny Sailors in Providence.

With these new arrangements in place, all that Podoloff could do was hope for the best.

The 1947–48 playoffs commenced on March 22, and the championship was won by Baltimore in a ferociously contested six-game series with Philadelphia. The Bullets, though, were considered a dull club that lacked any crowd-pleasing superstars. Their best players were Kleggie Hermsen, Chick Reiser, Buddy Jeannette, and Paul Hoffman—not exactly household names even then.

So it was that the BAA's sophomore season was another artistic and financial disaster, but help was on the way. In the summer of 1948, the BAA successfully raided the NBL of its most successful franchises. The new teams included these properties:

- The Rochester Royals, which starred Arnie Risen (the original Plastic Man) as well as a pair of flashy guards, Bobby Wanzer and Bob Davies (who was the first white player to master the behind-the-back dribble)
- The Fort Wayne Zollner Pistons
- The Indianapolis Jets
- Most important—the Minneapolis Lakers, with their dreadnought center, George Mikan, who would make professional basketball truly a big-time sport

Shortly after the 1948–49 season, the BAA absorbed several other NBL teams: the Syracuse Nationals, Tri-Cities Blackhawks, Sheboygan Redskins, Waterloo Hawks, Denver Nuggets, and Anderson Packers. Also, the Jets in Indianapolis were replaced by the Olympians, a team featuring several former all-Americans from the University of Kentucky—including Alex Groza and Ralph Beard. This expanded league was now renamed the National Basketball Association, today's NBA.

The NBL, reduced to franchises in Hammond, Oshkosh, and Dayton, disbanded for good. The ABL, however, persisted until 1953.

Al Cervi was a feisty, 5′11″ guard from Buffalo who had never played college ball but who excelled in the NBL with the Buffalo Bisons, Rochester Royals, and Syracuse Nationals. When the Nationals jumped to the BAA (cum NBA), Cervi went on to become one of the best guards, and then a superior coach, in the new league. He was elected to the Hall of Fame in 1985 and was always fiercely defensive of the old NBL and dismissive of the BAA. "The NBL had by far the best players," said Cervi. "Mikan, Jim Pollard, Bobby McDermott, Davies, Wanzer, and Risen. Compared to us, the BAA was like a high school league. If the BAA hadn't stolen ball clubs from us, then they were out of business."

Why, then, did so many NBL teams defect?

The reason was that the new league, with its metropolitan attractions, offered more publicity and more financial opportunities than did Oshkosh, Toledo, Youngstown, et al. In 1949, publicity was paramount in the mind of Fred Zollner, the millionaire industrialist who owned the Pistons. Paul Walk, the general manager of the Indianapolis team, which was owned by a wealthy florist, had a similar mind-set. So, when Fort Wayne and Indianapolis jumped to the BAA, the Minneapolis owner, Ben Berger, decided to go along with the times. Rochester was next, and the fait was accomplished.

From these humble, penny-pinching roots, the modern NBA has developed into a multibillion-dollar enterprise. These days, the lowliest scrub earns more than the entire BAA did in that first season.

And just how close to financial ruin was the neophyte BAA?

In Bulletin 99, issued on June 6, 1947, Podoloff summoned the owners to a meeting to discuss the league's future. Included in his memo was a comment that all the participants should "arrange to have lunch before the start of the meeting." Podoloff then incriminated himself—and summed up the true state of the league—when he wrote the following: "I am not trying to dodge a lunch bill."

Yes, he was.

Be that as it may, the true meaning of that first season has more to do with matters of the spirit than of finance. A ball game was, as Chuck Connors said, "a night in the flower of a young man's youth and enthusiasm." He concluded, "Playing basketball with a bunch of other guys you knew and respected, with people yelling and screaming for you to succeed—how could anything have been better?"

SOURCES

An invaluable guide was Leonard Koppett's *24 Seconds to Shoot* (Kingston, N.Y.: Total Sports Illustrated Classics, 1999).

Honey Russell: Between Games, Between Halves, by John Russell (Washington, D.C.: Dryad Press, 1986), is a thoughtful and entertaining memoir of the exploits of the author's father.

Another indispensable history of the pre-NBA era is *Cages to Jump Shots: Pro Basketball's Early Years*, by Robert Peterson (New York: Oxford University Press, 1990).

Let Me Tell You a Story, by John Feinstein and Red Auerbach (Boston: Back Bay Books, 2004), is a cover-to-cover delight.

Corrie Anderson and Rob Reheuser, eds. *Official NBA Guide: 2006–2007 Edition* (Chesterfield, Mo.: Sporting News Books, 2006).

Zander Hollander, ed. *The Modern Encyclopedia of Basketball* (New York: Four Winds Press, 1973).

Ken Shouler et al., *Total Basketball* (Toronto: Sport Classic Books, 2003).

INDEX